TEACHING READING

TEACHING READING
a decision making process

Nicholas J. Silvaroli, Ed.D.
Professor of Education
Director, Reading Education
Arizona State University

Warren H. Wheelock, Ed.D.
Professor of Education
Director, Reading Clinic
University of Missouri—Kansas City

KENDALL/HUNT PUBLISHING COMPANY
DUBUQUE, IOWA

contents

v

preface

Teaching Reading: A Decision Making Process consists of 12 chapters. Chapter 1 presents a rationale for why information is essential for decision making. The remaining 11 chapters are divided into three major sections: **Basic Teacher Skills, Classroom Applications,** and **Programmed Word Learning.**

Section One, **Basic Teacher Skills,** deals with those skills we feel teachers should possess in order to be effective in the classroom. Chapter 2 (Word Recognition) discusses the processes we believe are involved in the act of decoding words. Chapters 3 and 4 (Comprehension) discuss language development, how experience is related to comprehension, and the processes we believe are involved in acquiring meaning from print. Chapter 5 attempts to summarize the basic skills required in the areas of word recognition and comprehension. This section is concerned with what teachers need to know and understand rather than what children need to learn. This is based on the belief that if the teacher has acquired concrete skills he is likely to be more effective with children and should have the information necessary for making instructional decisions in the classroom.

Section Two, **Classroom Applications,** utilizes, in various ways, the basic skills presented in the previous section. Chapter 6 (Evaluation) discusses strengths and weaknesses of group reading achievement tests and individual Classroom Reading Inventory. For the most part, these measures evaluate word recognition and comprehension skill development. Therefore, we believe that if the teacher is to function as an effective decision maker, he must understand the basic skills he is attempting to evaluate. Thus, the section on basic teacher skills becomes a prerequisite for the evaluation chapter in the classroom application section. Chapter 7 (Improving Instructional Practices) is less dependent on the basic skills section. Here we discuss what has *not* been effective in our attempts to improve instruction in reading programs. Chapter 8 (Readiness for Reading) is another chapter which is less dependent on the basic skills section. Here we are attempting to identify those factors which we believe are essential in readiness or general preparation for learning to read. Chapter 9 (Classroom Environments) is essentially a discussion of curriculum and not reading. As such, it can be applied to any subject area, i.e., social studies, math, etc. Our purpose for including a discussion of pre-structured and emerging type classrooms is to establish concretely the type classroom environment which relates to different reading methods or reading approaches.

Chapter 10 (Pre-Structured Classroom) discusses reading methods which, in our judgment, are directly related to the pre-structured classroom. We provide recommendations that require teachers to make decisions and utilize basic word recognition and comprehension skill techniques. Chapter 11 (Emerging Classroom) discusses reading approaches, (notice here we use the word approach rather than method because emerging type reading programs tend to utilize interest and experience rather than commercially prepared reading programs) which, in our judgment, are directly related to the emerging classroom.

Chapter 12 (Special Reading Teacher) discusses what we believe is the appropriate role for today's special reading teacher, namely, one who functions as a resource person. We found it difficult to deal with the role of a reading resource specialist if we did not discuss alternative classroom environments, alternative reading programs, or reading approaches and basic teacher skills. Therefore, this final chapter assumes that both teachers and special reading teachers have a thorough understanding of what has been presented in the previous 11 chapters.

Section Three, **Programmed Word Learning**, is not really a chapter of the book. Yet, this section is essential because it attempts to actually teach teachers approximately 30 word recognition concepts. We use a programmed learning format which requires teachers to make a response to a programmed item, reinforce their responses, and, hopefully, learn these word recognition concepts. This section begins with a pretest, which is followed by programmed items in the word recognition categories of "readiness," consonants, vowels, and structure-syllables. The consonant, vowel, and structure-syllable categories all have one or more self-tests. After working through the programmed items and taking several self-tests, the teacher has an opportunity to take the posttest.

If we are successful, then your enthusiasm as a teacher, reflected in the reading achievement and reading enjoyment of your students, will be your reward as well as ours.

acknowledgments

First of all, the authors wish to express their gratitude to Mr. Jesse Roberson who read the entire manuscript and provided many useful suggestions.

Dr. Silvaroli is especially grateful to Mrs. Caroline M. Silvaroli, Diane, Christine and Pamela who have always been understanding and appreciative. Dr. Wheelock expresses his gratitude to Lara Lynn and Sean.

It is impossible for the authors to mention all of the individuals who in one way or another were of assistance. They desire, however, to make known the valuable part played by Mrs. Dorothy Norburg, Ms. Yvonne N. McCay, and Mrs. Virginia Blakey, who typed the manuscript in its various stages with patience and enthusiasm.

chapter 1

INFORMATION IS ESSENTIAL FOR
DECISION MAKING

Teaching Reading: A Decision Making Process hopes that teachers will be able to conceptualize how children function in the act of learning to read. *Teaching Reading: A Decision Making Process* also hopes that teachers will come to know a wide variety of specific instructional options and will become skillful in applying them.

Traditional approaches to teaching teachers how to teach reading might be described in terms of a "level of theory" and a "level of practice." A vast amount of information has been presented at both levels. However, we would like to discuss why we feel that these traditional approaches have failed to help classroom teachers become instructional decision makers when teaching reading.

At the "level of theory," that which goes on in university or college courses, publishing companies, and other places where people gather to better understand how children learn to read, we are likely to find a variety of practices which provide teachers with abstract principles or guidelines. These principles do little to help class-room teachers become instructional decision makers. We will use the area of word recognition to point out several problems at this level. Teachers take courses, read professional books, review research studies, use learning materials, etc. Reading educators have had difficulty agreeing on terms or concepts. Therefore, the term or concept of word recognition is often interchanged for such terms as decoding, phonics, word attack, sounding-out, unlocking, etc. Educational psychologists tend to agree on terms but are likely to present abstract theories or models which deal with how people learn. However, psychologists are usually unequipped to relate these abstract terms to concrete teaching situations. For example, if we were to ask how a child perceives a word during the act of identifying or recognizing a word, a Gestaltist is likely to provide one model, an Operant Conditioner another; but both might have difficulty in relating these descriptions to concrete situations.

The net result is to place the teacher in the position of having to integrate this and other types of abstract information when attempting to understand the area of word recognition. Also at this "level of theory" reading educators have presented abstract information in the areas of comprehension, language development, testing, evaluation, readiness, grouping, learning environments, etc. We can readily understand why many classroom teachers are long on abstract information, but sometimes find it difficult to

1

translate this theoretical or abstract information into effective classroom practices. In our judgment, we feel that classroom teachers lack simple concrete understandings, which make it almost impossible for them to make essential instructional decisions when teaching reading.

We would like to describe another problem, at the "level of theory," which seems to interfere with teacher decision making. Recently we were involved in a staff meeting with fellow reading educators. We made the point that in the introductory reading class, students were given a scope and sequence in word recognition. A faculty member, in the meeting, interrupted and pointed out that he could name at least six additional scope and sequences in word recognition and asked why we only presented one.

We indicated that we consciously made the decision to present only one scope and sequence despite the fact that other scope and sequences were available. In this introductory reading class we were only interested in providing students with a minimum, nonconflicting concrete understanding of a word recognition scope and sequence. We limited ourselves to only one scope and sequence, not because we felt that others were invalid or inadequate, but because we wanted to make our presentation as simple and concrete as possible. The faculty member acted as if we were about to destroy the sacred academic traditions of scholars since the time of the Greeks. Our discussion raised the unquestioned academic belief that *every* learning setting requires exposing students to all possible alternatives and allowing students to make appropriate choices. Rather than argue against this position, we're suggesting that at all levels of education, concepts, or information should be arranged in a hierarchy. We believe that learning is more effective if information is presented in gradual steps. This procedure, we feel, should enable a teacher to make appropriate instructional decisions.

Therefore, the person reading this book will be introduced to a number of *basic constructs,* ideas, or perceptions which result from the authors' observations, impressions, and experience. Assuming that these basic constructs provide teachers with simple concrete understandings, we will be able to introduce advanced understandings without confusing teachers.

Traditional teaching of reading, and teaching reading as a decision making process, also differ at the "level of practice."

The teacher as a decision maker is more than a technician or one who systematically follows published methods of reading. This is not to say that techniques and published methods are unimportant. They are important! However, published reading methods will only be effective to the extent that the teacher is able to conceptualize their particular function in the overall reading program, and apply these concepts in the classroom. Too often, teachers are led to believe that if they completely cover a published method their students will automatically learn to read. Our experience suggests that published methods only work well in certain classes and for certain teachers.

The teacher's emotional reaction seems to be a powerful factor at the "level of practice."

Teaching Reading: A Decision Making Process is based on the belief that as teachers acquire specific or concrete understandings they are more likely to utilize published methods more effectively. In short, basic constructs (concrete understandings) should enable teachers to manipulate published reading methods rather than to be manipulated by them. We are not suggesting that published reading programs are not important. We are merely suggesting that basic skill-development lessons are ineffective if compartmentalized and taught mechanically, without evaluation by the classroom teachers. Teachers can evaluate only if they have concrete understandings.

In the body of this book we have outlined specific procedural methods. We offer these, however, only as possibilities, not as absolute guidelines to be followed. The title of this book implies its major thrust: the teacher can function effectively in teaching students to read only if he has the necessary understandings and confidence to make appropriate decisions within whatever classroom environment he finds himself working, and using whatever published reading programs are available to him.

For example, in Chapter 9 (Classroom Environments) we describe in some detail the two major types of schools (and classrooms) presently existing in this country. We also describe the basic attitudes, methods, and procedures found in each of these environments, as well as the conditions and concepts which gave rise to these two essentially different environments within which you will find yourself functioning as a classroom reading teacher.

Our purpose in writing this book is twofold. One, we want to present and describe the *basic constructs* referred to above as a means of enabling the teacher to translate educational theory into workable classroom practice. Two, we hope to assist teachers in utilizing these constructs in whatever environment they find themselves working.

In implementing these two major purposes, we have tried to avoid evaluating either environment described in Chapter 9; instead we have sought simply to describe them.

On the basis of our own experience and understanding, gained both in public school classrooms and in teaching undergraduate and graduate students who are preparing themselves to teach reading in the public schools, we feel that what we have called the emerging environment is more adequate and effective. But we also recognize that the majority of schools and classrooms fit the pre-structured type.

When we view the emerging environment as a national educational force or movement, we can easily defend it over the traditional pre-structured environment. However, in view of the fact that it will take years to change schools from pre-structured to emerging types, we have emphasized the importance of the teacher as a decision maker in this book.

Despite our preference for the emerging over the pre-structured environment, we recognize that both types of environment, and the teaching practices and procedures required in each of these environments, afford functional learning environments. Thus the role of the teacher as decision maker becomes crucial.

Therefore, rather than becoming involved in the debate over the relative merits of either environment, we have deliberately chosen to emphasize the importance (and the possibility) of the teacher as decision maker. We feel that the *basic constructs* presented in this book should enable the teacher of reading to function effectively and comfortably in either environment.

Because the classroom teacher at present has little control over the type of environment in which he will be working, we have tried to conceptualize, define, and describe certain constructs, ideas, or perceptions which can be utilized in any classroom environment.

Granted the validity of these observations, you can perhaps understand both why we have chosen to restrict ourselves primarily to description, in simple, basic terms, and the importance of the constructs we have presented.

Beyond this, we have been motivated by a purely personal concern. It is both trite and a truism to say that teaching—and learning—can be exciting adventures. Nevertheless, both experiences are too often dull and laborious. But we feel that if prospective teachers acquire an understanding of the basic principles involved in both teaching and learning in the simplest possible form and manner, and learn to apply these principles, or insights, with skill and effectiveness, both students and teachers will profit in more than merely intellectual growth.

As mentioned in the introduction, Section One, Chapters 2, 3, 4, and 5 will present **Basic Teacher Skills**; Section Two, Chapters 6, 7, 8, 9, 10, 11 and 12 will present **Classroom Applications**. Section Three presents a separate programmed word recognition program for teachers. This simplified word recognition program begins with a pretest and provides lessons in the categories of "readiness," consonants, vowels, and structure-syllables; each of these four categories has its own self-test. Finally, we provide a posttest.

If we have succeeded in the above stated purposes, then your enthusiasm as a teacher, reflected in the enhanced learning achievements of your students, will be your reward as well as ours.

BASIC TEACHER SKILLS

chapter 2

WORD RECOGNITION—PART A

Reading education is concerned with a variety of instructional areas. We have selected two areas generally found in all basic reading programs. One area is the mechanical, automatic level commonly referred to as word recognition, "sounding-out," word analysis or word attack, etc. Today's literature refers to words in print as a code, and the learning and application of word recognition skills as the decoding process.

Reading, however, involves a great deal more than word recognition, even though the ability to recognize printed symbols is basic to learning to read. The other area is comprehension, or meaning. Meaning, or comprehension, is a basic function in reading. However, like word recognition, it is only one aspect of learning to read. Reading cannot take place unless the student can identify and recognize the printed symbol.

Reading education, then, focuses on two basic areas: one, word recognition, or the decoding process; and two, comprehension, or the meaning function.

Before getting into a discussion of the skills and concepts necessary for developing comprehension (Chapters 3 and 4), it will be necessary to consider the contructs related to word recognition (acquisition of printed symbols). When an individual encounters a page of printed material, he must first deal with the symbols, or code, he finds printed there. We will refer to letters and words as conventional, or arbitrarily agreed upon, symbols. They are conventional symbols because we believe they have no meaning of their own. The writer and the reader communicate only if they are able to decode these conventional symbols and then assign some common meaning to them.

If you accept the authors' position that words have no meaning of their own and that an individual has to decode those conventional printed symbols, it will be easy for you to understand the major difference between *word recognition* and *comprehension* when you "read" the following short paragraph:

> "Today I had Pungoes or Keswicks,
> I'm not really sure. If restaurant
> owners were wise they would serve
> either Red La Sodas or Red Pontiacs."

You "read" or "called" these words. This is basically word recognition where one makes automatic or mechanical responses to printed symbols. In all probability, however, you did not completely comprehend the author's intent or meaning. To do the one, word recognition, without the other, comprehension, is not reading—only word calling.

If we asked you, "Were you reading this?" you would have to answer that you were not reading the paragraph in the sense of completely comprehending the author's meaning. You were simple recognizing the printed symbols, or performing an automatic function generally referred to as word recognition, sounding-out, word analysis, word attack, decoding, etc.

However, the pertinent question is, To what extent did you understand the author's meaning? Meaning, or comprehension, is an elusive concept at best. For example, in the paragraph above, the meaning of that paragraph may have eluded you because you did not know that Pungoes, Keswicks, Red La Sodas, and Red Pontiacs are names for potatoes.

Consider, for the moment, the following passage:

"To be or not to be."

In this "simple" sentence all of the words are readily recognized and known. All of this is to say that information and ideas beyond the most elementary sort are not conveyed in print by single words. Meanings are expressed by particular interrelationships between and among words, and unless the reader takes to passages an adequate understanding of the ideas, events, or situations to which the passage refers, these interrelationships cannot be grasped.

To summarize, reading instruction generally consists of two basic areas—word recognition and comprehension. To be able simply to decode the printed symbols on a page without attaching some common meaning to those symbols is not reading—only word calling. On the other hand, to know the meaning of many words without the ability to recognize those same words as they are set down as printed symbols is not reading, either. Reading is the skillful blending of *both* comprehension and word recognition.

GENERALIZATION AND DISCRIMINATION LEARNING

Now that you realize that it is possible to decode words in print without comprehending the author's meaning, we need to deal with the decoding process itself.

We asked ourselves, is it possible that information, designed to clarify matters, might actually interfere with a teacher's understanding of what an individual does when he decodes words?

A number of respected psychologists have made contributions in the areas of generalization and discrimination learning. However, we have selected the following to make our point.

Dollard and Miller[1] presented three "levels" of generalization and discrimination learning. Their first "level" stated:

1. *Those based solely on innate similarities and differences.* After the subject learns a response to one cue, this response will tend to generalize to other similar cues, with more generalization occurring to cues that are more similar. This is called a *gradient of innate stimulus generalization.* For example, a child who is burned by one object will tend to fear other similar objects, showing more fear of objects that are more similar.

   If the response to the original cue is repeatedly reinforced and that to the dissimilar cue is repeatedly nonreinforced, the response to the former will tend to be strengthened while that to the latter will be weakened until a *discrimination* is established. With further experience of being burned by one object but not by others the child's fear will tend to become restricted to the hot object. Because of generalization, the difficulty in establishing a discrimination will be a function of the similarity of the cues, and if the cues are too similar, it will be impossible to establish a discrimination.[2]

GENERALIZATION LEARNING

Let us use a word learning example of the concept of learning to *generalize.* Consider the response (R) a first grader has to make to the stimulus (S) word **DOG**

---

1. John Dollard and Neal Miller, *Personality and Psychotherapy: An Analysis in Terms of Learning, Thinking, and Culture* (New York: McGraw-Hill Book Co., Inc., 1950), pp. 103-105.
2. Ibid., p. 103

The first grade youngster looks at the word that the teacher has printed on the board:

DOG ──────────────────────► (R)
  (S_1)

The teacher then tells the first grader that the word is "dog." The youngster has to associate the printed symbols **DOG** with the word "dog" in his language. (When we use the term "language" we will always mean oral language, or speaking and listening.)

At another time, the teacher writes the word "dog" on the board:

dog ──────────────────────► (R)
  (S_2)

The teacher then asks what is the word on the board. The learner might well be confused because he learned that the visual symbol **DOG**—not dog—represents "dog."

During this initial period the learner might see the stimulus word "dog" written several different ways. For example:

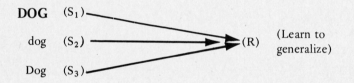

DOG (S_1)
dog (S_2) ────► (R) (Learn to generalize)
Dog (S_3)

For the learner to find any order in all of these printed symbols, obviously the learner must generalize that while all of these words appear to be different, they all refer to the animal we call—dog.

Although it is not related to the point we are making, you should be able to sense the importance of keeping the stimulus words *consistent* in form and appearance during the initial phases of learning the decoding process.

DISCRIMINATION LEARNING

Just as the learner must learn to generalize, so must he also learn to discriminate between the subtle differences in letters and word symbols.

Let us take an example of this concept of learning to discriminate. We now present our beginning reader with the letter *b,* the letter *d,* the letter *p,* and the letter *q.* Structurally, these letters—b, d, p, q—are all the same.

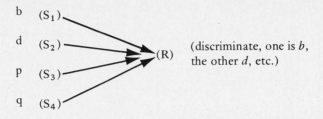

$$
\begin{array}{ll}
b & (S_1) \\
d & (S_2) \\
& \qquad\qquad (R) \quad \text{(discriminate, one is } b, \\
p & (S_3) \qquad\qquad\qquad\qquad \text{the other } d, \text{ etc.)} \\
q & (S_4)
\end{array}
$$

Because they are structurally the same, the youngster is likely to be confused by them. We manipulate these symbols by changing their basic position, but their structure remains the same. The youngster becomes confused because he has to realize that while the symbols are structurally the same they are, in fact, different. Primary grade teachers report that their students are constantly reversing and confusing these basic letter shapes of b-d-p-q. Popp's[3] study, for example, showed that the lower case letter pairs b-d and p-q are most confusing to prereading children.

Before a youngster starts to school, he operates in a three-dimensional environment. He sees such things as chairs, dishes, toys, animals, and whatever in a variety of positions. But he still retains the object's basic identity. The chair is still a chair even though it has tipped over. The cat is still a cat even though it is looking sideways. This is a three-dimensional environment where objects maintain their identity despite the fact that they change their basic positions.

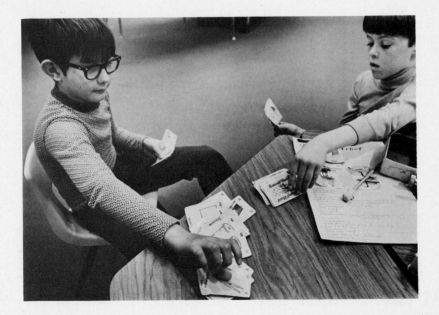

3. Helen M. Popp, "Visual Discrimination of Alphabet Letters," *The Reading Teacher*, 17:221-226, January, 1964.

Now the youngster starts to school. The teacher presents him with a *b*. The child calls it a *d*. He has not yet learned that the change in position of a letter also changes its identity. We take this symbol *b* where the circle part of the symbol faces to the right. In that position we call it a "b." Now we take that same basic symbol but this time we face the circle to the left—*d*. In this position we call it a "d." In that three-dimensional world of before school, a cat was a cat no matter which way it was facing.

Many of the daily lessons used in first grade are based on generalization learning. It is assumed that an equal number of daily lessons are based on discrimination learning. If we read basic texts in psychology, we are likely to find a number of experiments based on generalization and discrimination learning. As a result, the authors believe that teachers are likely to isolate these learning functions and view them as *separate learning functions.* We admit that these are separate learning functions, but our observations suggest that both functions must operate simultaneously during word recognition. We can provide separate generalization and discrimination lessons, however, the teacher must understand that both functions operate simultaneously during word recognition.

An understanding of the simultaneous function of generalization and discrimination learning appears to lead to the construct: *the ability to hold the whole word and simultaneously attend to the parts within the word.*

WHOLE WORD AND PART WORD LEARNING

Reading educators have discussed whole word learning ("Gestalt" Psychology) versus part word learning ("Stimulus-Response" Psychology) for the past several decades. Again, the authors believe that these attempts to clarify word recognition might actually interfere with a teacher's basic understanding of this process.

To enable us to illustrate what the learner appears to do during word recognition, we have placed a single word in a box on page 15. When you look at that word, think about what you did to *decode* that word. Please turn to page 15 now.

For those of you who responded with something like, "Father's Day is coming and I haven't gotten his present yet," or the like, you were making a meaning response and that is not what this chapter is about. We are dealing with a decoding response.

When you looked at the stimulus word in the box, you may have seen the whole word "father." On the other hand, you may have seen some part of the word. If we could poll the readers of this book as to their reaction to the stimulus word, we would probably find that reactions were equally divided. Some of you saw the whole word and some of you saw an "F," or were more conscious of the "th," or whatever.

For years, teachers have been confronted with the heated controversy as to whether people see parts ("Stimulus-Response" Psychology), or whether people see wholes ("Gestalt" Psychology).

If you tend to favor the "parts" theory, we would be more phonic-oriented or code-oriented. If you tend to favor the "whole-word" theory, you would be traditionally more basal or basic-reader oriented.

Rather than rehash a tired, old argument over part versus whole, we would like to postulate that it is neither part nor whole, but that we are, in fact, dealing simultaneously with parts and wholes.

We would like you to look at another stimulus word and think about what we have been saying here. We will attempt to make the point that when we look at words it is *both whole* and *part simultaneous recognition of symbols.* It is not a question of doing either part or whole. Rather, it is doing both whole *and* part simultaneously. Now look quickly at the stimulus word on page 16.

Here again, if we could poll the readers of this book we would probably find that they reacted in this way: First, they looked at the entire word and then had a frantic type of reaction—orin, ore, oco, loco, etc. We believe that the reader looks at the total stimulus word, and if he does not decode the whole word instantly, he holds the whole word in mind and begins finding systematic or consistent word parts within the word. When the reader does this, he is engaging in the function we call word recognition, decoding, "sound-out," etc.

The point is that the reader first "held" the total stimulus word in mind (usually called the "whole word" approach). Then, while he "held" the word in mind, simultaneously began attending to the parts within the word (usually called a phonic approach).

Consider youngsters in elementary or secondary school and what they do when they look at words that they don't understand and they are poor readers as well. Characteristically, they look at the stimulus word, they see the whole, get no instant response, and then they leave the word. Just that quickly, in that fleeting moment of frustration, just like that temporary feeling of frustration you felt with "Orinoco," they leave the word, and, for poor readers, the entire word recognition process.

The difference is that when you encountered that fleeting feeling of frustration, you held and delayed the frustration and then you went back and simultaneously worked on the parts. When a youngster with a reading problem has this slight, transient moment of frustration, he gives up, saying, "That's too hard for me." He no longer attempts to find consistent parts within the whole word.

To be able to decode, one must be able to hold the whole word, and tolerate minimal frustration, while attempting to find consistent parts within the word.

We believe that by constantly engaging in the whole-versus-part debate without pointing out that these are merely ways to explore word recognition, we are likely to mislead teachers. The authors take the position that in actual practice, it appears more reasonable to view word recognition as: (construct) *the ability to hold the whole word and simultaneously attend to the parts within the word.*

Realizing that we are repeating ourselves, we need to restate that there are two basic skill areas in reading education. One is the area of word recognition. This is not a very productive level of reading. It is essential, however, for the youngster must master word recognition. But as quickly as he can get by this mechanical level, it is then necessary for him to begin moving more toward the level of meaning function. Trying to read without understanding the author's meaning is simply a waste of time. There are youngsters in school who are essentially "word callers." That is, they can decode the symbols, they can sound exactly like the teacher, but they do not understand the author's meaning.

As a function of word recognition the learner has to be able to make a generalized *and* a discriminatory response to letter forms and word forms. That is, the learner has to be able to generalize and discriminate when he sees basic word symbols.

For example, when the student looks at a word such as "father," he has to learn about the orientation of the letters, and he has to be able to understand that the word proceeds from left to right. In addition, he has to be able to make an instantaneous reaction of the word and, in fact, decode it by finding stable word parts throughout.

Finally, it is our feeling that the whole word-versus-part word argument is a tired one and an overdone one in public education. In a classroom situation, it seems quite unrealistic to fight the outmoded battle of part versus whole. It really seems much more reasonable to try to deal with the concept of whole *and* part: *the ability to hold the whole word and simultaneously attend to the parts within the word.*

FATHER

```
┌─────────────────────┐
│                     │
│      ORINOCO        │
│                     │
└─────────────────────┘
```

WORD RECOGNITION—PART B

Research has shown that there is not one best method, or program, for developing independence in word recognition. The most ambitious instructionally-oriented research project was the Cooperative Research Program in first-grade reading instruction, summarized by Bond and Dykstra[1] and by Dykstra[2]. The latter stated one of the main findings of the first-grade studies as follows: "No method was especially effective or ineffective for pupils of high or low readiness as measured by tests of intelligence, auditory discrimination, and letter knowledge."

In discussing the implications of the first-grade studies, Dykstra noted "that future research should center on teacher and learning characteristics rather than on method and materials."

However, at the level of daily instructional practice there appears to be an agreed upon *sequence* of major word recognition skill lessons used to teach children to recognize or decode words. Stated another way, regardless of the reading method, or reading program used, authors tend to present a similar sequence of word recognition skill lessons to enable the learner to acquire the *ability to hold the whole word and simultaneously attend to the parts within the word.*

COMPARISON OF CURRENT READING PROGRAMS

All basal, or basics—oriented reading programs in use in schools today (See Bibliography—Part One, p. 21) use the following sequence of lessons presented by Botel, Heilman, Wilson and Hall, and many others:

Sequence of Skill Lessons

	Botel	Heilman	Wilson/Hall
"Readiness"		Chapter I	
Consonants	Level A	Chapter II	Chapter I
Vowels	Level B	Chapter III	Chapter II
Structure-Syllables	Level C	Chapter IV	Chapter III

A general review of sample phonic programs (See Bibliography—Part Two p. 21) such as; Economy Company, Phonovisual, Lippincott, and others, show a slightly different order but the same major word recognition concepts are introduced:

1. G.L. Bond and R. Dykstra, "The Cooperative Research Program in First-Grade Reading Instruction," *Reading Research Quarterly*, 1967, 2, 5-141.
2. R. Dykstra, "Summary of the Second-Grade Phase of the Cooperative Research Program in Primary Reading Instruction," *Reading Research Quarterly*, 1968, 4, 49-70.

Sequence of Skill Lessons

	Economy	Phonovisual	Lippincott
"Readiness"	Tag	Readiness Book	Not taught separately
Consonants	Tag* Dot and Jim	Steps I and II	Pre-Primer, Primer Book 1-1
Vowels	Dot and Jim All Around	Step III	Pre-Primer, Primer Book 1-1
Structure-Syllables	Along New Ways	Method Book	Book 2-1, 2-2

(*Tag book introduces vowels before consonants)

Several of the reading programs introduced in the past several years (See Bibliography—Part Three p. 21) such as: Programmed readers, i/t/a, SRA's Distar also present a slightly different order but tend to introduce similar word recognition (letter/word symbol—letter/word sound associations) lessons:

Sequence of Skill Lessons

	Programmed Reading (BRL)	i/t/a	Distar (SRA)
"Readiness"	Pre-reader	redy for reeding	
Consonants	Books—pre-reader, 1-6	Phase I	Reading I
Vowels	Books—pre-reader 2, 6-20	Phase II	Reading I
Structure-Syllables	Books—1-18	Phase III	Reading II

Obviously, all of the complexities of each current reading program listed (instructional assumptions, lesson sequence, etc.) are not given adequate attention in the following over-simplified, four-part word recognition construct: *Word recognition lessons should be limited to consistent high frequency word elements in the areas of:*

"Readiness"

Consonants

Vowels

Structure-Syllables

The limited number of reading programs used in the above comparisons were selected merely to illustrate the point that common word recognition skill lessons are taught in a similar manner on a daily basis. It is not our intention to praise, or find fault with, any existing reading method. In fact, we believe that the following assumptions are basic to teaching reading as a decision making process:

1. Teachers are the primary factor in any reading program. The commercial method employed is, at best, only a secondary factor.
2. Teachers must adapt or adjust any existing commercial reading program.
3. Teachers must be involved in selecting the commercial reading program used in their classroom.
4. In order for each teacher to make instructional decisions about the reading method used, he must understand what the learner does during the word recognition and comprehension processes, and be proficient with basic lessons used to assist the learner to grasp these processes.

Given these assumptions it follows then that we will present the specific word recognition elements which are related to our word recognition construct: *Word recognition tends to develop in the following sequence:*

"Readiness"

Consonants

Vowels

Structure-Syllables

The work of Clymer[1], Bailey[2], Emans[3], and others, made us aware of the notion that some phonics generalizations have greater utility (instructional consistency) than others.

PROGRAMMED WORD LEARNING

We presented two constructs (abstract ideas) in this chapter:

Word recognition requires the ability to hold the whole word and simultaneously attend to the parts within the word.

Word recognition tends to develop in the following sequence:

"Readiness"

Consonants

Vowels

Structure-Syllables

1. Theodore Clymer, "The Utility of Phonic Generalizations in the Primary Grades," *Reading Teacher*, vol. 16, Number 4, January, 1963.

2. Mildred Hart Bailey, "The Utility of Phonic Generalizations in Grades One Through Six," *Reading Teacher*, vol. 20, February, 1967.

3. Robert Emans, "The Usefulness of Phonic Generalizations Above the Primary Grades," *Reading Teacher*, vol. 20, February, 1967.

These constructs might also be called educational objectives. By this we mean educational objectives which are based on our beliefs and observations; they are not concrete and cannot be measured. Yet, these educational objectives are useful because they provide an overall understanding of a process that we are otherwise unable to explain.

In contrast to educational objectives, performance objectives are directly related to some aspect of instruction and are always stated in concrete terms.

Ideally, performance objectives identify what the learner would be doing when demonstrating his achievement of the objective. These instructional statements also suggest conditions relevant to the desired performance, and usually suggest how to tell when the objective has been achieved. It is the concrete nature of performance objectives which differentiates them from traditional educational objectives. For example, the first construct presented in this chapter, namely, *word recognition requires the ability to hold the whole word and simultaneously attend to the parts within the word*, is an example of an educational objective.

The concrete performance objective, which is related to the overall educational objective, can be stated as follows:

> *Given 24 groups of words (five words per group) you will be able to name the specific* **Consonant, Vowel,** *or* **Structure-Syllable** *elements common to all five words within the group.*

We have provided two sets of the 24 groups of words in the form of Pre- and Posttests. If you are able to identify the common "readiness," consonant, vowel, and structure-syllable elements in the Pretest, then we believe that the constructs presented in this chapter should be known to you. Please turn to pp. 193-195 and take the Word Recognition Pretest you find there. If you are unsuccessful with the Pretest, i.e., missed more than six of the 24 items, then it is recommended that you work through the programmed word learning lessons presented in Section Three, pp. 196-237.

After completion of the programmed word learning lessons, please turn to pp. 238-239 and take the Word Recognition Posttest you find there. Your performance on the Posttest will determine whether or not you have met the Performance Objective as italicized above. That is, the Posttest will determine how well you understood the material presented in this chapter. If you are unsuccessful on the Posttest, then it is recommended that you go back over the material in this chapter again.

SUMMARY

We attempted to make the point that the process of word recognition requires a simultaneous whole *and* part perception; and that in actual practice it appears reasonable to view word recognition as: *the ability to hold the whole word and simultaneously attend to the parts within the word.*

This chapter also attempted to present a sequence of highly consistent word recognition concepts. The construct for this sequence was limited to word elements or phonic concepts in the categories of—*"Readiness," Consonants, Vowels, and Structure-Syllables.*

The role of the teacher now becomes that of a decision maker. The teacher must ask: "What word recognition skills do I need to teach to children to enable them to recognize or decode words?" Regardless of the reading program or method used, the decision making teacher will adjust the program to meet the specific skill needs of the children. For example, if a reading program or method suggests that an obscure word recognition skill be taught, the teacher might decide not to introduce the skill. If a particular skill is extensively repeated, the teacher might decide to reduce the number of repetitions.

We believe that the success or failure of word recognition programs and ultimately overall reading programs are directly related to the extent to which classroom teachers are willing to make instructional decisions.

BIBLIOGRAPHY: COMPARISON OF CURRENT READING PROGRAMS
(Pages 17-18)

Part One:

Botel, Morton, *How to Teach Reading,* Follett Publishing Company, Chicago, Revised Edition, 1964.

Heilman, Arthur W., *Phonics in Proper Perspective,* Second Edition, Charles E. Merrill Publishing Company, Ohio, 1964.

Wilson, Robert M., and Hall, Mary Anne, *Programmed Word Attack for Teachers,* Charles E. Merrill Publishing Company, Ohio, 1968.

Part Two:

McCracken, Glenn and Walcutt, Charles C., *Basic Reading,* J.B. Lippincott Company, New York, 1966.

Harris, Theodore L., Creekmore, Mildred and Margaret Greenman, *Phonetic Keys to Reading,* The Economy Company, Oklahoma City, 1970.

Phonovisual Products, Inc. Washington, D.C.

Part Three:

Tanyzer, Harold J., and Mazurkiewicz, Albert J., *Early to Read i/t/a Program,* Revised Edition, Initial Teaching Alphabet (i/t/a) Publications, Inc., New York, 1966.

Englemann, Siegried and Brunner, Elaine C., *Distar Reading,* Science Research Associates, Inc., Palo Alto, California, 1970.

Programmed Reading, A Sullivan Associates Program from McGraw-Hill Book Company, New York.

REFERENCES FOR CHAPTER 2

Bond, Guy L., and Miles A. Tinker. *Reading Difficulties: Their Diagonisis and Correction.* New York: Appleton-Century-Crofts, 1973.

> *See:* Section IV (pp. 267-353) "Treatment of Word-Recognition Difficulties." This section contains three chapters dealing with (1) basic principles of remedial instruction, (2) correcting basic word-recognition difficulties, and (3) treating special word-recognition difficulties.

Fry, Edward B. *Reading Instruction for Classroom and Clinic.* New York: McGraw-Hill Book Company, 1972.

> *See:* Chapter 7 (pp. 114-134) "Phonics Teaching Materials." Presents a variety of good phonics materials to teach specific word recognition skills.

Gans, Roma. *Fact and Fiction: About Phonics.* New York: The Bobbs-Merrill Co., Inc., 1964.

> A paperback of 100 pages that should be read in its entirety.

Hafner, Lawrence E., and Hayden B. Jolly. *Patterns of Teaching Reading in the Elementary School.* New York: The Macmillan Company, 1972.

> *See:* Chapter 5 (pp. 89-117) "Patterns for Teaching Word-Identification Skills." Enumerates some basic word-identification tools and discusses alternative approaches to teaching them.

Harris, Albert J. *How To Increase Reading Ability.* New York: David McKay Co., Inc., 1970.

> *See:* Chapter 13 (pp. 315-348) "Developing Word Recognition Skills." Presents a program of word analysis and discusses scope and sequence in teaching word analysis.

> *See:* Chapter 14 (pp. 349-389) "Overcoming Difficulties in Word Recognition." Outlines strategies for correcting specific faults in word recognition and presents materials for improving word attack skills.

Heilman, Arthur W. *Principles and Practices of Teaching Reading.* Columbus, Ohio: Charles E. Merrill Publishing Company, 1967.

> *See:* Chapter 9 (pp. 259-287) "Phonics Instruction." Reviews past practices in phonics instruction and the tasks involved.

Otto, Wayne, Richard A. McMenemy and Richard J. Smith. *Corrective and Remedial Teaching.* Boston: Houghton Mifflin Company, 1973.

> *See:* Chapter 7 (pp. 155-184) "Word-Attack Skills in Reading." Lists a comprehensive guide of approaches to word attack.

Schneff, Virginia and Odessa Meyer. *Improving Your Reading Program.* New York: The Macmillan Company, 1971.

> *See:* Sequence Problem 1 (pp. 104-123) "Word-Attack Skills." Attempts to get teachers to analyze their own convictions about teaching the word-attack skills and not lose sight of individual differences among children.

Smith, Frank. *Understanding Reading.* New York: Holt, Rinehart and Winston, Inc., 1971.

> *See:* Chapter 12 (pp. 159-184) "Phonics—and Mediated Word Identification." Discusses the speech-writing relationship.

Spache, George D., and Evelyn B. Spache. *Reading in the Elementary School.* Boston: Allyn & Bacon, Inc., 1973.

> *See:* Chapter 12 (pp. 448-510) "Word Recognition Techniques and Skills." Discusses systematic approaches to teaching phonics, structural analysis, and contextual analysis.

Stauffer, Russell G. *Directing Reading Maturity as a Cognitive Process.* New York: Harper & Row, Publishers, 1969.

> *See:* Chapter 6 (pp. 241-291) "Developing Skill in Word Recognition." Discusses what is needed to keep phonics in perspective and to recognize its contribution to reading and to the learning-to-read process.

Teaching Word Recognition Skills. Reprinted from the Publications of the International Reading Association, Newark, Delaware, 1971.

> A collection of articles compiled by Mildred A. Dawson, dealing with all aspects of word recognition.

Wallen, Carl J. *Competency in Teaching Reading.* Chicago: Science Research Associates Inc., 1972.

> *See:* Section I (pp. 19-232) "Recognition Skills." Designed to help the teacher develop competency in designing and conducting tests and lessons suitable for specific reading-skill objectives.

Wilson, Robert M., and Maryanne Hall. *Reading and the Elementary School Child.* New York: Van Nostrand Reinhold Company, 1972.

> *See:* Chapter 7 (pp. 142-169) "Word Attack." Includes a detailed study of issues in word attack to assist the teacher to see advantages and limitations of different viewpoints.

Zintz, Miles V. *The Reading Process.* Dubuque, Iowa: Wm. C. Brown Company Publishers, 1970.

> *See:* Chapter 7 (pp. 131-179) "Word Recognition Skills." Contains a discussion of the skills in word recognition. Also summarizes the usefulness of phonic generalizations.

chapter 3

LANGUAGE DEVELOPMENT

Just as it is impossible for comprehension to occur without language and/or experience, it is also impossible to discuss comprehension without first discussing language and/or experience as well.

When a native English speaking child enters the first grade, he can understand much of the English language when he hears it spoken. This is sometimes called his listening vocabulary and is composed of all the words for which he assigns correct meaning when he hears them. In addition, he can pronounce with correct meaning many of the words in our language. This is the part sometimes called his speaking vocabulary. It is also true that a child can use simple, compound, complex, and compound-complex sentences at this early age. In speaking, he demonstrates an awareness of the structure of language.

Obviously, it will be impossible to deal with the vast field of language. This is a lifetime study for anyone.

DeLancey[1] attempts to answer the question—"What Is Language?"—in the following way:

"Language is a system of arbitrary vocal symbols organized for communication among human beings. This definition, while not perfect, includes those elements felt by contemporary writers on the subject to be significant:

"1. *Language is symbolic.* The elements of any language serve as symbols by which its speakers can represent or portray the world of their experience.

"2. *This symbolism is arbitrary.* The association of these symbols with the phenomena they represent is purely a matter of convention. No object in the real world of our experience exhibits characteristics obliging us to represent it symbolically by any specific sound or sounds.

"3. *Language is vocal.* An individual learns to speak before he learns to write; we assume that all peoples who have evolved or adopted a writing system were already using a language. Thus, the primary state of a language is speech; a writing system is a secondary, derived means of expression. This conclusion does not imply that writing is not important or that special conventions appropriate to writing do not evolve.

---

1. Robert W. DeLancey, "Linguistics and Teaching: A Manual of Classroom Practices," *Monograph Number Nine. The New York State English Council* 1965, p. 5.

"4. *The symbols of a language are systematically arranged.* We cannot, for example, in English say, 'Man on the air heard,' and expect ourselves to be understood. The symbols of any language must be arranged to the system, or grammar, of that language.

"5. *Language is for human communication.* Although much is being discovered about the extremely important conceptual function of language, the primary function of language is communication among members of a speech community. To the best of our knowledge, only human beings possess language as it is here defined."

Accepting this definition of language, we have arrived at the following construct: *language symbolizes our world of experience.*

In expanding this construct that language symbolizes our world of experience, we have arrived at another construct related to language: *print symbolizes our language.*

Stated another way, we can say that there exists a world of phenomena which surrounds us as we experience it. We symbolize this world of phenomena as we experience it with language (language symbolizes our world of experience). Man is also capable of writing down his language (print symbolizes our language). Therefore, the written word symbolizes not the object in the real world, but the spoken symbol. It is the spoken symbol that is the referent for the object in the experiential world.

If, for example, a child can pronounce with correct meaning the word "horse," it is because horse has been a part of his world of experience. He may have seen a horse, or ridden a horse, or have been shown pictures of a horse, etc. It is this spoken symbol "horse" which is the referent for horse in the experiential world of the child.

"Experience"   "Language"

Language Symbolizes Our World of Experience

We have a system which enables us to graphically represent the utterance "horse." This system is print or writing. But what we put into print merely represents the sounds of the utterance—not the meaning behind those utterances. The printed form of the word does not carry the meaning of that word. Meaning for the word must exist within us as a result of our having had some experience with the world of phenomena that encompasses us.

"Language"   "Print"

Print Symbolizes Our Language

All of which is to say that language (which symbolizes our world of experience) must precede print (which symbolizes our language) and, therefore, reading.

"Experience"   "Language"   "Print"

Since language must precede reading and writing (print) it seems quite useless to place a youngster in a reading program without previous adequate language development. A child's use of language in expressing his own thoughts reveals much about his language background and how well that background is suited to the task of learning to read.

Monroe[2] presented a scale for evaluating a child's language ability in interpreting pictures. She suggested that a picture be selected in which two or more characters are

2. Marion Monroe, "Necessary Preschool Experiences for Comprehending Reading," *Reading and Inquiry.* International Reading Association Conference Proceedings, vol. 10 (Newark, Delaware, 1965), pp. 45-46.

engaged in some interesting activity and that the pupil be asked to tell what the picture is about. His verbal response is recorded and classified as to the level according to the following steps:

Step 1. The child merely shrugs his shoulders and does not reply. He may venture to name some of the objects in the picture.

Step 2. The child describes what the characters are doing.

Step 3. The child expresses a relationship between the characters or objects.

Step 4. The child sees the picture as one part of a narrative. He gives relationships of time, place, cause-effect.

Step 5. The child reacts to the mood of the picture, perceives the emotional reactions of the characters and draws a conclusion or evaluates the actions.

Monroe postulates that children who have not reached Step 3 on this scale have not developed sufficient language ability to interpret a picture in a primer and react to the text that accompanies that picture.

The child who does not achieve Step 3 should then be placed in a language development program rather than in a reading program, since adequate language development must precede reading and writing.

One must also be cognizant of the fact that schools use a standard English language and assume the learner has all of the experience of the English speaking language community.

COMPREHENSION DEVELOPMENT

It should be obvious from the previous discussion about language development, that experience is basic to all communication. The order of the development of language abilities is from experience to the formation of concepts and ideas to the use of language labels to symbolize these ideas. There is no meaning in the language labels as such, but only in the experiences upon which they are based.

Following is a communication model:[3]

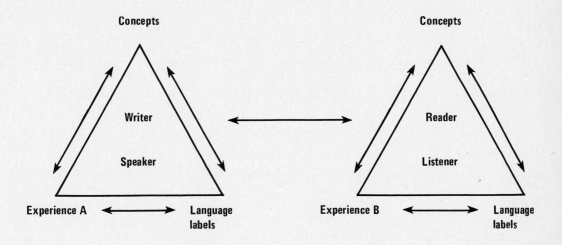

As the writer or speaker, I have had certain experiences which have led to the formation of concepts (ideas). In turn, these concepts (ideas) are translated into language labels to symbolize them.

Now, you as the reader or listener have also had certain experiences which have lead to the formation of concepts (ideas). Here again, these ideas and concepts are translated into language labels which symbolize them.

As the reader or listener you will understand me as the writer or speaker only to the extent to which there is some degree of similarity in our experience background, our ability to organize this experience and form ideas and concepts, and our use of the same language labels to symbolize these concepts (ideas).

For example, consider the line from Edward Lear's poem "The Owl and the Pussycat," where it says something about how they "took some honey and plenty of money wrapped up in a five pound note."

Lear was an Englishman and, of course, when he said "five pound note" he meant paper money having the equivalent of five pounds sterling silver, something like a twenty-dollar bill in America. Such was Lear's experience, his concept of five pound note, and, finally the language label he used.

Youngsters reading that same line today may have other ideas. "Hey, teacher, that's really a heavy note—a five pound note!"

3. Roy A. Kress, "Thinking and Comprehension Base of Communication," *Reading in Modern Communication.* Proceedings of the 1962 Annual Reading Institute at Temple University.

This illustrates the problem of communication. Even though the language labels are the same, the writer or speaker and the reader or listener have different concepts of what the language labels actually said. "Five pound note" means different things because of different experiences.

If we stick to language labels alone (words written or spoken) then the learner brings to the situation any concepts (ideas) that he may have previously acquired. Obviously, it is not just a matter of bringing in language labels and assuming that youngsters will have the same concepts (ideas) that we have.

Our social studies books, our health books, our science books, our reading books, do just that. There is very, very little communication going on in public schools because we keep centering only on the language labels. We never quite get around to checking to see whether the reader or listener has the same concepts and ideas that the writer or speaker has.

Consider, for a moment, this sentence from a story in a typical basal reader: "A launch with a strong motor was nosing along the Yukon River north of Dawson City."

Now, as teachers, we may be able to get a youngster to look at the sentence above, and put back into sounds the language labels (words) contained therein. However, we have seen from our communication model that there is no meaning in these language labels, as such. The meaning lies in the experiences upon which the language labels are based.

The question, then, is—does the reader have the same concepts (ideas) that the author has? If the reader does not, then there is only an exchange of language labels, or verbalisms.

The writer of the sentence, "A launch with a strong motor . . ." uses the language label "launch" to describe a type of boat. The reader of that sentence may associate the word "launch" with an entirely different concept—"launch" meaning to send a rocket into space. After having made this "incorrect" response to the label "launch," the reader may become hopelessly confused with what the story is all about even though he can decode the symbols he sees before him.

PRODUCT AND PROCESS COMPREHENSION

At the risk of repeating ourselves, it is necessary to remind you that organizing the complex area of comprehension is an extremely difficult task. We are going to develop an organizational scheme around a rather simplistic idea, which we have elected to call Product and Process Comprehension. Basically, **Product Comprehension** is that which is known, directly stated, or agreed upon in advance. In short, this type of comprehension requires the reader to answer questions on the basis of what the teacher and/or manual state are "correct answers." **Process Comprehension** is that which is relative, open for question and not easily agreed upon in advance. In short, it is that type of comprehension which requires that reader to go beyond the level of recall and interpret questions on the basis of his experience.

30

Another distinction between these two areas is that **Product** type questions tend to require single "correct" or "incorrect" responses as determined by the teacher or the manual. **Process** type questions have no real "correct" or "incorrect" responses; they are "correct" only if the reader can defend them in terms of his reasoning and experience.

Some authors[4] refer to what we call "product comprehension" as the "closed question." The closed question is structured in anticipation of one "right" answer. For example: "Who was David? Where did he live? What grade was he in?"

Youngsters who are asked to respond to questions like this find themselves trapped in an attempt to read the teacher's mind so they can give her the answer she wants. The "right" answer to one question closes a door which is seldom reopened. The closed question makes no attempt to arouse critical thinking or spark further questions.

The "open question" (or what we have been calling Process Comprehension) is phrased so as to admit a variety of answers and stimulate further questioning and supposition. Each open question leads to another and to deeper thinking. Thus, open questions draw the discussion to personal reactions and involvement. For example: "How do you think David felt when he failed his tests? Why was it difficult for David to get along in school?"

The nature and sequence of the questions depend upon the responses of the children, as well as the questions they raise along the way. It becomes a spontaneous network of supposition and personal reaction, rather than the time-honored game of fact retrieval.

To illustrate what we mean, allow us to use a question taken from a third grade test!

"Of the following four words, select the one word which you think does not belong with the other three:"

kitten	puppy	baby	cow

For those of you who have selected the word "cow" as the one that does not belong with the others—the authors of this book extend to you their congratulations. You are rewarded with a happy face ☺ . For those of you who have selected the word "baby" as the one that does not belong with the others—the authors of this book extend to you their condolences in the hope that maybe some day you will become as "smart" as some of our other readers. You are rewarded with an unhappy face ☹ . This may seem somewhat absurd to you, but isn't this what we are really

4. Nancy Larrick, "We Are Still Afraid," *IRA Perspectives in Reading Conference.* Atlantic City, 1971.

doing when we know in advance what the answer should be? We elicit responses—which word doesn't fit? What we are really saying is, what word doesn't fit according to the manual, or according to the teacher?

This approach to comprehension is what we are calling a **product** approach. We know in advance what the "right" answer is. The learner has as his charge to guess what the teacher has been thinking about or what it says in the teacher's manual.

Let's look at it another way! Those of you who selected "cow" probably did so because you were thinking that "cow" is an adult while the remainder are infants. There is nothing wrong with that response and you should be rewarded with a happy face ☺ for having made it. Those of you who selected "baby" probably were thinking homo sapiens versus other classifications of animals. That, too, was a good response and you should be rewarded with a happy face ☺ for having made it.

Some of you could have selected "baby" because a baby is a bi-ped and the other animals are quadrupeds.

It is entirely possible that some of you may have selected the word "puppy." Why? Because it is the only word containing the consonant "p." For those of you who did select "puppy" for this reason, we need to also reward you with a happy face ☺.

Taking the **product** approach—cow, or baby, or even puppy—we could have three possible *correct* alternatives. One can see the difficulty in this type of approach. The difficulty is that we are overly concerned with having a "right" and a "wrong" response. Just as there must be a "right" response—so must there be a "wrong" one.

Now, however, we must become concerned with the individual's ability to reason. Essentially, this is the case with modern math. Modern math's basic concern is with the youngster's ability to reason; not that two plus two equals four, instead, how did you arrive at four as your answer? Basically, this is what we in reading education should be concerned with, but, so far, have not. We should be thinking more about alternative answers; not only what answer did you get, but how did you arrive at the answer?

All of this might make for a good discussion; but what does it mean in terms of classroom practices? It is our feeling that much of what masquerades as comprehension teaching in the classroom is essentially a product approach to comprehension.

We believe that we need a **product** approach but that each teacher must be willing to balance comprehension lessons with a **process** approach to comprehension.

The following chapter is devoted to transforming classroom practices from almost exclusive product approaches to comprehension to a balance between **product** *and* **process** approaches. The key to both approaches is not something inherent in **product** or **process** types of comprehension questions, but in the **Teacher's Ability to Recognize When Either Approach Is Possible.**

SUMMARY

There exists a world of phenomena which surrounds us as we experience it. We symbolize this world of phenomena as we experience it with language. Therefore, the following construct is derived: *language symbolizes our world of experience.*

We have a system which enables us to graphically represent our language. This system is print or writing. Therefore, the following construct is derived: *print symbolizes our language.*

It follows, then, that language must precede writing and, therefore, reading. A child's use of language in expressing his own thoughts reveals much about his language background and how well that background is suited to the task of learning to read.

The comprehension basis of communication lies in the richness of the life experience of the individual. The exactness with which one person understands another is always dependent upon the degree of similarity found in their bank of life experience, in the content of their concepts, and in their agreement upon the language labels used to symbolize these concepts.

Finally, a good deal of comprehension development in schools today uses a product approach when they should be using *balance* between a product and process approach to comprehension development. We realize that it is not really an approach we're dealing with but rather the teacher's ability to recognize when either approach is possible.

chapter 4

COMPREHENSION—PART B

In Chapter 3, we attempt to make the point (construct): *experience is basic to all communication.* The order of the development of language abilities is from experience to the formation of concepts and ideas to the use of language labels to symbolize these ideas. There is no meaning in the language labels as such, but only in the experiences upon which they are based. As the reader you will understand us as the authors only to the extent to which there is some degree of similarity in our experience background, our ability to organize this experience and form ideas and concepts, and our use of the same language labels to symbolize these concepts and ideas. The comprehension basis of communication lies in the richness of the life experience of the individual.

The first major construct basic to this chapter is: *the development of comprehension skills requires a balance between process and product approaches.* That is, there must be a balance between the development of those comprehension skills that are structured in anticipation of one "right" answer (product), and the development of those comprehension skills structured so as to admit a variety of answers and stimulate further questioning and supposition (process).

Since process comprehension and product comprehension are teaching strategies, it is essential that the teacher has the ability to recognize when either approach is possible. Thus, the second major construct basic to this chapter is: *the teacher has the ability to recognize when either a process approach or a product approach is possible.*

Accepting the position that lessons related to the development of comprehension skills need to be balanced between process and product type teaching strategies, we will now attempt to introduce you to these two main aspects of comprehension skill development.

PROCESS COMPREHENSION

Process comprehension is that which is relative, open for question and not easily agreed upon in advance. In short, that type of comprehension which requires the reader to go beyond the level of recall and interpret questions on the basis of his experience.

Recall, if you will, the question: "Of the following four words, select the one word which you think does not belong with the other three:"

kitten	puppy	baby	cow

Following a product comprehension approach, the "correct" answer to this question is "cow." However, if we go beyond the level of recall and allow possible alternatives on the basis of experience and reason, other "correct" answers might be "baby" because the respondent was thinking biped as opposed to quadrupeds, etc. All answers are acceptable because they are based upon reason rather than mere recall.

Almost all comprehension lessons used by teachers are product type because the correct answer is known in advance. The process approach is different because there is no manual and the teacher is unable to control how the child will reason based on his experiences.

We would like to introduce several teaching strategies which would enable a teacher to utilize a process comprehension approach in the classroom. Simply stated, such strategies might be identified as:

Type I

    a.   multiple meanings of words
    b.   specific meanings of words
    c.   words which signal time
    d.   words which signal identity
    e.   words which signal author bias

Type II

    In addition to the five types of lessons listed above, we would also like to introduce one aspect of the cloze procedure which can be used as a process comprehension lesson.

The following paragraph about Ramon Magsaysay is representative of teaching material found in the classroom.

While the Type I strategies are confined to this paragraph, a teacher could use any paragraph at any level of reading difficulty to help develop process comprehension.

Read the paragraph below and the lesson related to the stated performance objective.

Following are the **Performance Objectives** related to **Process Comprehension** (Type I).

Given a paragraph the teacher will be able to:

    a.   Select five words which have multiple meanings and give at least two different meanings for each word.

b. Select three words which have specific meaning.
c. Select five words which indicate or "signal" time (tense: past, present, future).
d. Select five words which indicate or "signal" identity (pronoun).
e. Select five words which indicate or "signal" author bias (usually associated with propaganda techniques).

These, while not the full range of possible process type lessons, represent several teaching strategies for the development of comprehension skills using a process type approach.

RAMON MAGSAYSAY

"Why was Ramon Magsaysay, former president of the Philippines, recently honored on a United States postage stamp? America has always been the champion of liberty. From 1776 to the present day we have upheld the principles of freedom. Maysaysay was also a champion of liberty. He fought with us against the Japanese in the Second World War. He fought to drive communist guerilla forces out of his country, and he fought constantly against any form of totalitarianism. He wanted to help the Philippine people in every way, but most of all he wanted them to be free, to have liberty. We honor him on an American stamp as a defender of and fighter for freedom."

Select five words which have multiple meanings and give at least two different meanings for each word.

Example:

Present

1. a gift _____
2. here, in attendance _____

1. _____   1. _____
                            2. _____

2. _____   1. _____
                            2. _____

3. _____   1. _____
                            2. _____

4. _____   1. _____
                            2. _____

5. _____   1. _____
                            2. _____

37

It is not possible in a process approach to control the words you select or the multiple meanings you assigned, however, we can select several words that we would have chosen. Also, any word selected is neither "correct" nor "incorrect." It is a matter of comparing your results with some degree of group consensus.

Following are examples of words selected by a class of graduate students (N=50) in a reading methods course at Arizona State University during the second summer semester of 1972:

1. stamp:
   a. to place one's foot down
   b. postage

2. champion:
   a. fighter for a cause
   b. winner of an event

3. drive:
   a. to operate a motor vehicle
   b. to herd

4. country:
   a. nation, state
   b. rural area

5. liberty:
   a. freedom
   b. free time for a sailor

6. free:
   a. no charge
   b. state of being without restrictions

7. forces:
   a. pressures or weights
   b. a group of people

8. wanted:
   a. wished, desired
   b. hunted by the law

It is important that you understand that many words in our language have multiple meanings and when comprehending material the reader must select the *"appropriate"* meaning from among the possible alternatives.

Select three words which have specific meaning.

Example:

Ramon Magsaysay   <u>A person's name</u>

1. _____   _____

2. _____   _____

3. _____   _____

The specific words selected by the aforementioned graduate class at Arizona State University are:

1. Japanese: The people of Japan.
2. United States: A country in North America.
3. Philippines: A group of Islands in Southeast Asia.
4. Second World War: A specific war.
5. Totalitarianism: Rule by a dictatorship.

With lessons on multiple meanings and specific meaning, the learner will be able to analyze more adequately words in paragraphs and hopefully acquire two aspects of process comprehension; i.e., to recognize that some words have multiple meanings while other words have specific meaning.

Select five words which indicate or "signal" time (tense: past, present, future).

Example:

former

1. _____
2. _____
3. _____
4. _____
5. _____

The specific words selected by the graduate class at Arizona State University are:

1. former
2. present
3. always
4. recently
5. was
6. has
7. day
8. constantly
9. fought
10. wanted

With the lesson on time signals the learner would be able to analyze paragraphs for *"appropriate"* words that signal past, present, and future time relationships.

Select five words which indicate or "signal" identity (pronoun).

Example:

We

1. _____
2. _____
3. _____
4. _____
5. _____

The specific words selected by the graduate class at Arizona State University are:

1. he
2. we
3. his
4. them
5. him
6. us

With lessons on time and identity signals, the learner should then be able to better understand the settings (time-oriented) and characters (identity-oriented) of the materials he reads. One might raise the question that the learner had acquired these understandings during grammar/language arts lessons in a classroom. Therefore, it would be unnecessary to rename the lesson, i.e., time signals, when in fact we have called the identical lesson *verb tense*—past, present, and future.

The authors' reason for introducing "grammar" in this manner is that we believe most learners *do not* transfer lessons in grammar to their reading—comprehension development. That is, the learner acquires knowledge of grammatical structure in isolation and does not necessarily transfer these structures to the reading—comprehension development.

Select four words which indicate or "signal" author bias (usually associated with propaganda techniques).

Example:

Champion

1. _____ 3. _____
2. _____ 4. _____

The specific words selected by the graduate class at Arizona State University are:

1. champion
2. honor
3. totalitarianism
4. liberty
5. freedom
6. communist
7. always
8. defender
9. fighter
10. guerilla

With lessons on author bias the learner can become more critical of what he reads. The learner can also understand that anything that is set down in print is influenced by the subjectivity of the author.

Another type of process lesson is related to cloze procedure. Wilson L. Taylor generally is regarded as being the originator of the cloze procedure. His definition of cloze is "a method of intercepting a message from a 'transmitter' (writer or speaker), mutilating its language patterns by deleting parts, and so administering it to 'receivers' (readers and listeners) that their attempts to make the patterns whole again potentially yield a considerable number of cloze units."[1]

Simply, cloze procedure is carried out by deleting every *nth* word from a passage and replacing each deleted word with an underlined blank space of standard length. Subjects, who have not previously read the passages from which the cloze units are made, are given the units and instructed to figure out what word was taken from each space and write it in.

There are many variations on cloze procedure, e.g., some would argue that responses are scored correct when they exactly matched the deleted words; others that the deletions should be only noun verb deletions, etc. However, we have selected a procedure where every *fifth* word from a passage has been deleted, and the learner is asked to substitute *any* word he thinks will be appropriate for the deleted word.

Our purpose in suggesting this *one* variation is to help the learner utilize words from his experiential background which appear "*appropriate*," and allow him to think about the relationships of words and their meanings in the paragraphs.

The following paragraph about the surface of the moon is representative of teaching material found in the classroom!

While the Type II strategy (cloze procedure) is confined to this paragraph, a teacher could use any paragraph at any level of reading difficulty to help develop process comprehension.

1. Wilson L. Taylor, "Cloze Procedure: A New Tool for Measuring Readability," *Journalism Quarterly,* 30 (Fall, 1953), 415-33.

Read the paragraph below and the lesson related to the stated performance objective.

Following is the **Performance Objective** related to **Process Comprehension** (Type II):

Given a paragraph of approximately one-hundred words, with every fifth word deleted, the teacher will be able to supply the word deleted, or an appropriate synonym for each deleted word.

THE MOON

"The moon's surface is _____ pockmarked, looking as if _____ had been bombarded by _____ host of large celestial _____. And this is very _____ just what happened. At _____ time it was thought _____ the lunar craters were _____ volcanoes, but for the _____ reasons this now seems _____. Some of the craters _____ over a hundred miles _____, and the big ones _____ almost the same structure _____ the small ones. Terrestrial _____ craters, on the other _____, are only a few _____ across and do not _____ the same uniformity of _____. Besides, it is certain _____ volcanic activity on the _____ is quite negligible at _____ present time."

Supply the word deleted, or an appropriate synonym, for each deleted word. There are twenty-two deleted words in the paragraph.

Following are the exact deleted words and some appropriate synonyms selected by a class of graduate students (N=50) in a reading methods course at Arizona State University during the second summer semester of 1972.

Deleted Words	Appropriate Synonyms (ASU)
1. severely	1. extremely, very, quite, deeply, heavily, virtually, all, literally, completely, greatly, noticeably, highly, considerably, unusually, and badly
2. it	2. all responses = it
3. a	3. all responses = a
4. missiles	4. objects, bodies, masses, meteors, stones, bombs, rockets, planets, and rocks

Deleted Words	Appropriate Synonyms (ASU)
5. likely	5. nearly, probably, much, and possibly
6. one	6. the, that, some
7. that	7. all responses = that
8. extinct	8. old, actually, huge, large, inactive, small, dead, sunken, active, ancient, and dormant
9. following	9. above, obvious, evident, and geodetic
10. unlikely	10. false, outdated, untrue, wrong, improbable, impossible, obsolete, erroneous, illogical, incorrect, and inaccurate
11. are	11. stretch, measure, run, extend, range, and expand
12. across	12. wide, long, out, and horizontally
13. show	13. have, are, resemble, were, had, and possess
14. as	14. all responses = as
15. volcanic	15. type, and meteor
16. hand	16. all responses = hand
17. miles	17. kilometers
18. show	18. have, possess, display, exhibit and form
19. structure	19. size, shape, formation, and configuration
20. that	20. all responses = that
21. moon	21. all responses = moon
22. the	22. all responses = the

Following is another paragraph of approximately one-hundred words with every fifth word deleted. The **Performance Objective** for this exercise is that the teacher will be able to supply the word deleted, or an appropriate synonym for each deleted word.

ALEXANDRIA

"Alexandria is the one _____ of Alexander that has _____ to the present day. _____ or four other new _____, likewise adorned with his _____, perished in Asia, as _____ sons of his body _____; his wives and mother _____ all killed too. Gone _____ the boundary stone he _____ up on the Hydaspes _____ India to show posterity _____ far the first king _____ the Mediterranean had advanced. _____ Alexandria was not just _____ port on the Mediterranean _____ in harbors. It was _____ stroke of genius, a _____ form, the first modern _____ of the Old World, _____ at the same time _____ model of what harbors _____ to become."

Supply the word deleted, or an appropriate synonym, for each deleted word. There are 22 deleted words in the paragraph.

Following are the deleted words and some appropriate synonyms selected by a class of graduate students (N-50) in a reading methods course at the University of Missouri—Kansas City during the fall semester of 1972.

Deleted Words	Appropriate Synonyms (UMKC)
1. creation	1. monument, contribution, city achievement, accomplishment and providence
2. survived	2. remained, lived, lasted, existed, endured, stood, withstood, and persisted
3. three	3. all responses = three
4. cities	4. ports, harbors, monuments, communities, and towns
5. name	5. crown, title, symbol, crest, and emblem
6. the	6. all responses = the
7. did	7. had, perished, and died
8. were	8. all responses = were
9. is	9. was
10. set	10. put

11. in	11. all responses = in
12. how	12. all responses = how
13. of	13. all responses = of
14. but	14. port, however, Egyptian, so, this, now, great, certainly, for, and beautiful
15. another	15. all responses = another
16. abounding	16. rich, set, teeming, resplendent, and lined
17. a	17. all responses = a
18. new	18. perfect, innovative, creative, masterful, genuine, modern, model, super, planned, rare, true, and unique
19. city	19. port
20. and	20. while, functional, but, portraying
21. a	21. all responses = a
22. were	22. all responses = were

We could introduce additional process type lessons for the development of the comprehension skills. However, our purpose in presenting the above sample lessons is to ask the teacher to gain additional practice in understanding the central aspect of process comprehension, i.e., *the answers are relative and are based on the experiences of a given time.*

It is also believed that if the learner acquires this process he would be more likely to engage in the "guessing" strategy usually associated with product type comprehension. For without process—comparing one's ideas with another's—it seems almost impossible to learn to communicate with an author.

PRODUCT COMPREHENSION

Basically, product comprehension is that which is known, directly stated, or agreed upon in advance. In short, this type of comprehension requires the reader to answer questions on the basis of what the teacher and/or manual state are "correct answers."

Recall, if you will, the question posed in Chapter 3: "Of the following four words, select the one word which you think does not belong with other three:"

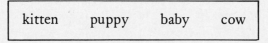

kitten	puppy	baby	cow

If you remember, the "correct" answer to this question is "cow." This approach to comprehension is what we are calling a product approach. We know in advance what the "correct" answer is. The learner has as his charge to guess what the teacher has been thinking about, or what it says in the teacher's manual.

We would like to introduce the teacher to several teaching strategies which would enable the teacher to utilize a product comprehension approach in the classroom. Simply stated, such strategies might be identified as:

a. Finding the main idea.
b. Finding related details.
c. Finding the sequence.

The following paragraph **New Shoes** is representative of teaching material found in the classroom.

NEW SHOES

"The old bus bumped and jerked down a long hill. Ed held tightly to his seat, but he was not thinking of the rough ride. He was dreaming of a pair of shoes, one for his left foot and one for his right foot—a pair he did not have to share with his brother Frank."

Read the paragraph above and do the lesson related to the stated performance objective.

Following are the **Performance Objectives** related to **Product Comprehension**: Given several paragraphs the teacher will be able to:

a. Select the author's main idea.
b. Select at least two specific facts or details related to these main ideas.
c. Organize ideas or details in a specific sequence.

These, while not the full range of possible product type lessons, represent several teaching strategies for the development of comprehension skills using a product type approach.

Select the author's main idea.

_____ The bus gave the boys a rough ride.

_____ Ed and Frank shared one pair of shoes.

_____ Ed wanted a pair of shoes of his own.

The correct main idea, according to the author and the manual, is that Ed wanted a pair of shoes of his own. This is the manner in which comprehension is developed in most published reading programs. That is, the reader is asked to read a specified amount of material. He is given a specified number of alternatives, and then is required to select the appropriate alternative according to a fixed response.

46

Select at least two specific facts or details related to the author's main idea.

1. What were the boys riding on?_____

2. What was Ed dreaming of?_____

The correct answer to question 1, according to the author and the manual, is that the boys were riding on a bus. The correct answer to question 2, according to the author and the manual, is that Ed was dreaming of a pair of shoes.

Organize the following ideas or details in the sequence in which they occurred in the story.

1. Ed was dreaming of a pair of shoes.
2. The bus bumped and jerked.
3. Ed has a brother named Frank.
4. Ed held tightly to his seat.

The correct sequence in which the above listed details occurred in the story, according to the author and the manual, is 2, 1, 4, 3. Be aware that there are other sequence alternatives. For example, #2 and #4 occurred at the point in time of the story; #1 occurred throughout the story and #3 occurred before, during, and after all the others.

Now, read the following paragraph **Mr. Revere**, and do the lesson related to the stated performance objective.

MR. REVERE

"Every few days some grinning countryman would appear at the kitchen door bearing a heavy basket of vegetables, fruit, or eggs; sometimes a chicken or two or a leg of mutton. They were all former soldiers of the King, all still eager to express their gratitude to Mr. Revere and his family. They were all staunch Patriots. Most of them had joined the Colonial Militia, where their training made them most valuable. Enoch Sawtell the shepherd was now a Sergeant."

Select the author's main idea.

_____The soldiers expressed their gratitude to Mr. Revere.

_____The countrymen brought eggs and meat.

_____Enoch Sawtell joined the colonials.

Select at least two specific facts or details related to the author's main idea.

1. What did Enoch Sawtell do before becoming a Sergeant?_____
_____

2. What did most of the men join?_____

Organize the following ideas or details in the sequence in which they occurred in the story.

1. The men brought food to Mr. Revere.
2. Enoch Sawtell was now a Sergeant.
3. The men came to the kitchen door.
4. Most of the men joined the Colonial Militia.

Following are correct answers according to the author and the manual.

Main Idea:	The soldiers expressed their gratitude to Mr. Revere
Related Details:	1. he was a shepherd
	2. the Colonial Militia
Organizing Sequence:	3, 1, 4, 2

From the three types of product lessons you will note that in every case the learner was asked to read a specified amount of material, and then select an appropriate alternative according to the author and/or the manual. The burden for selecting the appropriate alternative (correct answer) is placed exclusively on the learner. Under a product comprehension approach, the learner has no way of knowing how others arrived at their answers or what process was employed to select the appropriate response.

Our major constructs for this chapter are:

1. *The development of comprehension skills requires a balance between process and product approaches.*
2. *The teacher's ability to recognize when either a process approach or a product approach is possible.*

Given these two main constructs let's take exactly the same reading material used to find the author's main idea and develop it using a process orientation, i.e., to help the learner know how others arrive at an appropriate response.

NEW SHOES

"The old bus bumped and jerked down a long hill. Ed held tightly to his seat, but he was not thinking of the rough ride. He was dreaming of a pair of shoes, one for his left foot and one for his right foot—a pair he did not have to share with his brother Frank."

You will recall that the main idea of this paragraph is that Ed wanted a pair of shoes of his own. The teacher could now switch from a product approach to a process approach by merely helping the learner to recognize how others arrived at the appropriate response. For example, the paragraph stated that Ed was dreaming of a pair of shoes; that he wanted one shoe for each foot; and that he did not want to share them with his brother. Taken together, one might conclude that the main idea is that he wanted a pair of shoes of his own.

Following is an example of a balance between a product and process approach to comprehension development for finding the main idea.

"Ed worked for the baker, stacking big pieces of wood near the oven. But the baker did not give him money—he gave Ed two loaves of bread as his pay. The druggist would not give Ed a job. The grocer would not trust him to take a box of apples to sell—he wanted a deposit."

(This is an example with all the blanks filled in.)

Select the author's main idea.

Product	Process
1. The main idea according to the author and the manual is: *Ed tried, but he could not earn money.*	1. Ed worked for the baker, but he got paid with bread—no money. 2. Ed tried for a job with the druggist but the druggist would not give him a job. 3. Ed tried to sell apples, but the grocer would not trust him.

For additional practice on your ability to determine product and process comprehension, read the paragraph below and do the exercises.

FARMING IN MEXICO

"Only about one fourth of the land in Mexico is really good for farming. The mountains with steep slopes make much of the land difficult to farm. Most of the tools, which the people must use for working the land, are awkward and slow. We can raise large crops in our country because the machines do most of the work, and because much of the land is flat. Many areas in Mexico, which are now used for grazing cattle, could be used for farming if there were more rainfall."

Select the author's main idea.

Product	Process
____ The U.S. has large plains	1.
____ Farming is difficult in Mexico	2.
____ Mexico needs more rain	3. etc. . . .

Following are the correct responses according to the author and the manual and some appropriate items selected by the authors of this text.

Product	Process
✓ Farming is difficult in Mexico	1. Only one-fourth of the land in Mexico suitable for farming.
	2. Much of the land mountainous with steep slopes.
	3. Lack of modern farming tools and machines.
	4. Lack of adequate rainfall.

Organizing the complex area of Comprehension is an extremely difficult task. In this Chapter, we have attempted to develop an organization scheme which we have elected to call Product and Process comprehension. Basically, **Product Comprehension** is that which is known, directly stated or agreed upon in advance. In short, this type of comprehension requires the reader to answer questions on the basis of what the teacher and/or manual state are "correct" answers.

Process Comprehension is that which is relative, open for question and not easily agreed upon in advance. In short, that type of comprehension which requires the reader to go beyond the level of recall and interpret questions on the basis of his experience.

Another distinction between these two areas is that **Product** type questions tend to be single "correct" or "incorrect" responses as determined by teacher or manual. **Process** type questions have no real "correct" or "incorrect" responses, they are "correct" only if the reader can defend them in terms of his reasoning and experience.

The first major construct basic to this chapter is: *the development of comprehension skills requires a balance between the process and product approaches.* That is, there must be a balance between the development of those comprehension skills that are structured in anticipation of one "correct" answer (Product), and the development of those comprehension skills structured so as to admit a variety of answers and stimulate further questioning and supposition (Process).

Since process comprehension and product comprehension are teaching strategies, it is essential that the teacher develop the ability to recognize when either approach is possible. Thus, the second major construct basic to this chapter is: *the teacher has the ability to recognize when either a process approach or a product approach is possible.*

REFERENCES FOR CHAPTERS 3 AND 4

Bush, Clifford L., and Mildred H. Huebner. *Strategies for Reading in the Elementary School.* London: The Macmillan Company, 1970.

See: Chapters 5 and 6 (pp. 95-158) "Comprehension: Basic Factors," and "Comprehension: Skills." Stresses the importance of high-level reading comprehension and through the procedures of task analysis shows how the teacher can structure the type of lesson that will ensure efficient performance for each learner.

Carter, Homer L.J., and Dorothy J. McGinnis. *Diagnosis and Treatment of the Disabled Reader.* London: The Macmillan Company, 1970.

See: Chapter 13 (pp. 233-261) "Treatment of Individuals Who Have Difficulty in Reading for Meaning." Discusses a hierarchy of skills ranging from sentence reading to reading in math, science, social studies, and literature.

Developing Comprehension—Including Critical Reading. Reprinted from publications of the International Reading Association, Newark, Delware, 1968.

A valuable source of articles dealing with comprehension skills compiled by Mildred A. Dawson.

Durr, William K. (editor). *Reading Instruction: Dimensions and Issues.* Boston: Houghton Mifflin Company, 1967.

See: Section 5 (pp. 126-143) "Improving Comprehension." Olive S. Niles' article *Comprehension Skills,* is must reading.

Harris, Albert J., and Edward R. Sipay. *Effective Teaching of Reading.* New York: David McKay Co., Inc., 1971.

See: Chapter 11 (pp. 294-332) "Developing Comprehension Reading." Ten different kinds of comprehension skills are discussed and ways of developing them are described.

Harris, Larry A., and Carl B. Smith. *Reading Instruction Through Diagnostic Teaching.* New York: Holt, Rinehart and Winston, Inc., 1972.

See: Chapter 11 (pp. 238-280) "Reading Comprehension." Discusses four components of reading comprehension: thinking skills, background experience, language skills, and purposes for reading.

Jones, Daisy Marvel. *Teaching Children to Read.* New York: Harper & Row, Publishers, 1971.

See: Chapter 10 (pp. 173-192) "Comprehension." Emphasizes that an adequate background of understanding is necessary for comprehension of material to be read.

McKee, Paul. *Reading: A Program of Instruction for the Elementary School.* New York: Houghton Mifflin Company, 1966.

See: Chapters 8, 9, and 10 (pp. 254-404) "Coping with Meaning Difficulties," "Studying Informative Material" and "Critical Reading." A very thorough discourse on the subject of reading comprehension.

May, Frank B. *To Help Children Read.* Columbus, Ohio: Charles E. Merrill Publishing Company, 1973.

> *See:* Module 6 (pp. 193-227) "Developing Children's Reading Comprehension and Thinking Skills." Guides the reader by means of performance objectives to help develop comprehension skills.

Russell, David H. *The Dynamics of Reading.* Waltham, Massachusetts: Ginn—Blaisdell, 1970.

> *See:* Chapter 7 (pp. 151-177) "Comprehension: Literal and Interpretive." Discusses the nature of meaning and understanding.

Stauffer, Russell G. *Teaching Reading As A Thinking Process.* New York: Harper & Row, Publishers, 1969.

> *See:* Chapter 10 (pp. 374-396) "Concept Development." Presents the theory that the reader's level of conceptual development and his cognitive functioning determines what he will get (or expects to get) from what he reads.

Strang, Ruth, Constance M. McCullough and Arthur E. Traxler. *The Improvement of Reading.* New York: McGraw-Hill Book Company, 1967.

> *See:* Chapter 6 (pp. 212-263) "Teaching Basic Reading Skills." Of particular interest is the section dealing with the teaching of vocabulary.

Tinker, Miles A., and Constance M. McCullough. *Teaching Elementary Reading.* New York: Appleton-Century-Crofts, 1968.

> *See:* Chapter 9 (pp. 185-203) "Comprehension and Interpretation." Discusses how reading comprehension should equal, or even exceed, what is comprehended through listening.

Wallen, Carl J. *Competency in Teaching Reading.* Chicago: Science Research Associates Inc., 1972.

> *See:* Chapter 16 (pp. 412-436) "Teaching Strategies for Paragraph-Meaning Skills." Provides the teacher with simulation practice for paragraph-meaning skills.

Wilson, Robert M. *Diagnostic and Remedial Reading for Classroom and Clinic.* Columbus, Ohio: Charles E. Merrill Publishing Company, 1967.

> *See:* Chapter 8 (pp. 157-188) "Remediation of Comprehension Difficulties." Discusses remedial techniques and some pitfalls of remediation.

Zintz, Miles V. *The Reading Process.* Dubuque, Iowa: Wm. C. Brown Company Publishers, 1970.

> *See:* Chapter 8 (pp. 180-210) "Comprehension Skills." Presents an outline of comprehension skills and illustrative exercises for teaching the skills of comprehension.

chapter 5

SUMMARY: BASIC TEACHER SKILLS

In his recent book, *Understanding Reading,* Frank Smith emphasizes a concept which serves as an excellent summary for the first four chapters of this book. He states, "Information is the reduction of uncertainty."[1] This concept suggests that if we use consistent terminology and/or terminology which is consistent with the materials we use during instruction, we are likely to reduce the learner's uncertainty. When attempting to teach a child to read, or when attempting to train a teacher to teach reading, to what extent do we in Reading Education or Educational Psychology honestly attempt to reduce the learner's uncertainty?

Even in a reading course designed to reduce your uncertainty about Reading Education we are forced to use multiple words to describe the basic process of word recognition. For example, in Chapters 1 and 2, we interchanged the following terms to describe what we believe the reader does when recognizing words:

Word Recognition
Decoding
Sounding-Out
Word Analysis
Word Attack
Phonics or Phonetic Analysis
Whole Word Approach
Generalization Learning
Part Word Approach
Discrimination Learning

We use these terms because we are unable to agree upon the actual word recognition process. Unfortunately, we are likely to confuse rather than inform you when we use all the above terms.

If you accept the fact that not enough is known about what humans actually do when reacting to printed symbols (words), and that Reading Education will continue to interchange terms and Educational Psychology will continue to study isolated aspects of learning, you might be able to develop your own perceptions about what

1. Frank Smith, *Understanding Reading* (Holt, Rinehart and Winston, Inc., 1971), p. 16.

readers do in the process of word recognition. It appears to be more helpful in this stage of your training to carefully consider the word recognition process you used to interpret the unknown word **ORINOCO**. We believe that you followed this construct during that process:

> *The ability to hold the whole word and simultaneously attend to the parts within the word.*

In dealing with the implications of this construct, we attempted to teach you a minimal number of phonetically oriented descriptive parts of words (Chapter 2). This leads to another construct:

> *"Readiness"*
> *Consonants*
> *Vowels*
> *Structure-Syllables*

In addition to providing you with a minimal number of descriptive word parts, we suggested some ways in which word recognition lessons might be presented in a class-room.

The essential idea to be learned, however, is that the teacher must be willing to make instructional decisions in order to reduce the uncertainty for the learner. Imagine the dilemma children are likely to have if their teacher is systematically "covering" the word recognition portion of the required reading program, without ever deciding to eliminate obscure descriptive parts of words or emphasizing descriptive parts within the "readiness," consonant, vowel, structure-syllable construct. In addition to this "robot like" lesson-by-lesson approach, the terms used to describe these various word parts in required programs are likely to be different in supplementary readers, e.g., "phonic rule charts," weekly news-type supplemental materials, etc. As a teacher you can reduce the child's uncertainty if you are willing to present fewer word parts and keep what is presented consistent.

At this point you need to ask, "Do I conceptualize what the learner has to learn to do when recognizing words? Do I know a minimum number of descriptive parts of words? Am I willing to make essential instructional decisions and thereby reduce the learner's uncertainty in learning to recognize words?"

We were again forced to use multiple words in attempting to present our constructs in Chapters 3 and 4:

> Comprehension Development
> Meaning
> Understanding
> Product Comprehension
> Process Comprehension

As background for the area of comprehension development (or any word you might use) we emphasized the belief that it is impossible for comprehension to occur without adequate language development. We again offer these constructs:

Language symbolizes our world of experience.
Print symbolizes our language.

Despite the fact that these constructs appear logical, many of our schools continue to ignore them. For example, a child who speaks and listens in a language other than English is usually required to read and write English, rather than be given an opportunity to learn to speak and listen in English. When schools engage in this practice, they are requiring nonspeakers of English to associate a secondary system— **Print** (in almost all cases **English Print**) with a different primary system—**Language** (depending on the learner, Spanish, Navajo, etc.). A survey of children who speak a language other than English will quickly reveal a disproportionate number of reading disability cases. In short, before presenting English print to children we need to be certain they speak English at a reasonable level.

If a child speaks and listens in English (primary system) he has a reasonable chance of being successful in learning to read and write in English (secondary system).

Another background area for comprehension development, or whatever you choose to call it, is the child's need for adequate experience. Since language and experience appear to be so closely related, we can apply quite similar ideas. That is, unless the learner has some direct or indirect experience with the selection he is reading, he is not able to really comprehend the words he calls from the printed page.

We can reduce the learner's uncertainty about the meaning of print if we are willing to provide him with adequate experiences. Let's assume again that the teacher is "covering" all of the text materials assigned to her grade level. This "covering tendency" usually takes the form of a textbook for reading, math, social studies, spelling, language, and science. The total pages in these books are likely to add up to over 1,000 of printed material. We believe that it is not possible for any teacher to provide the essential experiences and concepts related to all of this text material. Therefore, for improved comprehension and less student uncertainty about what is actually read, we recommend that the teachers and students become extremely selective regarding the amount of material introduced in the classroom. What is selected should be presented as completely as possible, and adequate time should be given to each presentation. In developing the learner's ability to comprehend, it is important that words are not merely recognized as meaningless ends in themselves, but as reorganizations of the learner's experience and conceptual structure.

In Chapter 4 we presented two constructs:

The development of comprehension skills requires a balance between process and product approaches.

The teacher has the ability to recognize when either a process approach or a product approach is possible.

We're urging a balance between process and product approaches because process lessons tend to provide the learner with more feedback than traditional product lessons. For example, in a product approach the learner is asked to read material and answer questions. In turn, he marks his answers, correct or incorrect, according to the answer guide. If he marks the "incorrect" answer, the feedback he receives is that his answer is wrong and he loses credit. In a process approach responses are discussed, the learner is required to evaluate the adequacy of those responses, and, in turn, learn why certain responses were given.

We believe that if the teacher has the ability to balance these approaches, the learner will acquire sufficient feedback to handle traditional product oriented comprehension questions.

Note again our emphasis on the teacher as an instructional decision maker. Very few reading materials in schools today utilize a process approach. But it is quite easy for teachers to turn product type questions into process types by merely withholding the "correct or incorrect answer" and discussing a wide variety of possible alternatives.

Our experience suggests that most children will not automatically engage in a process approach. They are not accustomed to searching for alternatives or know how to ask essential questions. This approach will need considerable development by classroom teachers.

In the final part of this summary chapter we would like to explore this question:

What am I, the teacher, really attempting to accomplish when I present word recognition and comprehension lessons to children?

We'll attempt to answer this basic question by presenting a diagram in three separate parts.

Part I

LANGUAGE (Speaking-Listening) SYSTEM

The learner comes to school with an acquired language (speaking-listening) system. This system contains the basic sounds, sentence structures and meanings essential for communication with others.

Scientists are not in agreement as to how this language is acquired, how it develops, or exactly what it contains. However, we are all able to observe that the phenomenon of language does occur.

Part II

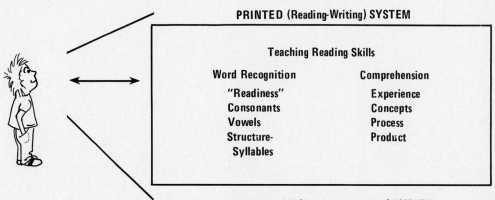

PRINTED (Reading-Writing) SYSTEM

LANGUAGE (Speaking-Listening) SYSTEM

Schools have been assigned the responsibility of helping the child acquire a Printed (reading-writing) System. This system contains graphic representations (letters-words) of the sounds, sentence structures, and meanings used to communicate in print. As in language, the learner must acquire the phenomena of communicating in print if he is to learn to read and write.

Part III

Now for the question:

What am I, the teacher, really attempting to accomplish when I present word recognition and comprehension lessons to children?

PRINTED (Reading-Writing) SYSTEM

Teaching Reading Skills

Word Recognition	Comprehension
"Readiness"	Experience
Consonants	Concepts
Vowels	Process
Structure-	Product
Syllables	

LANGUAGE (Speaking-Listening) SYSTEM

By encountering consistent skill lessons in both the word recognition and comprehension areas, the learner should grasp the relationship between his acquired Language (speaking-listening) System and the existing Printed (reading-writing) System. We are hoping that at some point he will discover what a six year old discovered when she said: "Hey! Reading is only talk written down."

How teachers present simplified basic skill lessons is obviously an individual matter. We hope that the information presented in the preceding chapters provided a series of starting ideas. Stated another way, this information should help teachers make instructional decisions in the reading program.

As authors, we recognize the complexities involved in every aspect of Reading Education. However, we were willing to make these arbitrary judgments, presented in the form of constructs, to give teachers specific points of reference in the decision-making process. If these arbitrary judgments are accepted, fine. If not, then we can assume that teachers have considered other alternatives for helping the learner acquire the relationship between his language system and the system of print.

CLASSROOM APPLICATIONS

chapter 6

EVALUATION IN READING

Reading Achievement Tests. Standard school practice utilizes group reading achievement tests to measure a student's reading ability. This kind of measurement can be identified as *classification* testing. The results tend to classify the student according to a global reading achievement level which is frequently interpreted as the student's instructional reading level. On the other hand, an informal reading inventory takes the form of *diagnostic* testing and attempts to detect the student's specific reading abilities.

Global reading achievement scores on standardized group reading achievement tests are used to classify students of comparable ages or grade groups according to above average, average, and below average reading ability. However, results from these kinds of tests do not provide classroom teachers with the information necessary to establish an *independent* and *instructional*[1] reading program for the student. Therefore, if the classroom teacher does not have information regarding the student's specific reading needs, it becomes impossible to determine the types of instructional programs best suited for each student.

Therefore, let us introduce the main construct for this section—Construct: *group reading achievement tests only classify students and compare groups—they do not diagnose.*

Group reading achievement tests may be part of a total battery of tests that deal with math, social studies, science, language arts, etc. On the other hand, group reading achievement tests may deal only with reading achievement, per se. In any case, group reading achievement tests attempt to measure reading achievement in two primary areas. One area is word recognition. The other area is comprehension.

Many of these group reading achievement tests include subsections dealing with visual discrimination, or different kinds of letter recognition. These subsections, however, come under the word recognition category. There are also subsections labeled vocabulary, but vocabulary comes under the comprehension category.

Group reading achievement tests are administered in approximately 95% of American schools. One problem here is the misunderstanding of the function and purpose of these tests. Basically, group reading achievement tests are designed to

---

1. For a definition of the terms "independent" and "instructional," see page 68.

compare groups. Unfortunately, teachers, administrators, and parents use them in individual comparisons as well.

Imagine, if you will, all the fifth grade classes in your school district. School X's fifth grade reading achievement can be compared to school Y's fifth grade reading achievement by use of one of the many group reading achievement tests. From this we can determine if a particular fifth grade class is at, above, or below the norm established for fifth grade students. But such a procedure cannot help us to determine an individual student's competence.

As a hypothetical example, let us invent a youngster we shall call Ira. Ira is a fifth grade student who is a nonreader. Today, Ira is going to take a group reading achievement test designed for grades fourth, fifth, and sixth. We might take special precautions so that Ira won't accidentally do well on the test. Even though we are sure that he is a nonreader, we will blindfold him. Then we will guide Ira so that he can make random marks on the test answer sheet. What would you predict Ira's reading achievement score to be once we have graded his answer sheet? Did you predict that Ira's score would be zero? After all, he is a nonreader. We also know that he is blindfolded and marking his answer sheet at random. But wait a minute! Would Ira's score be zero?

Following is the scoring profile for a group reading achievement test designed for fourth- fifth- and sixth-grade students.

	Sample Test Result								
Items Correct →	25	40	50	65	80	90	105	115	120
Grade Placement	2.0*	3.0	4.0	5.0	6.0	7.0		8.0	

*2.0 is the lowest possible grade placement

By inspection, we can see that Ira would be assigned a reading achievement score of 2.0. That is, we can take this to mean that Ira is reading as well as the students in the sample population who had a score of 2.0—students reading two years, no months, in terms of reading achievement. Simply stated, Ira is supposedly doing as well as a second grader even though we *know* him to be a nonreader. The reason Ira has a grade equivalency score of 2.0 is that this particular test does not go any lower. Ira's grade equivalency score of 2.0 represents the floor, or base, of this test.

The example of a student taking a test blindfolded is an absurd one used to dramatize our point. However, let us now assume that Ira, a nonreader, is taking the test without being blindfolded. Let us also assume that Ira as a fifth grade student has had some previous experience in taking group achievement tests, reading or other kinds. This particular test has 120 test items. Statistically, Ira is bound to make some correct responses in taking this test. If he scores 45 items as correct out of the total 120 items, this would now give him a grade equivalency score of 2.9. That is, he starts with a grade equivalency score of 2.0 for the floor, or base; and if you add the 45 correct responses for guessing to this floor of 2.0, you now arrive at a total grade equivalency score of 2.9. This means that Ira is reading as well as the sample population of two years, nine months—or almost as well as a third grader.

Keep in mind that Ira is a nonreader. The conscientious teacher then looks at Ira's grade equivalency score of 2.9, and says to the librarian: "Give me a few books with a low third grade or upper second grade readability level because Ira has difficulty reading."

The teacher presents these books to Ira. Ira looks at these books and exclaims, "I can't read them!" At this point, our conscientious teacher throws up his hands in dismay and wonders, "What in the world am I going to do now? Ira can't even measure up to what he did on the test!"

This is an obvious problem and teachers must be sensitive to the floors built into group reading achievement tests.

What is more frustrating is that Ira will show a major gain in reading despite the fact that he may not have had any additional reading assistance. This will occur when

Ira gets to seventh grade. At this point he will show a massive leap ahead in reading achievement because at this level the floor of the test has been raised to 4.0. So Ira will show a gain in reading achievement not because his reading skills have improved, but because the group reading achievement test has bumped him along. Again, if we add some correct responses for guessing, Ira, by the time he is in junior high, will show a grade equivalency score to indicate that he is doing as well as a fifth grader. And Ira may still be a nonreader! Consequently, it is very important that teachers be aware of the meaning and limitations of group reading achievement test scores.

Whereas Ira, a nonreader, was scored as a low level reader, the reverse situation can also occur. For example, consider the possible results of a test which has a ceiling, or a top. On this test, a student has to have 120 correct responses out of a possible 120 to achieve a grade equivalency score of 8.0. If he misses a mere 15 items (he only has about 35 minutes to complete the test), his grade equivalency score will plummet to 6.0.

The point in this discussion is that these tests, *at best,* classify. They classify a student as high, average, or low. Beyond classification, group reading achievement tests cannot give the teacher any information regarding the achievement level of a particular, individual student. The group reading achievement test cannot tell the teacher whether Ira's grade equivalency score of 2.9 indicates that he could independently read "hard" second grade material, that he needs instruction at the second grade level or that he is frustrated with second grade material.

There are other misconceptions regarding group reading achievement tests. For example, Brian comes to school in September. Brian has a grade equivalency score of 5.4 in reading achievement. By the end of the school year in May, Brian has a grade equivalency of 5.7. Brian's teacher may be inclined to think, "Well, it isn't much, but at least he has gained three months!" This gain, however slight, may satisfy the teacher and give her something positive to report to Brian's parents.

Now, let's have Brian come at this in another way. He comes to school in September. Brian has a grade equivalency score of 5.7 in reading achievement. By the end of the school year in May, Brian has a grade equivalency of 5.4. Did Brian *lose* three months? No! All that the difference of three months indicates, whether plus or minus, is what is called the error of measurement. Differences so slight, as in Brian's case, are the result of chance and are nonsignificant.

The problem that teachers face is that quite often they are at a loss to explain how Brian could lose three months after putting in a year of work. Unless the student has shown a difference, plus or minus, of six months, the teacher should not be concerned about interpreting the score. To insure that Brian did, in fact, make some growth in reading achievement, the teacher should look for a change of six months or more in his grade equivalency score. And then only after she has checked to see that this gain is not accounted for by the fact that the floor, or base, of the test had come up.

64

Another problem with group reading achievement tests is the question of whether or not they are diagnostic.

Following is a group reading achievement test with a series of items purporting to be diagnostic.

Sample: Analysis of Reading Achievement

Decoding

1. *Form*

    1-15 Lower case letters
    16-19 Upper case letters
    20-25 Various type faces

2. *Phonics*

    1-15 Consonants
    16-25 Vowels

3. Etc.

The youngster is required to look at each item and then decide whether the two words presented are the same or different. He is instructed to mark an S for same, and a D for different. If he scores correctly on items 1 through 15, we assume that he knows the lower case letters of the alphabet. If the student scores correctly on items

16 through 19, we assume that he knows the upper case letters of the alphabet. Finally, if the student scores correctly on items 20 through 25, we assume that he knows various type faces. But do we really know this?

The student has three minutes to respond to those items. If the student is a slow worker and completes only the first fifteen items, which we will assume he scored correctly, does that mean that he doesn't know his upper case letters—items 16 through 19? Or does it mean that *time* ran out on him?

It is fortunate, however, that very few teachers ever use group reading achievement tests in an attempt to describe what would be called a *diagnostic* interpretation of a student's reading. The only thing that group reading achievement tests can do is compare groups and classify students as either high, average, or low in respect to their reading achievement. Beyond that—comparison and classification—it is virtually impossible for group reading achievement tests to do anything else.

When the time comes for teachers to report students' progress to parents, extreme caution should be taken when discussing grade equivalency scores. We have seen situations where parents have come to a parent-teacher conference and said, "Last year, Scott had 4.3 on his reading test. What did he get this year?" The parents actually record these grade equivalency scores and refer to them from year to year.

We urge teachers and administrators to observe extreme caution in giving out grade equivalency scores. It would be much better to talk to parents in terms of above average, slightly above average, outstanding—words such as this rather than the actual score.

As teachers, if you have ever heard, at one time or another, your own youngster's I.Q. score or reading achievement score, it would be a safe bet that you still recall that score no matter how long ago it was reported to you. These scores that we deal with have a tremendous impact on each of us as human beings. When reporting scores to parents, remember that they are very sensitive to numbers. Moreover, we really aren't sure what these numbers mean. A good rule to follow is to try to avoid numbers in all cases.

Before moving on to the next section in this chapter let us restate the main construct introduced at the outset—Construct: *group reading achievement tests only classify students and compare groups—they do not diagnose.*

Informal Reading Inventories: As noted above, group reading achievement tests rate a particular student's performance *as compared* to the performance of other students. The informal reading inventory, however, rates a particular student's performance in reading without comparing him to what other students do. It is specifically designed to determine how well that particular student can read.

The most important question a teacher has to answer about a student's reading is: "How difficult a book can this child read?" The answer to this important question depends not only on the classification of pupils into instructional groups (below average, average, or above average), which is determined by the group reading achievement tests, but also on the choice of basal reader and supplementary reading material. If reading instruction has as its goal helping a student improve his reading performance, instruction must start at the particular student's present instructional level. The main purpose of the informal reading inventory, therefore, is to find the correct level for instruction.

An informal reading inventory is an unconventional way of appraising certain abilities and skills. The word *informal* may be confusing. *Informal* means that the testing is nonstandardized in the usual sense of test construction and administration. In the use of informal reading inventories no attempt is made to administer and score them under standardized conditions. However, *informal* does not mean that the scoring is subjective. Standards and procedures for testing with an informal reading inventory have been determined. Nevertheless, no norms have been predetermined for one student's performance to be compared with what other students can do. A student's ability is judged against the material in the test rather than compared with what the majority of children might do if presented with the same task.

An informal reading inventory, therefore, gives the teacher the opportunity to evaluate a student's actual reading behavior as he deals with material of varying difficulty.

Most informal reading inventories are composed of two main parts. Part I is comprised of graded word lists, and Part II is comprised of graded oral paragraphs. The words and oral paragraphs are generally similar to the type of reading material found in various grade levels throughout school. The paragraphs selected are evaluated for their readability level.

Some teachers prefer to make their own informal reading inventories from basal readers. Other teachers prefer to use informal reading inventories prepared by various publishing companies. In either case, informal reading inventories are used to determine the student's independent reading level, instructional level, frustration level, and hearing capacity level. We discuss the meaning and criteria for each of these levels later in this chapter.

Betts has shown that several levels of reading competence should be identified.[2] The teacher using an informal reading inventory can identify the level at which the student can read independently, the point at which he can profit from instruction, the level where he experiences total frustration, and the student's level of hearing comprehension. It is important to know the level of material the student can handle easily when working on his own because a great deal of a student's school work is done on an independent basis. Unless the student is provided with material at the proper level, he cannot reasonably be expected to do a satisfactory job in independent work. All instructional tasks must be provided at a level where the student is challenged to learn and, at the same time, exhibits the readiness for such learning. This means that the

2. Emmett A. Betts, *Foundations of Reading Instruction* (New York: American Book Company, 1946), Chapter 21.

student must be able to assimilate the material presented. On the other hand, to instruct the student in material which he can handle on his own would serve no real purpose.

Another purpose for administering an informal reading inventory is the diagnosis of the student's specific strengths and weaknesses in terms of word recognition and comprehension. Only in terms of such evaluation of specific word recognition and comprehension skills of the student can an appropriate instructional program be formulated and implemented. Teaching at the right level is only part of the task. An instructional program must also be geared toward the removal of any specific weaknesses that exist.

Criteria for Levels

1. *Independent Level:* The independent reading level is the highest level at which a student can read easily and fluently without any help from the teacher, parents, etc., with almost no word recognition errors (word recognition = 99%) and very good comprehension (comprehension=90%). That is, at the independent level, the student (on the average) makes only *one* word recognition error per every 100 running words of the story, and his comprehension and recall are 90% accurate or better.

Attention to the independent level is very important. Books selected for the student's own library should be at his independent level. Reference material to be read in order to complete an assignment should be at the independent level. Homework should also be assigned at this level. It is through wide reading at the independent level that the student has the opportunity to bring his reading ability to the point where it will provide him with genuine satisfaction.

2. *Instructional Level:* The instructional reading level is the highest level at which a student can do satisfactory reading with help from a teacher. Word recognition errors are not excessive (word recognition = 95%) and comprehension is satisfactory (comprehension = 75%). That is, at the instructional level, the student (on the average) makes only *five* word recognition errors per every 100 running words of the story, and his comprehension and recall are 75% accurate or better.

It is in guided work at the instructional level that the student will have ample opportunity to establish new word recognition and comprehension skills. It is essential, therefore, that the teacher know each student's instructional level.

3. *Frustration Level:* The frustration level is the lowest level at which the student's reading skills break down. Word recognition errors are numerous (word recognition = 90% or less) and comprehension is faulty (comprehension = 50% or less). That is, at the frustration level, the student (on the average) is making one word recognition error for every ten running words in the story, and his comprehension and recall are only half or less. Awareness of the frustration level can give the teacher some idea about the kinds of material to avoid for a particular student's program.

4. *Hearing Capacity Level:* The hearing capacity level is the highest level at which the student can satisfactorily understand material when it is read to him (comprehension = 75% or better). That is, at the hearing capacity level, the student is able to understand the meaning of material read to him.

The hearing capacity level gives the teacher an indication of the level at which the child should be reading. The aim of the teacher of reading, therefore, is equivalence of the instructional and the hearing capacity levels.

The construct for this section is as follows: Construct: *Informal Reading Inventories distinguish the several levels of reading competence, and they are diagnostic.* They are designed to enable the teacher to understand each student's achievement level and to indicate the next level to which he is ready to be introduced.

Classroom Reading Inventory: [3] For the purpose of clarification, let us state at the outset that the Classroom Reading Inventory is an informal reading inventory. It is called Classroom Reading Inventory to distinguish it from all other published informal reading inventories.

Elsewhere in this chapter, we indicated that standard school practice utilizes group reading achievement tests to measure student's reading ability. This approach toward measurement might be identified as *classification* testing. The results tend to classify the student according to a global reading achievement level which is frequently interpreted as the student's instructional reading level. An informal (or classroom) reading inventory takes the form of *diagnostic* testing and attempts to detect the student's specific reading abilities.

The differences between classification and diagnostic testing can be illustrated by the reading performance of two fifth grade boys, Roger and Flip. Both boys were reading below the average of their fifth grade class.

Both Roger and Flip had taken a group reading achievement test prior to an administration of the Classroom Reading Inventory. The results of the group reading achievement test are as follows:

1. Roger—Chronological age = 11 years, 5 months—group reading achievement test score = 4.1 (fourth grade, one-month level).

2. Flip—Chronlogical age = 10 years, 10 months—group reading achievement test score = 4.3 (fourth grade, third-month level).

Since the results of the group reading achievement test indicated that both Roger and Flip were "reading" at the early fourth grade level, most teachers and administrators would be likely to expect considerable similarity in their reading performance. But the use of the Classroom Reading Inventory showed that the reading performance of Roger and Flip tended to be quite dissimilar.

Roger was able to effectively read and comprehend the selection at the first grade reader level. However, his word recognition skills were inadequate for much of the

3. Nicholas J. Silvaroli. *Classroom Reading Inventory* (Dubuque, Iowa: Wm. C. Brown Company Publishers, 1973).

second grade reader material. Therefore, his responses to the Graded Word List and the Oral Reading Paragraphs indicated that his reading disability might be attributable to inadequate word recognition, decoding, phonetic analysis, etc., skills.

The results of the Classroom Reading Inventory also indicated that Roger was able to read typical first reader material (Roger's independent level) and that he would profit from word recognition development at the second reader level (Roger's instructional level). This estimate of the need for word recognition instruction at the second reader level (approximately two years below the level suggested by the group reading achievement test) is an indication of the student's frustration level and not his instructional level.

On the Graded Word List, Flip was able to pronounce most of the twenty representative words selected from sixth grade reader material. With only minor exceptions, Flip adequately understood the fundamental letter-form, letter-sound relationships involved in phonetic and structural analysis. However, he was unable to effectively comprehend what he read at the primer reading level. The results of the Classroom Reading Inventory also indicated that Flip's word recognition skills were firmly established. The Inventory indicated that Flip needed specific instruction which would enable him to associate meaning with words. Since the use of "experience stories" seems appropriate for Flip's instructional program, no specific grade or level was recommended.

It should be recalled that the results of the group reading achievement test classified Roger and Flip at the beginning fourth grade reader level. Yet the results of the Classroom Reading Inventory suggested that no specific level be identified until Flip received instruction in fundamental comprehension skills and Roger received assistance in word recognition at the level of beginning reading.

Global reading achievement scores on group reading achievement tests are able to classify children of comparable ages or grade groups according to above average, average, and below average reading ability. However, results from these types of measures do not provide information necessary to establish an *independent* and *instructional* reading program for the student. Therefore, if the teacher does not have information relevant to the student's specific reading needs, it becomes impossible to determine the types of instructional programs best suited to each student.

Informal reading inventories provide useful information for *independent* and *instructional* reading programs. However, the *time* required to administer these measures frequently discourages teachers from using them. The Classroom Reading Inventory was designed to provide the teacher with an informal reading inventory while keeping individual test administration time to a minimum.

To gain this time advantage for the teacher it was necessary to modify procedures usually found in other informal reading inventories. For example: only untimed responses to words in isolation (Part I—Graded Word Lists) are required; the number of questions in the comprehension check, per selection, was held to five; and only oral reading selections are recommended.

The modifications in the Classroom Reading Inventory tend to reduce the overall effectiveness of informal inventory testing in reading. However, this quick inventory should enable the teacher to realistically assess the reading performance of most children in the classroom.

The Classroom Reading Inventory is a diagnostic tool for use by teachers. The following questions and answers should provide sufficient general information about the Classroom Reading Inventory.

What is it?

Each form of the Classroom Reading Inventory is composed of two main parts: Part I—Graded Word Lists, and Part II—Graded Oral Paragraphs. The words and oral paragraphs used in this inventory are similar to the type of reading material found in various grade levels throughout the elementary school. The paragraphs selected for the Inventory have been evaluated for their readability level.

Is the Inventory used with groups or individuals?

The Inventory is designed for use with an individual student. However, the Classroom Reading Inventory also contains an additional section—Part III (Spelling Survey), which may be used with groups and individuals. The procedure used in the Spelling Survey is similar to those used in the classroom. Therefore, we will not provide additional comments.

Is the teacher expected to test every student?

The Inventory should be administered only to those students who need further testing in reading. Either the results of a group reading achievement test or the teacher's knowledge of the class group should reveal those students who appear to be in need of further testing.

How long does it take to administer the Inventory?

On the average, Part I (Graded Word Lists) can be administered to a student in five minutes. Part II (Oral Paragraphs) can be administered to a student in seven minutes. Excluding the Spelling Survey (Part III), the teacher should be able to test one student in approximately twelve minutes.

Can the Inventory be administered during the class time?

Yes. The student is expected to work with the teacher, at his desk, while the other students are engaged in quiet seat activities.

In what specific ways do the results of the Classroom Reading Inventory benefit the teacher?

The Inventory provides the teacher with information concerning the student's *independent, instructional, frustration* and hearing capacity reading levels. In addition to identifying realistic reading levels, the teacher is able to assess the student's specific word recognition and comprehension abilities. This information should enable the teacher to provide independent and instructional reading programs for the students in his classroom.

Specific Instructions: Following are the specific instructions for administering Form A, Form B, and Form C of the Classroom Reading Inventory.

Part I—Graded Word Lists

Purpose: To identify specific word recognition errors and to estimate the approximate starting level where the student begins reading the oral paragraphs in Part II.

Procedure: Present the graded word lists, starting at the PP (Pre-Primer) level, and say: "Pronounce each word. If you are not sure, or do not know the word, then say what you think it is."

Discontinue at the level at which the student mispronounces or indicates he does not know 5 of the 20 words in a particular grade level (75%). Each correct response is worth five points.

As the student pronounces the words at each level, the teacher should record all word errors on the Inventory Record. Corrected errors are counted as acceptable responses on Part I.

	Example		
1. was	saw		(error)
2. day	+		
3. three	d.k. (don't know)		(error)
4. farming	+		

After the student reaches the cut-off point (75%), his *oral reading* level should be *started* at the highest level in which he successfully pronounced all (100%) 20 words in the list.

Part II—Graded Paragraphs

Purpose: (1) To estimate the student's independent and instructional reading levels.

(2) To identify word recognition errors made during oral reading and to estimate the extent to which the student actually comprehends what he reads.

Procedure: Present the graded oral paragraphs starting at the highest level at which the student successfully recognized all 20 words in a word list on Part I.

Ask the student to read "out loud" for you and tell him that you will ask him to answer several questions about what he has just read when he is finished reading the story.

Each oral reading selection is accompanied by a picture and a brief background description that is called motivation. Listening to all or some aspect of the motivation and a brief inspection of the picture should provide the child with a measure of readiness for the oral selection which he is asked to read. This information (picture and motivation) has been checked to make certain that answers are not supplied for the comprehension questions which follow each oral reading selection.

Word Recognition: As the student reads each selection orally, record his word recognition errors on the separate Inventory Record. The student makes a word recognition error when he repeats, substitutes, omits, or needs teacher assistance in pronouncing words.

The following symbols will enable the teacher to quickly record the type of word recognition errors made during the oral reading:

Common Error	Symbol	Notes
Repetition	R͡	Mark word(s) repeated
Insertion	∧	Add additional word(s)
Substitution	—	Add substituted word
Omission	⬭	Circle word(s) omitted
Needs Assistance	P	Pronounce word when it's apparent that child does not know the word(s)

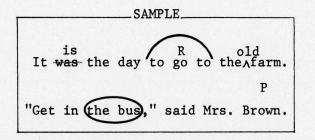

SAMPLE

It ~~was~~ the day to go to the ∧farm.
(is) (R͡) (old)

"Get in ⬭the bus," said Mrs. Brown.
(P)

Comprehension: After each oral selection the student is asked to answer five questions about what he has just read. The questions deal with the facts, inferences, and vocabulary contained in each selection. The questions for each selection are in the separate Inventory Record and labeled; F (fact), I (inference), and V (vocabulary). Answers provided for each question are merely guides or probable answers to the question. Therefore, the teacher must judge the adequacy of each response made by the student.

A full credit response is scored with a +. Partial credit (1/2 or 1/4) is allowed for responses to questions and is scored as 1/2 or 1/4. If a child answers a question incorrectly, the response is scored with a 0. If a child makes no response to the question, or says he doesn't know, the response is scored with a d.k. (don't know). In some cases it is helpful to record the child's response(s).

Example

(F) 1. __0__   Is there more than one kind of spider?
                (Yes—many more)   no

(F) 2. __+__   What two things do plant spiders quickly learn?
                (Hunt for food—build new nests)

(F) 3. __1/2__ What color was the spider in this story?
                (Black and green)   black

(F) 4. __+__   What size feet does a (plant) spider have?
                (Small—little)

(I) 5. __d.k.__ At what time of year do we see more spiders?
                (Check answer in your area—usually more
                are seen during the warm weather—spring
                and summer)

Testing with the CRI—Specific Illustrations

Typically, reading problems in the classroom fall into three categories. The first category could be designated: (I). *Basic Skills in Reading.* This category has two sub parts. Part (a) could be designated: *Inadequate Word Recognition Development.* The student with this type of reading problem is deficient in the basic word recognition skills. Part (b) could be designated: *Inadequate Comprehension Development.* The student with this type of reading problem is deficient in the basic comprehension skills.

The second category could be designated: (II) *Application of Basic Skills in Reading.* The student who seems to be having a reading problem is found *not* to be deficient in either of the basic skills areas—word recognition or comprehension. This student has

74

the necessary word recognition and comprehension skills, but cannot or will not apply them in a typical classroom reading situation.

The designation for the third category could be: (III) *Attitudes Toward Reading.* This student does not seem to turn to reading as a means of acquiring information as readily as he turns to listening for the purpose of acquiring information.

Following are some specific illustrations of reading problems falling into the category designated as: (I) *Basic Skills in Reading.*

The second and third categories of reading problems—(II) *Application of Basic Skills in Reading,* and (III) *Attitudes Toward Reading*—will be dealt with in greater detail in subsequent chapters in this book.

I. *Basic Skills in Reading*

A. *Inadequate Word Recognition Development:* Todd B. is a fourth-grade student whose chronological age = nine years, two months. His Full Scale I.Q., as measured by the Wechsler Intelligence Scale for Children, is 106, giving Todd a mental age of nine years, nine months. In his class, Todd is in the lowest reading group. His grade equivalency score in reading is 3.7, as measured by a group reading achievement test.

Todd's teacher, Mrs. Ada Larson, administered Todd Form A of the Classroom Reading Inventory. See a copy of Todd's Inventory Record at the end of Chapter 6, pp. 85-94.

By inspection, we can see that Todd's Instructional Level is at the beginning reading level. His Independent Level was not determined (N.D.). Todd reaches the Frustration Level with first grade material. Upon examination of Todd's Inventory Record, we can see that his problem is with the word recognition skills. He appears to have particular difficulty with blends and ending sounds: e.g., Todd read grade for garden, story for strong, etc.: e.g., Todd read crowl for crawl, crowed for crowd, etc., and other irregular vowel combinations, e.g., Todd read herd for head, etc.

There is no problem with comprehension. Even at the point where his word recognition skills reach the Frustration Level on the Graded Oral Paragraphs, Todd is able to get enough of the gist of the story to answer the questions about that story. Todd is what is termed a "context" reader.

B. *Inadequate Comprehension Development:* Lisa T. is a fifth-grade student whose chronological age = ten years, six months. Her Full Scale I.Q., as measured by the Wechsler Intelligence Scale for Children, is 98, giving Lisa a mental age of ten years, four months. In her class, Lisa is in the middle reading group. Her grade equivalency score in reading is 4.8, as measured by a group reading achievement test.

Lisa's teacher, Mr. Wilbur Millston, administered Lisa Form A of the Classroom Reading Inventory. See a copy of Lisa's Inventory Record at the end of Chapter 6, pp. 77 to 84.

Upon examination of Lisa's Inventory Record, we can see that her problem is with comprehension. She appears to have difficulty with questions of all types—factual, vocabulary, and inferential. There is no problem with word recognition skills. Lisa is what is called a "word caller." That is, she is a girl who can sound out almost any word presented to her. However, she does not associate any meaning with the words she decodes.

In this chapter we have discussed a way of evaluating reading problems having to do with the basic skills in reading—either inadequate word recognition development, or inadequate comprehension development. Chapters 1 and 2 of this book presented some basic constructs and some specific means of helping a student in your classroom to overcome a problem with word recognition. Chapters 3 and 4 of this book presented some basic constructs and some specific strategies for helping a student in your classroom to overcome a problem with comprehension. We feel that the material presented in these chapters should enable you, the teacher, to make some decisions about how to proceed with either type of problem.

SUMMARY

Standard school practice utilizes group reading achievement tests to measure a student's reading ability. However, *group reading achievement tests only classify students and compare groups—they do not diagnose.*

On the other hand, *informal reading inventories distinguish the several levels of reading competence* (Independent, Instructional, Frustration, and Hearing Capacity), *and they are diagnostic.*

For the purposes of being explicit, we introduced the Classroom Reading Inventory. The CRI provides the teacher with information concerning the student's *independent, instructional, frustration,* and *hearing capacity* reading level. In addition to identifying realistic reading levels, the teacher is able to assess the student's specific word recognition and comprehension abilities. This information should enable the teacher to provide independent and instructional reading programs for the students in his classroom.

Finally, we suggested a model for categorizing reading problems in the classroom:

I. Basic Skills in Reading
    A. Inadequate Word Recognition Development
    B. Inadequate Comprehension Development
II. Application of Basic Skills in Reading
III. Attitudes Toward Reading

Examples of the first category—(a) Word recognition and, (b) Comprehension problems were presented in some detail. Application problems and attitudinal problems will be dealt with in subsequent chapters.

FORM A
INVENTORY RECORD

Student's Name: _.LiSa T._____ Grade: _6_ Age (Chronological): _10 6_
                                                              yrs. mos.

Date: _2/15/73_ School: _Central_ Administered by: _Mr. Millstron_

GRADE		PART I	PART II—ORAL			ESTIMATED LEVELS		
		% of words correct	WR	COMP	H.C.		GRADE	
1	PP	100						
	P	100	Ind.	Ind.		INDEPENDENT	P	
	1	100	Ind.	Inst.				
2		100	Ind.	Frust		INSTRUCTIONAL	1	(range)
3		100	Ind.	Frust				
4		100				FRUSTRATION	2	
5		100						
6		90				(Hear. Capacity)	N.D.	
7								
8								

Check consistent WORD RECOGNITION ERRORS (Parts I, II, and III)

consonant

{ _____ Consonant sounds (e.g.; p, b, etc.) _____ Digraphs (e.g.; th, ch, etc.) _____ Compounds
{ _____ Blends (e.g.; bl, sm, etc.)   _____ Endings (e.g.; s, ed, ing)   _____ Contractions

vowel

_____ Long vowels (Name)   _____ Short vowels (Sound)
{ _____ Long/Short oo   _____ Vowels plus r
{ _____ a plus l or w (e.g.; call, saw) _____ Diphthongs (e.g.; ou, oi, etc.)
{ _____ Lacks vowel rule understanding   Vowel combinations (e.g.; oa, ai, etc.)

syllable

{ _____ Visual Patterns of syllables (e.g.; vccv, vcv, c+le)   _____ Prefix
{ _____ Auditory Syllable elements   _____ Suffix

Check consistent COMPREHENSION ERRORS (Part II-Questions)

_✓_ Fact question (F) _✓_ Inference question (I) _✓_ Vocabulary question (V)
_✓_ "Word caller" (reads words without associating meaning)
_✓_ Poor memory or recall _✓_ Unable to utilize visual images while reading

Summary of Specific Needs:

FORM A, PART I-Graded Word List (Teacher's Worksheet)

	(PP)			(P)			(1)			(2)	
1.	for	+	1.	was	+	1.	many	+	1.	stood	+
2.	blue	+	2.	day	+	2.	painted	+	2.	climb	+
3.	car	+	3.	three	+	3.	feet	+	3.	isn't	+
4.	to	+	4.	farming	+	4.	them	+	4.	beautiful	+
5.	and	+	5.	bus	+	5.	food	+	5.	waiting	+
6.	it	+	6.	now	+	6.	tell	+	6.	head	+
7.	helps	+	7.	read	+	7.	her	+	7.	cowboy	+
8.	stop	+	8.	children	+	8.	please	+	8.	high	+
9.	funny	+	9.	went	+	9.	peanut	+	9.	people	+
10.	can	+	10.	then	+	10.	cannot	+	10.	mice	+
11.	big	+	11.	black	+	11.	eight	+	11.	corn	+
12.	said	+	12.	barn	+	12.	trucks	+	12.	everyone	+
13.	green	+	13.	trees	+	13.	garden	+	13.	strong	+
14.	look	+	14.	brown	+	14.	drop	+	14.	I'm	+
15.	play	+	15.	good	+	15.	stopping	+	15.	room	+
16.	see	+	16.	into	+	16.	frog	+	16.	blows	+
17.	there	+	17.	she	+	17.	street	+	17.	gray	+
18.	little	+	18.	something	+	18.	fireman	+	18.	that's	+
19.	is	+	19.	what	+	19.	birthday	+	19.	throw	+
20.	work	+	20.	saw	+	20.	let's	+	20.	own	+

Teacher note: As soon as the child misses five words in any column-stop Part I. Begin oral paragraphs, Part II, (Form A), at highest level in which child recognized all 20 words.

FORM A, PART I.

	(3)			(4)			(5)			(6)	
1.	hour	+	1.	spoon	+	1.	whether	+	1.	sentinel	+
2.	senseless	+	2.	dozen	+	2.	hymn	+	2.	nostrils	+
3.	turkeys	+	3.	trail	+	3.	sharpness	+	3.	marsh	*march*
4.	anything	+	4.	machine	+	4.	amount	+	4.	sensitive	+
5.	chief	+	5.	bound	+	5.	shrill	+	5.	calmly	+
6.	foolish	+	6.	exercise	+	6.	freedom	+	6.	tangle	+
7.	enough	+	7.	disturbed	+	7.	loudly	+	7.	wreath	+
8.	either	+	8.	force	+	8.	scientists	+	8.	teamwork	+
9.	chased	+	9.	weather	+	9.	musical	+	9.	billows	+
10.	robe	+	10.	rooster	+	10.	considerable	+	10.	knights	+
11.	crowd	+	11.	mountains	+	11.	examined	+	11.	instinct	+
12.	crawl	+	12.	island	+	12.	scarf	+	12.	liberty	+
13.	unhappy	+	13.	hook	+	13.	muffled	+	13.	pounce	+
14.	clothes	+	14.	guides	+	14.	pacing	+	14.	rumored	+
15.	hose	+	15.	moan	+	15.	oars	+	15.	strutted	+
16.	pencil	+	16.	settlers	+	16.	delicious	+	16.	dragon	+
17.	meat	+	17.	pitching	+	17.	octave	+	17.	hearth	*heart*
18.	discover	+	18.	prepared	+	18.	terrific	+	18.	shifted	+
19.	picture	+	19.	west	+	19.	salmon	+	19.	customers	+
20.	nail	+	20.	knowledge	+	20.	briskly	+	20.	blond	+

Teacher note: As soon as the child misses five words in any column-stop Part I. Begin oral paragraphs, Part II (Form A), at highest level in which child recognized all 20 words.

W.P.M.
___/1440

FORM A, PART II—Level PP (24 words)

MOTIVATION: All the family drove to the airport to see father off on a plane trip. Read to find out what the children are looking at.

THE WORK CAR

"Look over there," said Jane.

"See the funny little car.

Can you see it?"

"I see it," said Bob.

"It is a work car."

Scoring Guide: Pre-Primer

WR Errors		COMP Errors	
IND	0	IND	0-1
INST	1-2	INST	1½-2
FRUST	3+	FRUST	2½+

COMPREHENSION CHECK

(F) 1. ___ Who are the children in the story?
(Bob and Jane)

(F) 2. ___ What did they see?
(funny little car)

(I) 3. ___ Who saw the car first?
(Jane)

(F) 4. ___ What is the car called?
(Work car or help car)

(I) 5. ___ What does the work car do?
(Helps or carries baggage, etc.)

FORM A, PART II—Level P (33 words)

W.P.M.
___/1980

MOTIVATION: Most people like to fly. Read this story to find out what it would look like if you were in an airplane in the sky.

JACK'S FIRST AIRPLANE RIDE

Jack and his father got on the airplane.

Away they flew.

"How high we are," said Jack.

"The trees look small."

"And so do the animals," said Father.

Jack said, "This is fun!"

Scoring Guide: Primer

WR Errors		COMP Errors	
IND	0	IND	0-1
INST	1-2	INST	1½-2
FRUST	3+	FRUST	2½+

COMPREHENSION CHECK

(F) 1. + Who was with Jack on the airplane?
(Father)

(F) 2. + What words in the story tell that Jack liked his ride?
(This is fun)

(V) 3. + What does the word "high" mean in this story?
(Way up in the air, above the buildings, trees, etc.)

(I) 4. + What in the story tells you that Jack and his father are up high?
(The trees and animals looks small)
(they are flying)

(I) 5. dK How many airplane rides did Jack have before this one?
(None)

*It is recommended that the "language" of the Inventory be adapted to conform to the age of the child being tested.

80

FORM A, PART II-Level 1 (43 words)

W.P.M.
_____/2580

MOTIVATION: This story is about a type of spider that builds its web between flowers or plant stalks. Read this selection to find out more about this type of spider.

PLANT SPIDERS

There are all kinds of spiders.

This black and green one is called the plant spider.

A plant spider has small feet.

All spiders have small feet.

Plant spiders live in nests.

They soon learn to hunt for food and build new nests.

COMPREHENSION CHECK

(F) 1. **0** Is there more than one kind of spider?
(Yes-many more)

(F) 2. **½** What two things do plant spiders quickly learn?
(Hunt for food and <u>build new nests</u>)

(F) 3. **½** What color was the spider in this story?
(Black and <u>green</u>)

(F) 4. **+** What size feet does a (plant) spider have?
(Small) (little)

(I) 5. **+** At what time of year do we see more spiders?
(Check answer in your area-usually more are seen during the warm weather-spring and summer)

Scoring Guide: First

WR Errors		COMP Errors	
(IND)	0	(INST)	0-1
INST	2	(INST)	1½-2
FRUST	4+	FRUST	2½+

FORM A, PART II—Level 2 (49 words)

W.P.M.
___/2940

MOTIVATION: This story takes place at a rodeo. At a rodeo cowboys show their skill with horses, steers, and ropes. Read to find out more about the horse and cowboy in this story.

THE RODEO

The people at the rodeo stood up.

They were all waiting for the big ride.

Everyone came to see Bob Hill ride Midnight.

Bob Hill is a top rider.

Midnight is the best horse in the show. He is big and fast.

Can Bob Hill ride this great horse?

COMPREHENSION CHECK

(F) 1. + What did the people do?
(Stood up, were waiting, etc.)

(F) 2. dk What was the name of the horse?
(Midnight)

(F) 3. + What did he (Midnight) look like?
(Big, black, strong, etc.)

(F) 4. dk Why do you think that Bob Hill was a good rider?
(Story said he was a top rider, he had practice)

(I) 5. O Did the story say that Bob Hill rode Midnight? yes
(No, he did later, only in the picture)

Scoring Guide: Second

WR Errors		COMP Errors	
(IND)	0	IND	0-1
INST	3	INST	1½-2
FRUST	5+	(FRUST)	2½+

82

FORM A, PART II—Level 3 (100 words)

W.P.M.
___/6000

MOTIVATION: Some people say birds are smart and some say they are silly. See if you will agree with the author when he says that most birds are smart.

SMART BIRDS

Everyone knows that birds like to eat seeds and grain. Birds also like to eat little stones called gravel. Birds have to eat the gravel because they don't have teeth to grind their food. The gravel stays in the bird's gizzard which is something like a stomach. When the bird eats seed the gravel and the seed grind together. All of the seed is mashed up.

Tame birds must be given gravel. Wild birds find their own gravel on the road sides. Now you can see how smart birds are.

COMPREHENSION CHECK

(F) 1. Name two things birds like to eat. (Seeds, grain, gravel stones, sand)

(F) 2. Why do birds have to eat sand or gravel? (Grind their food)

(V) 3. What does the word "grind" mean? (Crush, make smaller, etc.)

(I) 4. What do you think would happen to birds that can't get any gravel in their food? (Probably die, get sick)

(I) 5. A bird's gizzard works somewhat like what part of your body? (Stomach)

Scoring Guide: Third

WR Errors		COMP Errors	
IND	2	IND	0-1
INST	5-6	INST	1½-2
FRUST	11	FRUST	2½+

83

FORM A, PART II—Level 4 (98 words)

MOTIVATION: Everything changes, even sports. A new growing sport is called Sky Diving. Have you ever seen a Sky Diver in action? (TV, movies, etc.) If so, then you might enjoy reading this selection to find out more about this new sport.

SKY DIVING

An exciting new sport in the world today is sky diving. Sky divers do tricks, make falls, and take interesting pictures. This sport takes you away from your everyday life into a wonderful world you have never known. It is almost like being in a dream. Once out of the airplane, you feel as if you can climb walls or float over mountains.

Sky divers work to develop each of their jumps. Men and women are interested in sky diving. In fact, more people learn to sky dive each year. This relaxing sport is one of man's newest adventures.

COMPREHENSION CHECK

(F) 1. ___ Tell two things that sky divers do.
(Tricks, make falls, take pictures)

(I) 2. ___ Why is sky diving like being in a dream?
(You float, weightlessness, falling, etc.)

(F) 3. ___ Is it true that only men are sky divers?
(No, it is false; no, women, too)

(F) 4. ___ When diving, do sky divers climb walls?
(No)

(V) 5. ___ Sky divers "work to develop each jump"—what does this mean?
(Do it many times, practices, learn more about it, improves, etc.)

Scoring Guide: Fourth

WR Errors		COMP Errors	
IND	1-2	IND	0-1
INST	5	INST	1½-2
FRUST	9+	FRUST	2½+

Teacher note: Hearing Comprehension should have begun at this level, if the examiner elected to use this optional measure.

Student's Name: _Todd B._ _____ Grade: _4_ Age (Chronological): _9_ _2_

yrs.   mos.

Date: _2/15/73_ School: _Central_ _____ Administered by: _Mrs. Larson_ _____

GRADE		PART I	PART II—ORAL			ESTIMATED LEVELS	
		% of words correct	WR	COMP	H.C.		GRADE
1	PP	95	Inst.	Ind.		INDEPENDENT	Not Determined (N.D.)
	P	95	Inst.	Ind.			
	1	80	Frust	Ind.			
2		70			100	INSTRUCTIONAL	PP-P (range)
3		55			80		
4					100	FRUSTRATION	1
5					80		
6					60	(Hear. Capacity)	5
7							
8							

Check consistent WORD RECOGNITION ERRORS (Parts I, II, and III)

consonant

{ _____ Consonant sounds (e.g.; p, b, etc.) _____ Digraphs (e.g.; th, ch, etc.) _____ Compounds
{ _✔_ Blends (e.g.; bl, sm, etc.)   _✔_ Endings (e.g.; s, ed, ing)   _____ Contractions

vowel

{ _____ Long vowels (Name)   _✔_ Short vowels (Sound)
{ _✔_ Long/Short oo   _✔_ Vowels plus r
{ _____ a plus 1 or w (e.g.; call, saw)   _✔_ Diphthongs (e.g.; ou, oi, etc.)
{ _____ Lacks vowel rule understanding   _✔_ Vowel combinations (e.g.; oa, ai, etc.)

syllable

{ _____ Visual Patterns of syllables (e.g.; vccv, vcv, c+le)   _____ Prefix
{ _____ Auditory Syllable elements   _____ Suffix

Check consistent COMPREHENSION ERRORS (Part II—Questions)

_____ Fact question (F) _____ Inference question (I) _____ Vocabulary question (V)
_____ "Word caller" (reads words without associating meaning)
_____ Poor memory or recall _____ Unable to utilize visual images while reading

Summary of Specific Needs:

FORM A, PART I—Graded Word List (Teacher's Worksheet)

	(PP)			(P)			(1)			(2)	
1.	for	+	1.	was	+	1.	many	+	1.	stood	d.K.
2.	blue	+	2.	day	+	2.	painted	paint	2.	climb	clĭmb
3.	car	+	3.	three	+	3.	feet	+	3.	isn't	+
4.	to	+	4.	farming	+	4.	them	+	4.	beautiful	+
5.	and	+	5.	bus	+	5.	food	+	5.	waiting	wanting
6.	it	+	6.	now	+	6.	tell	+	6.	head	herd
7.	helps	+	7.	read	+	7.	her	+	7.	cowboy	+
8.	stop	+	8.	children	+	8.	please	+	8.	high	+
9.	funny	+	9.	went	+	9.	peanut	+	9.	people	+
10.	can	+	10.	then	them	10.	cannot	+	10.	mice	+
11.	big	+	11.	black	+	11.	eight	eat	11.	corn	+
12.	said	+	12.	barn	+	12.	trucks	tricks	12.	everyone	+
13.	green	+	13.	trees	+	13.	garden	grade	13.	strong	story
14.	look	+	14.	brown	+	14.	drop	+	14.	I'm	+
15.	play	+	15.	good	+	15.	stopping	+	15.	room	+
16.	see	+	16.	into	+	16.	frog	+	16.	blows	+
17.	there	three	17.	she	+	17.	street	+	17.	gray	+
18.	little	+	18.	something	+	18.	fireman	+	18.	that's	+
19.	is	+	19.	what	+	19.	birthday	+	19.	throw	d.K.
20.	work	+	20.	saw	+	20.	let's	+	20.	own	+

Teacher note: As soon as the child misses five words in any column-stop Part I. Begin oral paragraphs, Part II, (Form A), at highest level in which child recognized all 20 words.

FORM A, PART I.

	(3)			(4)			(5)			(6)	
1.	hour	*+*	1.	spoon	___	1.	whether	___	1.	sentinel	___
2.	senseless	*D.K.*	2.	dozen	___	2.	hymn	___	2.	nostrils	___
3.	turkeys	*truckeys*	3.	trail	___	3.	sharpness	___	3.	marsh	___
4.	anything	*+*	4.	machine	___	4.	amount	___	4.	sensitive	___
5.	chief	*D.K.*	5.	bound	___	5.	shrill	___	5.	calmly	___
6.	foolish	*+*	6.	exercise	___	6.	freedom	___	6.	tangle	___
7.	enough	*D.K.*	7.	disturbed	___	7.	loudly	___	7.	wreath	___
8.	either	*D.K.*	8.	force	___	8.	scientists	___	8.	teamwork	___
9.	chased	*+*	9.	weather	___	9.	musical	___	9.	billows	___
10.	robe	*Rode*	10.	rooster	___	10.	considerable	___	10.	knights	___
11.	crowd	*Crowed*	11.	mountains	___	11.	examined	___	11.	instinct	___
12.	crawl	*Crowl*	12.	island	___	12.	scarf	___	12.	liberty	___
13.	unhappy	*+*	13.	hook	___	13.	muffled	___	13.	pounce	___
14.	clothes	*+*	14.	guides	___	14.	pacing	___	14.	rumored	___
15.	hose	*+*	15.	moan	___	15.	oars	___	15.	strutted	___
16.	pencil	*+*	16.	settlers	___	16.	delicious	___	16.	dragon	___
17.	meat	*+*	17.	pitching	___	17.	octave	___	17.	hearth	___
18.	discover	*D.K.*	18.	prepared	___	18.	terrific	___	18.	shifted	___
19.	picture	*+*	19.	west	___	19.	salmon	___	19.	customers	___
20.	nail	*+*	20.	knowledge	___	20.	briskly	___	20.	blond	___

Teacher note: As soon as the child misses five words in any column—stop Part I. Begin oral paragraphs, Part II (Form A), at highest level in which child recognized all 20 words.

W.P.M.
___/1440

FORM A, PART II-Level PP (24 words)

MOTIVATION: All the family drove to the airport to see father off on a plane trip. Read to find out what the children are looking at.

THE WORK CAR

"Look over there," said Jane.

"See the funny little car.

Can you see it?"

"I see it," said Bob.

"It (is) a work car."

Scoring Guide: Pre-Primer

WR Errors		COMP Errors	
IND	0	(IND)	0-1
(INST)	1-2	INST	1½-2
FRUST	3+	FRUST	2½+

COMPREHENSION CHECK

(F) 1. + Who are the children in the story?
(Bob and Jane)

(F) 2. + What did they see?
(funny little car)

(I) 3. + Who saw the car first?
(Jane)

(F) 4. + What is the car called?
(Work car or help car)

(I) 5. + What does the work car do?
(Helps or carries baggage, etc.)

FORM A, PART II-Level P (33 words)

W.P.M.
___/1980

MOTIVATION: Most people like to fly. Read this story to find out what it would look like if you were in an airplane in the sky.

JACK'S FIRST AIRPLANE RIDE

Jack and his father got on the airplane.

Away they flew.

"How high we are," said Jack.

"The trees look small."

"And so do the animals," said Father.

Jack said, "This is fun!"

Scoring Guide: Primer

WR Errors		COMP Errors	
IND	0	(IND)	0-1
(INST)	1-2	INST	1½-2
FRUST	3+	FRUST	2½+

COMPREHENSION CHECK

(F) 1. + Who was with Jack on the airplane?
(Father)

(F) 2. + What words in the story tell that Jack liked his ride?
(This is fun)

(V) 3. + What does the word "high" mean in this story?
(Way up in the air, above the buildings, trees, etc.)

(I) 4. + What in the story tells you that Jack and his father are up high?
(The trees and animals looks small)
(they are flying)

(I) 5. + How many airplane rides did Jack have before this one?
(None)

*It is recommended that the "language" of the Inventory be adapted to conform to the age of the child being tested.

88

FORM A, PART II-Level 1 (43 words)

MOTIVATION: This story is about a type of spider that builds its web between flowers or plant stalks. Read this selection to find out more about this type of spider.

PLANT SPIDERS

There are all kinds of spiders.

This black and green one is called the plant spider.

Foot
A plant spider has small feet.

All spiders have small feet.

Plant spiders live in nests.

live hurt
They soon learn to hunt for food and build new nests.

COMPREHENSION CHECK

(F) 1. _+_ Is there more than one kind of spider?
(Yes-many more)

(F) 2. _+_ What two things do plant spiders quickly learn?
(Hunt for food and build new nests)

(F) 3. _½_ What color was the spider in this story?
(Black and green) *Black*

(F) 4. _+_ What size feet does a (plant) spider have?
(Small) (little)

(I) 5. _+_ At what time of year do we see more spiders?
(Check answer in your area-usually more are seen during the warm weather-spring and summer)

Scoring Guide: First

WR Errors		COMP Errors	
IND	0	(IND)	0-1
INST	2	INST	1½-2
(FRUST)	4+	FRUST	2½+

89

FORM A, PART II—Level 2 (49 words)

W.P.M.
____/2940

MOTIVATION: This story takes place at a rodeo. At a rodeo cowboys show their skill with horses, steers, and ropes. Read to find out more about the horse and cowboy in this story.

THE RODEO

The people at the rodeo stood up.

They were all waiting for the big ride.

Everyone came to see Bob Hill ride Midnight.

Bob Hill is a top rider.

Midnight is the best horse in the show. He is big and fast.

Can Bob Hill ride this great horse?

COMPREHENSION CHECK

(F) 1. +_What did the people do?
(Stood up, were waiting, etc.)

(F) 2. +_What was the name of the horse?
(Midnight)

(F) 3. +_What did he (Midnight) look like?
(Big, black, strong, etc.)

(F) 4. +_Why do you think that Bob Hill was a good rider?
(Story said he was a top rider, he had practice)

(I) 5. +_Did the story say that Bob Hill rode Midnight?
(No, he did later, only in the picture)

100%

Scoring Guide: Second

WR Errors		COMP Errors	
IND	0	IND	0-1
INST.	3	INST	1½-2
FRUST	5+	FRUST	2½+

*Teacher note: Hearing Comprehension began at this level.

FORM A, PART II-Level 3 (100 words)

W.P.M.
___/6000

MOTIVATION: Some people say birds are smart and some say they are silly. See if you will agree with the author when he says that most birds are smart.

SMART BIRDS

Everyone knows that birds like to eat seeds and grain. Birds also like to eat little stones called gravel. Birds have to eat the gravel because they don't have teeth to grind their food. The gravel stays in the bird's gizzard which is something like a stomach. When the bird eats seed the gravel and the seed grind together. All of the seed is mashed up.

Tame birds must be given gravel. Wild birds find their own gravel on the road sides. Now you can see how smart birds are.

COMPREHENSION CHECK

(F) 1. + Name two things birds like to eat.
(Seeds, grain, gravel stones, sand)

(F) 2. + Why do birds have to eat sand or gravel?
(Grind their food)

(V) 3. + What does the word "grind" mean?
(Crush, make smaller, etc.)

(I) 4. ± What do you think would happen to birds that can't get any gravel in their food?
(Probably die, get sick)

(I) 5. + A bird's gizzard works somewhat like what part of your body?
(Stomach)

80%

Scoring Guide: Third

WR Errors		COMP Errors	
IND	2	IND	0-1
INST	5-6	INST	1½-2
FRUST	11	FRUST	2½+

FORM A, PART II-Level 4 (98 words)

MOTIVATION: Everything changes, even sports. A new growing sport is called Sky Diving. Have you ever seen a Sky Diver in action? (TV, movies, etc.) If so, then you might enjoy reading this selection to find out more about this new sport.

SKY DIVING

An exciting new sport in the world today is sky diving. Sky divers do tricks, make falls, and take interesting pictures. This sport takes you away from your everyday life into a wonderful world you have never known. It is almost like being in a dream. Once out of the airplane, you feel as if you can climb walls or float over mountains.

Sky divers work to develop each of their jumps. Men and women are interested in sky diving. In fact, more people learn to sky dive each year. This relaxing sport is one of man's newest adventures.

COMPREHENSION CHECK

(F) 1. + Tell two things that sky divers do.
(Tricks, make falls, take pictures)

(I) 2. + Why is sky diving like being in a dream?
(You float, weightlessness, falling, etc.)

(F) 3. + Is it true that only men are sky divers?
(No, it is false; no, women, too)

(F) 4. + When diving, do sky divers climb walls?
(No)

(V) 5. + Sky divers "work to develop each jump"—what does this mean?
(Do it many times, practices, learn more about it, improves, etc.)

100%

Scoring Guide: Fourth

WR Errors		COMP Errors	
IND	1-2	IND	0-1
INST	5	INST	1½-2
FRUST	9+	FRUST	2½+

FORM A, PART II-Level 5 (128 words)

MOTIVATION: This story tells about a different type of school. Read to find out more about this special school.

AN UNDERWATER SCHOOL

A team of experts proved that seals had

a keen sense of hearing. These men trained

blind seals to expect food when they

heard sounds. The seals always began

snapping when a shrill signal was sounded.

It was proved that even a soft signal,

a considerable distance away, could make

these sea mammals respond. That should

make the fisherman who splashes his oars,

or talks loudly, start thinking.

The same team of experts also trained

seals to recognize different sounds. One

bell-tone meant food, two bell-tones meant

no food. In the beginning, the seals made

mistakes when the two-bell tones were

sounded. They were given a light tap after

each mistake. The seals were good learners.

They easily learned to tell the difference

between the sounds.

COMPREHENSION CHECK

(F) 1. +__ What animals or sea mammals did the experts train?
(Seals)

(F) 2. +__ What did the seals do when they heard the shrill signal?
(Began snapping, came for food)

(I) 3. dK__ Why was it necessary to use blind seals?
(Unable to use sight for clues)

(F) 4. +__ When the seals made mistakes, what happened?
(They were given a light tap)

(F) 5. +__ What did the seals learn?
(To tell the difference between bell sounds and when to come)

80%

Scoring Guide: Fifth

WR Errors		COMP Errors	
IND	2	IND	0-1
INST	6	INST	1½-2
FRUST	12	FRUST	2½+

FORM A, PART II-Level 6 (110 words)

W.P.M.
___/6600

MOTIVATION: This story is about a beaver and his unusual home. Read this story to learn more about the beaver's home and his problems with it.

A BEAVER'S HOME

A beaver's home, called a lodge, always has a

flooded lower room. These homes are built in large

ponds or streams. Mud and sticks are the main

building materials. One room is built above the

water level and another room is located under

water. The only way a beaver can get into the

house is to submerge and enter through an

opening in the flooded room. This room serves two

purposes: a storage area and a sanctuary from

enemies.

Occasionally the lower room becomes dry be-

cause the beaver's dam has been destroyed. This

energetic animal has to quickly repair the dam, or

begin building a new home in another place.

COMPREHENSION CHECK

(F) 1. _+_ What is the name of the beaver's home?
(Lodge)

(F) 2. _+_ Where do beavers build their homes?
(Ponds or streams)

(V) 3. _+_ What does the word "submerge" mean?
(Go under water, duck under, dive, etc.)

(I) 4. _dk_ What would happen to the beaver if there wasn't water in the stream?
(Home would dry up, couldn't live, etc.)

(I) 5. _dk_ How does the flooded lower room help the beaver?
(Storehouse, escape from enemies, helps him get into house)

60%

Scoring Guide: Sixth

WR Errors		COMP Errors	
IND	2	IND	0-1
INST	5-6	INST	1½-2
FRUST	11	FRUST	2½+

ORAL READING TESTS

1. Gilmore Oral Reading Test, 1968, Harcourt Brace & Jovanovich, Inc.
2. Gray Oral Reading Test, 1967, Bobbs-Merrill Co., Inc.
3. Slosson Oral Reading Test, 1963, Slosson Educational Publications.
4. Classroom Reading Inventory, 1973, Wm. C. Brown Company Publishers. Second edition.
5. Durrell Analysis of Reading Difficulty, 1955, Harcourt Brace & Jovanovich, Inc.
6. Diagnostic Reading Scales, 1972, McGraw-Hill.
7. Reading Miscue Inventory, 1972, Macmillan Publishing Company.

Tests	1	2	3	4	5	6	7
Grades	1-8	1-10	1-8	2-8	1-8	1-8	K-8
Forms	2	4	1	2	1	1	1
Time	15 (20)		3	12 min.	30-45	No Limit	Unlimited
Reading Paragraphs	$3.50	1.60		2.95	3.00	1.40	14.52
Record blanks per quantity	$5.50 35	3.20 35	.75 20		8.00 35	12.30 35	3.84 100
Specimen set	$1.50	50¢			8.00	2.80	None
Manual	$1.00				1.00	1.00	4.85

READING READINESS TESTS

1. Test of Basic Experiences, 1970, McGraw-Hill.
2. Gates-MacGinitie Readiness Skills Test, 1969, Teachers College Press.
3. Harrison-Stroud Reading Readiness Profiles, 1956, Houghton Mifflin Company.
4. Lee Clark Reading Readiness Test, 1962, McGraw-Hill.
5. Metropolitan Readiness Test, 1969, Harcourt Brace & Jovanovich, Inc.
6. Murphy Durrell Reading Readiness Analysis Test, 1965, Harcourt, Brace & Jovanovich.
7. Clymer-Barrett Prereading Battery, 1969, Personnel Press, Inc.

Tests	1	2	3	4	5	6	7
Levels	K-1	K-1	K-1	K-1	K-1	Gr.1	K-1
Forms	1	1	1	1	2	1	2
Time	25	120	80-90	20	60	60	90
Cost per quantity	$9.00 30	4.25 35	3.85 35	5.00 35	8.20 35	6.20 35	5.00 25
Specimen set	$3.00	75¢	80¢	75¢	1.50	1.50	1.00

PRIMARY READING TESTS

1. California Reading Test, 1963, McGraw-Hill.
2. California Reading Test, 1963, McGraw-Hill.
3. Comprehensive Tests of Basic Skills: Reading, 1970, McGraw-Hill.
4. Durrell Listening-Reading Series, 1970, Harcourt Brace & Jovanovich, Inc.
5. Gates-MacGinitie Reading Test, Primary A, 1965, Teachers College Press.
6. Gates-MacGinitie Reading Test, Primary B, 1965, Teachers College Press.
7. Metropolitan Achievement Tests, Reading, 1971, Harcourt Brace & Jovanovich, Inc.
8. Monroe's Standardized Silent Reading Test, 1959, The Bobbs-Merrill Co., Inc.
9. New Development Reading Tests, 1965, Lyons & Carnaham, Inc.
10. SRA Achievement Series, 1968, Science Research Association Inc.
11. SRA Achievement Series, 1968, Science Research Association Inc.
12. Stanford Achievement Test: Reading, 1973, Harcourt Brace & Jovanovich, Inc., Primary I.
13. Stanford Achievement Test: Reading, 1973, Harcourt Brace & Jovanovich, Inc., Primary II.

Tests	1	2	3	4	5	6	7	8	9	10	11	12	13
Total Scores	X	X	X	X	X	X	X			X	X		
Vocabulary			X	X						X	X	X	X
Word Meaning							X					X	X
Word Recognition							X		X			X	X
Comprehension	X	X	X		X	X		X	X	X	X	X	X
Following Directions									X				
Paragraph Meaning				X								X	X
Grades	1-2	2-4	2-4	1-2	1	2	2.5-3.4	3-5	1-3	1-2	2-4	1.5-2.4	2.5-3.9
Time	23	40	49	140	40	40	48	40	40	120	90	90	90
Forms	1	1	2	2	2	2	2	3	2	2	2	2	2
Cost per quantity	$5.50	5.50	5.75	10.50	3.60	3.60	6.50	3.50	5.80	5.85	3.75	8.15	8.15
Specimen Set	$1.25	1.25	1.75	1.40	60¢	60¢	2.00	50¢	60¢			2.00	2.00

INTERMEDIATE READING TESTS

1. American School Achievement Tests, Part I, Reading, 1963, Bobbs-Merrill Co., Inc.
2. California Reading Test, 1970, McGraw-Hill.
3. New Developmental Reading Tests, 1968, Lyons & Carnaham, Inc.
4. Durrell-Sullivan Reading Capacity and Achievement Tests, 1944, Harcourt Brace & Jovanovich, Inc.
5. Gates Basic Reading Tests, 1965, Teachers College Press.
6. Gates Reading Survey, 1960, Teachers College Press.
7. Iowa Silent Reading Test, 1942, Harcourt Brace & Jovanovich, Inc.
8. Metropolitan Achievement Tests: Reading, 1970, Harcourt Brace & Jovanovich, Inc.
9. Stanford Achievement Test, 1966, Harcourt Brace & Jovanovich, Inc.
10. SRA Achievement Series, 1969, Science Research Association, Inc.
11. Sequential Tests of Education Progress (STEP), 1963, Cooperative Test Division.

Tests	1	2	3	4	5	6	7	8	9	10	11
Total	X	X		X		X				X	
Vocabulary		X	X		X	X		X			
Word Meaning	X			X			X		X		
Comprehension		X	X		X	X	X				
Accuracy						X					
Factual reading			X								
Paragraph Comp.				X				X	X		
Appreciation			X								
Evaluation			X								
Reference Skills								X		X	
Reading Charts										X	
Rate					X	X					
Grades	3-6	4-6	4-6	3-6	4-6	4-6	4-12	4-8	5-6	4-5	4-9
Time	25	45	50	35	45	50	49	39	40	70	70
Forms	4	1			3	3	4	3	3	2	2
Cost per quantity	$3.00 35	$6.00 35	$6.00 35	$8.60 35	$3.60 35	$2.75 35	$3.20 35	$4.60 35	$6.20 35	$10.35 25	$4.00 20
Specimen Set	50¢	$2.00	$1.00	$1.65	60¢	50¢		40¢	$1.75		$2.00

JUNIOR AND SENIOR HIGH READING TESTS

1. American School Achievement Tests, 1958, Public Schools Publishing Co.
2. California Reading Test, 1970, McGraw-Hill.
3. Reading Comprehension; Cooperative English Test, 1960, Cooperative Test Division.
4. Gates Reading Survey, 1965, Teachers College Press.
5. Metropolitan Achievement Tests, 1969, Harcourt Brace & Jovanovich, Inc.
6. Nelson Reading Test, 1962, Houghton Mifflin Company.
7. SRA Achievement Series, 1969, Science Research Association, Inc.
8. Sequential Tests of Educational Progress (STEP), 1963, Cooperative Test Division.
9. Stanford Achievement Test, 1966, Harcourt Brace & Jovanovich, Inc.
10. Tests of Academic Progress: Reading, 1966, Houghton Mifflin Company.
11. Traxler High School Reading Test, Revised, 1967, Bobbs-Merrill Co., Inc.

Tests	1	2	3	4	5	6	7	8	9	10	11
Reading					X						
Comprehension		X	X	X		X	X		X	X	X
Word Meaning	X				X						
Paragraph Meaning	X					X					
Vocabulary		X	X	X		X	X				
Speed			X	X							X
Total Tests	X	X	X		X	X	X				X
Grades	7-9	6-9	9-12	7-9	5-7	3-9	4-9	7-9 10-12	9-12	9-12	10-12
Time	30	50	40	44	40		70	70	45	60	50
Forms	4	1	3	3	2		2	2	2	1	3
Cost per quantity	$2.00	6.00	4.00	3.60	2.80	4.00	8.70	4.00	8.20	30¢ per test	4.60
Specimen Set	35¢	2.00	2.00	60¢	2.00	1.00		2.00	2.00	3.00	60¢

TESTS OF MENTAL ABILITY

1. California Test of Mental Maturity, 1963, McGraw-Hill.
2. California Short Form Test of Mental Maturity, 1963, McGraw-Hill.
3. Cooperative School and College Ability Tests, Cooperative Test Service.
4. The Lorge Thorndike Intelligence Tests, 1966, Houghton Mifflin Company.
5. Otis Lennon Mental Ability Tests, 1970, Harcourt Brace & Jovanovich, Inc.
6. SRA Primary Mental Abilities, 1962, Science Research Association, Inc.
7. Stanford-Binet Intelligence Scale, 3rd Revision, 1964, Harcourt Brace & Jovanovich, Inc.
8. Wechsler Adult Intelligence Scale, 1955, The Psychological Corporation.
9. Wechsler Intelligence Scale for Children, 1949, The Psychological Corporation.
10. Slosson Intelligence Test, Slosson Educational Publications Inc.

Mental Ability Tests	1	2	3	4	5	6	7	8	9	10
Vocabulary	X	X	X					X	X	
Number	X	X	X							
Spacial relationship	X	X								
Memory	X	X								
Reasoning	X	X								
Language	X	X								
Non-Language	X	X		X						
Total	X	X	X					X	X	X
Grades	K-16	K-16	K-14	12-13	K-12	K-16	2-A*	16-A	5-15	K-16
Forms	1	1		2	2	1	1	1		1
Cost per quantity	$7.50	5.75	7.00	6.00	6.80	4.15	4.65	2.70	2.75	6.00
Specimen Set			3.00	2.25	2.25	1.00				1.25
Time	48	34		62	30		30	40	40	10-20

*Adult

REFERENCES FOR CHAPTER 6

Buros, Oscar Krisen. *Reading Tests and Reviews.* Highland Park, New Jersey: The Gryphon Press, 1968.

Provides frankly critical evaluations of tests, written by competent specialists representing a variety of viewpoints, to assist test users to choose the tests which will best meet their needs.

Bush, Clifford L., and Mildren H. Huebner. *Strategies for Reading in the Elementary School.* London: The Macmillan Company, 1970.

See: Part 4 (pp. 279-327) "Evaluation of Progress in Reading." Discusses informal classroom techniques and standardized techniques.

Carter, Homes L.J., and Dorothy J. McGinnis. *Diagnosis and Treatment of the Disabled Reader.* London: The Macmillan Company, 1970.

See: Chapter 8 (pp. 129-152) "Making Use of Informal Inventories." A thorough treatment of the informal reading inventory.

Dechant, Emerald. *Diagnosis and Remediation of Reading Disability.* West Nyack, New York: Parker Publishing Company, 1968.

See: Chapter 2 (pp. 26-53) "The Diagnostic Process—Diagnostic Testing." Discusses the formal and informal inventory, the oral reading test, and the diagnostic reading test.

Della—Piana, Gabriel M. *Reading Diagnosis and Prescription.* New York: Holt, Rinehart and Winston, Inc., 1968.

See: Chapter 7 (pp. 75-86) "Assessing Level of Reading Achievement." Uses a case study approach to illustrate the comparison of reading potential with achievement levels in a number of skills.

Durr, William K. (editor). *Reading Instruction—Dimensions and Issues.* Boston: Houghton Mifflin Company, 1967.

See: Chapter 13 (pp. 311-327) "Evaluating Reading." Contains three excellent articles on this topic.

Fry, Edward B. *Reading Instruction for Classroom and Clinic.* New York: McGraw-Hill Book Company, 1972.

See: Chapter 2 (pp. 8-37) "Measuring Reading Achievement." In addition to discussions of informal and standardized reading tests, this chapter contains an alphabetical list of reading tests and a list of test publishers and their addresses.

Hafner, Lawrence E., and Hayden B. Jolly. *Patterns of Teaching Reading in the Elementary School.* New York: The Macmillan Company, 1972.

See: Chapter 2 (pp. 9-36) "Measurement and Evaluation." Contains an excellent discussion of informal inventories and a strategy for establishing reading profiles.

MacGinitie, Walter H. (editor). *Assessment Problems in Reading.* Newark, Delaware: International Reading Association, 1973.

A compilation of articles on this topic.

Russell, David H. *Children Learn to Read.* Boston: Ginn and Company, 1961.

See: Chapter 16 (pp. 526-568) "Evaluation of Growth in and Through Reading." Discusses evaluation of the reading program.

Sebesta, Sam Leaton and Carl J. Wallen. *Readings on Teaching Reading.* Chicago: Science Research Associates, Inc., 1972.

See: Chapter 8 (pp. 424-481) "Evaluation in Reading." Contains five articles on this topic.

Veatch, Jeanette. *Reading in the Elementary School.* New York: The Ronald Press Company, 1966.

See: Chapter 12 (pp. 434-480) "Evaluation, Record Keeping, and Testing." Stresses the importance of record keeping for evaluation.

chapter 7

THE IMPROVEMENT OF INSTRUCTIONAL PRACTICES IN READING

When educators talk about improving instructional practices in reading, they tend to limit the discussion to organizational plans for schools (usually referred to as grouping) and the purchase of newly developed commercial reading programs. Obviously there are a variety of things to consider when educators intend to improve instruction. Our point is that as educators we have behaved as if instructional practices in reading can be improved by finding the ultimate organizational plan or finding the ultimate commercial reading programs.

We would like to present what we humorously call a "limited view" of educational attempts to improve instructional practices in reading. We call this a "limited view" because our purpose is not to present a comprehensive or precise listing of readings, but rather to select typical historical practices which show that as educators we have tended and continue to be guided by this concept: if one organizational plan or commercial reading method doesn't work, try another. We hope that the following "limited view" of organizational practices, followed by a discussion, will enable you to reconsider the practice of repeating ourselves and begin to search for significant ways to improve instructional practices in reading.

Brief History of Organizational Plans and Practices

During what Nila B. Smith[1] calls the Period of Religious Emphasis in Reading Instruction (1607-1776), the popular organizational plan was the Dame School. Under this instructional system children attended school during off-season agricultural periods to learn the basic skills of reading, writing, and arithmetic. The school was church supported. "Teachers" were hired because they understood what the church, that is, the community, expected them to teach. Oral reading was emphasized. This allowed "teachers" to engage in such tasks as sewing or shoe repair during the instructional sessions. Education was not complex, schools played a limited institutional role, and the pattern for American education was formed. By "pattern" we mean that education *followed* the community. At the risk of oversimplification: if the community needed help in peak agricultural periods, school was let out; if religious values were to be taught, teachers taught them; if only basic skills were needed, the curriculum was

---

1. Nila B. Smith, *American Reading Instruction* (Newark, Delaware: International Reading Association, 1962), p. 449.

limited to the three R's. We can go on but the point is, the school as an institution learned to follow rather than lead the community.

In a later era the Reverend Andrew Bell (1753-1832) and Joseph Lancaster (1778-1838) both claimed to have established the organizational plan called the Monitorial System.[2] This educational system was introduced in the United States in 1818 to meet the increased demands created by enormously large groups of students, in rapidly developing communities. The essence of this system was to employ a principal teacher, who in turn recruited older and brighter students to serve as monitors for groups of children. The principal teacher gave the assignments and the monitors would hear other students recite their lessons.

We note again that local communities and local educators adopted this system because, in our opinion, it served increased student populations without significantly increasing local school costs or educational practices.

2. Merritt M. Thompson, *The History of Education* (New York: Barnes & Noble Books, 1961), p. 72.

Colonel Francis W. Parker (1837-1902), Principal, Cook County Normal School, Chicago, Illinois, made a number of significant contributions to American education. His most significant contributions were the reorganization and redirection of elementary education.[3] Colonel Parker reorganized the large monitoral rooms into individual classrooms and recommended that children be assigned to these rooms according to age. This reduced the noise and confusion of the monitorial room, but created the graded lockstep found in schools today. In time the principal teacher became known as the principal and the monitors became classroom teachers.

This structure gave rise to a variety of organizational plans. Around the turn of the century the Cambridge Double—Track Plan was introduced. The regular classroom structure was maintained and study replaced recitations. Brighter, more able students completed six years of education in four years. Slower, less able students completed six years in eight years. During the early 1900s, the Platoon System was inaugurated. This was a "departmentalized" plan whereby basic skills or "fundamentals" were taught in a homeroom, with other rooms for art, music, etc. The history of education is replete with different kinds of schemes and strategies educators devised in their attempts to effect improvement of instructional practices by reorganizing students in one way or another.

By the second decade of the 1900s standardized group achievement testing gained a foothold in educational practice in this country. As a result of large scale and wide spread standardized testing, educators developed a scheme for homogeneous (ability) grouping. One such organizational plan was introduced in Detroit. Superior students were placed in the X Group. Average students were assigned to the Y Group, and below average students to the Z Group.

It wasn't long before opposition to the homogeneous grouping strategy developed. Educators felt that this plan was socially and psychologically undesirable. They found that there was much overlapping of achievement even with this arrangement.

We believe that as a counter thrust to the homogeneous grouping of the 1920s, the 1930s ushered in the era of heterogeneous grouping. Educators proposed the self-contained heterogeneous classroom, with homogeneous groups (usually three) within each heterogeneously arranged classroom. Basal reading instructional programs were rapidly developed to fit into the three-group self-contained classroom. Under this concept, any given classroom would have its share of superior, average and below average students. In this way, the objections voiced against a homogeneous grouping arrangement were nullified. However, a new set of objections took their place. Teachers felt that under the heterogeneous strategy, the variations in achievement were too wide, and that it took too much time to plan for this diversification. In addition, too much material at different levels was required.

3. Ibid., p. 75.

During the past ten or fifteen years, schools combined both homogeneous and heterogeneous plans by assigning students to a heterogeneous room for part of the day and then reassigning them to a homogeneous (ability grouped) room for subjects such as reading or math.

The point is that we have been rearranging students, hoping to bring about the improvement of instructional practices in public education. Today's classrooms are still influenced by the homogeneous grouping strategy of the 1920s, the heterogeneous grouping strategy of the 1930s, and the combination plans of the 1960s.

Thus, we arrive at our basic construct for this chapter: *the improvement of instructional practices occurs when teachers and administrators make appropriate instructional decisions. School organizational plans are not necessarily related to the improvement of instructional practices.*

We have presented most organizational and/or grouping stategies devised in education. They all had as their goal the improvement of instructional practices. Their emphasis has always been on changing organizational patterns. As such, the teacher has not been cast in the role of a decision maker. Traditionally, the teacher has been dependent upon a given administrative arrangement that happened to be present. And so we renew our search for that one scheme—that one panacea—for the improvement of instructional practices, even when a "limited view" tells us that this is not possible. Nongraded plans, team teaching, modular scheduling, etc., all are organizational plans that will get us exactly nowhere—unless the teacher becomes a decision maker. We believe that education in the 1970s cannot be improved by organizational schemes or strategies. Instructional improvement can come about only by changing teacher and administrator attitudes, altering our established school traditions, and learning to observe how children learn.

It is discouraging to note that despite our history of organizational plans for improvement of instructional practices and our stated conclusions regarding improvement of instructional practices, schools continue to assume that "better" organizational plans will result in increased learning achievement.

The Role of Commercial Reading Programs or Methods

The search for the panacea for the improvement of instructional practices does not stop with organizational schemes and strategies; it continues into the area of *method* where the sought after panacea takes the form, "What is the ideal/best method to employ?"

Confusion about the teaching of reading at all levels of public education appears to result from the constant repetition of the charge that schools employ, or fail to employ, certain methods of reading instruction. Newspapers frequently champion a single published method for teaching reading. Publishers and their representatives enthusiastically support their particular method for the teaching of reading. Parents observe their children, or other children in the neighborhood, profiting from reading instruction and quickly attribute their reading growth to the method employed. We believe that school administrators and classroom teachers become enamored with a particular method and then assume that the method itself teaches the student to read.

With so much discussion of method versus method, cost of methods, results of methods, or even the suggestion to use a combination of methods, how can we fail to conclude that the method is the single most important factor in teaching reading? And what is more, that there is *one* method superior to all other methods?

The authors of this text take the position that the method used to teach reading is only *one* factor in a reading program, and that the use of any given method will not of itself result in a student's learning to read.

The widespread emphasis on the importance of published reading methods must make the position of the authors of this text appear to be almost incredible.

We all have had the experience, at one time or another, of listening to somebody who has become a devotee of a particular method of reading instruction. If we listen only to what the person says, it appears that the method being described is *the* method for all students. If this is an adequate method for all students, then why shouldn't all teachers use this method? But, if we analyze the speaker's behavior rather than listen to his words, we might discover why he is convinced that the method he uses is the ultimate method.

Excitement over or emotional involvement in the method selected may have caused him to select it. Interest in this method may have caused him to analyze carefully or, stated another way, to learn thoroughly what the method entails. Better knowledge of the method may have resulted in improved communication with students. We also believe that the informed, enthusiastic person feels the need to encourage children to become involved in learning by this newly identified method. It appears that if this person is convinced that he has identified the "best" approach to teaching reading, he is likely to do all that is humanly possible to help students learn to read in order to support his biased position.

Let us look at a hypothetical situation. Teacher A, an experienced master teacher, has selected a particular method for teaching reading. If he behaves in the manner described above, we soon might hear him say "This method is the best I've ever used," or "This method seems to develop the skills necessary for reading." If we analyze these statements, we can see that the method caused the teacher to react in ways that probably created a more favorable learning environment for the students.

The point we wish to emphasize is that *methods affect teachers who in turn affect learning situations.* We believed that methods do not teach students to read. The teacher is more important than the method used.

Since our hypothetical teacher probably would be successful, administrators and parents would be likely to conclude that all teachers should use this method. This line of reasoning appears to contribute most to our method debate. We have no assurance that a method which stimulates one teacher will stimulate other teachers. Indeed, if a teacher is forced to employ a method he dislikes, he probably will create a flat, unenthusiastic environment for students. The fact that the teacher selects a method is *excellent* because he is acting in a decision making capacity. The problem arises when we force *other* teachers to use that same method and prevent them from acting in a decision making capacity.

We have looked to methods to solve our reading problems and we have consistently ignored one of the most important factors in the total process—the teacher. If a teacher is enthusiastic and informed about a method for teaching reading, that method will probably be successful for that teacher. Enthusiasm can neither be written into a teacher's manual nor can it be imposed from outside. Enthusiasm is a feeling which is highly individualistic. It is a necessary ingredient of every successful reading program.

Reading methods are not substitutes for qualified teachers who know the field of Reading Education, who are enthusiastic, and who understand the learning needs of children. So often, in unsophisticated research, we mistake the method as the successful ingredient, instead of recognizing the enthusiastic teacher as the successful ingredient. As long as education centers its attention on finding *the* ideal method, instead of on the teacher who will employ the method, we are merely continuing to search for a nonexistent panacea.

Thus, the other construct for this chapter: *the improvement of instructional practices occurs when teachers and administrators make appropriate instructional decisions. Selections of reading materials are not causes for the improvement of instruction.*

Since it is apparent that organizational plans and selection of reading materials are *not* causes for the improvement of instructional practices, where are we now? It is just as apparent that the only hope for the improvement of instructional practices is in the individuality, leadership, and decision making capabilities of teachers and administrators.

A good question at this point might be, "Where, in what areas, should teachers be making decisions regarding the improvement of instructional practices in reading?"

In Unit I (Chapters 1-5) we presented constructs as guides to decision making in the areas of basic word recognition and comprehension skill development. Chapter 6 presented constructs as guides to decision making in the areas of group and individual tests. At this point we might say that teachers have a minimum understanding of basic skills and are now ready to consider possible ways to apply these skills in actual classroom situations.

Chapters related to the application of basic skills will be developed throughout the remaining parts of this book.

SUMMARY

Educators have attempted to effect the improvement of instructional practices in education by employing a wide variety of organizational (grouping) plans, and through the selection of reading material. However, organizational grouping plans and selection of reading material are not causes for the improvement of instructional practices. The improvement of instructional practices occurs when teachers and administrators make appropriate instructional decisions. Traditionally, the teacher has been dependent upon whatever administrative arrangement was in effect.

The method used to teach reading is only one factor in a reading program, and it is not the method that teaches a child to read. The teacher is more important than the method he employs. Methods affect teachers who in turn affect learning situations.

The improvement of instructional practices lies in the individuality, leadership, and decision making capabilities of teachers and administrators, and not in nonexistent panaceas such as organizational plans and published methods.

REFERENCES FOR CHAPTER 7

Betts, Emmett Albert. *Foundations of Reading Instruction*. New York: American Book Company, 1957.

See: Chapter 4 (pp. 35-49), "Attempts to Break the Lock Step." Discusses various grouping plans and evaluates them.

Durr, William K., (Editor). *Reading Instruction: Dimensions and Issues*. Boston: Houghton Mifflin Company, 1967.

See: Chapter 9 (pp. 205-236), "Organizing for Instruction." Five excellent articles dealing with this topic.

Figurel, J. Allen (editor) *Reading and Inquiry*. Newark, Delaware: International Reading Association, 1965.

See: Sequence VI (pp. 128-145) "A New Look at Organizing the Classroom." Presents articles dealing with all levels of instruction: K-college.

Fitzgerald, James. A., and Patricia G. Fitzgerald. *Fundamentals of Reading Instruction*. Milwaukee: The Bruce Publishing Company, 1967.

See: Chapter 4 (pp. 94-126) "A Developmental Reading Program." Discusses grouping for reading instruction.

Gray, William S., *On Their Own in Reading*. New York: Scott, Foresman and Company, 1948.

See: Chapter 1 (pp. 3-33), "Changing Viewpoints." Some historical background on the teaching of reading—especially during the 1900s.

Harris, Albert J. (editor) *Readings on Reading Instruction*. New York: David McKay Co., Inc., 1963.

See: Section VI (pp. 134-169), "Grouping for Effective Reading Instruction." Presents seven articles covering many different aspects of this topic.

Sebesta, Sam Leaton and Carl J. Wallen. *Readings on Teaching Reading*. Chicago: Science Research Associates, Inc., 1972.

See: Chapter 3 (pp. 151-179), "Organizing for Instruction—Procedures." Specifies alternatives for solving procedural problems related to phonics, grouping, primary-class organization, and comprehension.

Smith, Nila Banton. *American Reading Instruction*. Newark, Delaware: International Reading Association, 1965.

See: The book in its entirety is recommended to gain perspective on movements in the field of reading instruction.

————. *Reading Instruction for Today's Children*. Englewood Cliffs, New Jersey: Prentice-Hall, Inc., 1963.

See: Chapter 6 (pp. 108-128), "Grouping Plans Take on New Forms." Comes to the conclusion that maintaining faith in the child and creating opportunities for him to experience success are more essential and hence more basic than any form of grouping.

Wilson, Robert M., and Maryanne Hall. *Reading and the Elementary School Child*. New York: Van Nostrand Reinhold Company, 1972.

See: Chapter 12 (pp. 264-286), "Individualization and Grouping." Discusses common grouping practices.

chapter 8

READINESS FOR READING

Reading readiness has been succinctly defined as: "That stage of developmental maturity when a child can learn to read easily, effectively, and efficiently, without much personal disturbances."[1]

Defined as such, readiness for reading is a developmental stage at which inherited (biological) and learned (environmental) factors have prepared the child for a program of formal reading instruction. Readiness for reading is a blending of these interdependent factors.

Because there are many factors, both inherited and learned, that may interfere with the child's readiness for reading, the teacher must be aware of the factors that foster or inhibit satisfactory reading performance. In addition, the teacher must have the ability to measure or evaluate these factors, and on the basis of that ability identify each pupil's specific readiness for reading. Finally, the teacher must be competent in providing the training and creating the environment which will enhance development of the skills involved in learning to read.

We are aware of the skills and understandings required of teachers in this area of readiness or beginning reading. We are also aware of the enormous and often conflicting amount of literature which, we believe, tends to confuse rather than assist teachers in gaining these skills and understandings. Consistent with our other chapters, we have formulated a three-stage construct to simplify and summarize the complex area of readiness or beginning reading. Reading readiness Construct:

Stage   I—Underlying Readiness Factors.

Stage   II—Evaluating Significant and Very Significant Readiness Factors.

Stage III—Training Significant and Very Significant Readiness Factors.

Most developmental textbooks in Reading Education devote at least one chapter to the topic of Reading Readiness. Research and research reviews also discuss the topic of Readiness. The problem, as we see it, is that there are too many terms or categories used to organize this vast amount of data. We feel that it might be useful to identify those factors which are most frequently discussed—hence, Stage I. In addition, we feel

---

1. Lawrence W. Carrillo, *Informal Reading—Readiness Experiences* (San Francisco: Chandler Publishing Company, 1964), p. 4.

that if we make simple, direct statements about each factor, this will provide you with an understanding of those readiness factors we call "significant" and "very significant," which lend themselves to evaluation (Stage II) and training(Stage III). You will note that the factors of age and sex have been eliminated from Stage II and Stage III because they are biological "givens" and cannot be evaluated or trained.

STAGE I: UNDERLYING READINESS FACTORS

The Age Factor: Chronological age, in and of itself, has practically no significance in determining a youngster's readiness for reading.

The Sex Factor: There is a widespread belief concerning the superiority of girls over boys in attaining readiness for reading. Contained within this notion is the idea that this presumed superiority of girls over boys is due to biological differences favoring the development of girls. When we realize that many more boys than girls experience difficulty learning to read in this country, it is easy to understand why this notion is given credence by many reading experts. However, differences in readiness which can be attributed to sex tend to be slight, as demonstrated through various tests. Furthermore, these differences do not always favor the girls. In America, most primary teachers are women, and it is possible that their attitudes towards boys are different from their attitudes toward girls. All of which is to say that possibly environmental factors, such as pupil-teacher relationships and expectations, are more important as determiners of reading achievement than are the biological factors when it comes to sex differences and their presumptive relationship to measurable learning achievement.

The Language Factors: Sufficient language development is necessary for progress in reading. The major factors of language that seem most significant in reading readiness are:

1. *Speaking Vocabulary:* The child's speaking vocabulary consists of the number of words used in oral communication, and is one indication of reading readiness level.
2. *Auditory Vocabulary:* The child's auditory vocabulary consists of the number of words that he recognizes when he *hears* them.
3. *Auditory Comprehension:* The child's auditory comprehension refers to the ability to answer questions about material read to him.
4. *Sentence Structure:* The child's mastery of sentence structure is shown most clearly in his spontaneous conversation; and it is an indication of the readiness level suggested in the preceding three factors.[1]

---

1. Albert J. Harris, *How To Increase Reading Ability* (New York: David McKay Co., Inc., 1970), p. 32.

5.   *Articulation:* The child's clarity of pronunciation, or his tendency to use baby talk and make substitutions for certain sounds is related to his early reading readiness.[2]

Kindergarten: More and more kindergarten teachers are starting to teach prereading and beginning reading skills. However, this earlier emphasis on reading in the kindergarten has not yet been shown to result in higher primary reading scores or more favorable attitudes toward reading and school than a well-planned program without this emphasis.

Physical Development: While it is impossible to make individual predictions, it is generally true that children whose parents provide adequate medical care and a proper diet tend to experience greater success in school.

Vision: Any marked departure from normal vision is likely to interfere with beginning reading. Thus the visual skills of the youngster are quite significant to his early reading success.

Visual Discrimination: Visual discrimination, or perception, is the ability to discern similarities and differences among letter shapes and word forms. The child may have normal vision and yet not be able to discern the difference between b-d or *was—saw,* for example. The ability to perceive visual similarities and differences is essential for progress in reading.

Hearing: Poor hearing, as well as poor vision, is likely to interfere with the development of reading skills.

Auditory Discrimination: Auditory discrimination, or perception, is the ability to distinguish likenesses and differences among letter sounds as they occur in words. The youngster may have normal auditory acuity (hearing), but may not have learned to detect the differences between the sounds of words, e.g., *pen—pin.* This inability to hear the differences between words which sound somewhat alike is likely to create a difficulty in learning to read.

The Intellectual Factors: It has been a long-standing belief that a mental age of approximately six years is necessary for success in beginning reading. If a teacher is unable or unwilling to meet individual pupil needs, then this concept of a minimum mental age is probably accurate. However, if it is possible to structure instruction according to individual pupil needs and readiness, children of a lower mental age can learn to read adequately. It is not possible to set a definite minimum mental age for learning to read because too many other factors are involved. Intelligence tests results are not highly predictive of early reading success, despite their value in other areas.

2. Ibid.

Directionality: Directional confusion, shown in inability to identify left and right correctly, and delay in establishing a consistent preference for one hand, seem to be significantly related to difficulty in learning to read.

Experience: The adequacy of the child's background of knowledge and experience is certainly helpful in creating a readiness for reading. By an adequate background of knowledge and experience we mean the type of knowledge and experience assumed by the printed material generally used in schools. If a child lacks this assumed background of knowledge and experience, he is likely to have difficulty in learning to read, especially in comprehending what he reads.

Emotional and Social Maturity: Harris[1] has identified three aspects of emotional and social maturity as being significant in reading readiness:

The first of these is *emotional stability.*

The second factor is *self-reliance,* or the ability and desire to help oneself.

The third factor is the ability to *participate actively* and *cooperatively* in group activities.

Interest in Books: The desire to learn to read is one of the most important factors of readiness. Youngsters who have been read to, and enjoy looking through picture books, and have come to realize that books give pleasure, usually look forward to learning to read with excitement and anticipation.

In Stage I, we have identified fourteen factors, both inherited (biological) and learned (environmental), that may interfere with the child's readiness for reading. At the beginning of this chapter, we pointed out that these factors are interdependent, and that reading readiness is a combination of many different characteristics. Some of these factors can be measured by standardized tests, some can be judged from information given by the youngster's parents, and some can be noted only by observing the child in his everyday behavior.

With the full realization that these factors are interdependent, we have, nevertheless, attempted to group them in three categories: Mildly Significant, Significant, and Very Significant.

Mildly Significant: The factors in this group will receive no further consideration in this chapter because they are biological "givens:"

1. The Age Factor.
2. The Sex Factor.

Significant: The factors included in this group are, for the most part, inherited

---

1. A.J. Harris, *How to Increase Reading Ability* (New York: David McKay Co., Inc., 5th ed., 1970), pp. 33-34.

characteristics, and are not readily susceptible to the intervention of a systematic program of training:

3. Vision.
4. Hearing.
5. Physical Development.
6. The Intellectual Factors.
7. Kindergarten.

Very Significant: The factors included in this group are, for the most part, learned or environmental characteristics and are readily susceptible to the intervention of a systematic program of training:

8. The Language Factors.
9. Visual Discrimination.
10. Auditory Discrimination.
11. Directionality.
12. Experience.
13. Emotional and Social Maturity.
14. Interest in Books.

STAGE II: EVALUATING SIGNIFICANT AND VERY SIGNIFICANT READINESS FACTORS

Vision: In most schools, vision testing is limited to far-point tests, usually the Snellen chart. This procedure provides only about one-third of the necessary visual data. The Snellen chart only measures visual acuity at far point (20-foot distance). Teachers need information regarding the near point reading distance (14-inch distance), and the extent to which the child has binocular coordination. Since visual development proceeds from far point to near point, most children are likely to pass a test that measures far-point acuity. Many youngsters who pass the Snellen test may have a vision problem that goes undetected, and which will limit their success in reading if the problem is not detected and corrected. About 50% of youngsters who successfully pass the Snellen are in need of visual correction of some kind.

What is needed is better vision testing in schools so that visual difficulties can be detected. Students who have visual deficiencies should be referred to a professional in the field of vision for a complete eye examination.

Many schools have set up screening programs which are administered by school nurses who train parents to detect those students who need professional care. There are several effective commercial vision screening tests available. Those that are most frequently recommended by specialists are:

Keystone Visual Survey Tests, Keystone View Company, Meadville, Pennsylvania.

Orthorater, Bausch and Lomb Optical Company, Rochester, New York.

Professional Vision Tester, Titmus Optical Company, Petersburg, Virginia.

Spache Binocular Reading Test, Keystone View Company, Meadville, Pennsylvania.

In the classroom, the teacher, by careful observation of students, will be able to spot certain behaviors that may indicate visual difficulties. Both observation and screening should be used to determine which youngsters need to be referred to an eye specialist. Among the more signigicant symptoms that may be observed by teachers are these:

1. Eyes tear or become bloodshot.
2. Frequent rubbing of eyes.
3. Squinting.
4. Closing one eye to see better.
5. Avoiding close work.
6. Holding book close to face.
7. Complaining of headaches.

Hearing: Youngsters in school today fare much better when it comes to auditory acuity testing because more adequate procedures are used to determine hearing capacity than to test vision. Many schools have set up screening programs in which a youngster's auditory acuity is checked on an audiometer test. *Auditory acuity* is the ability to hear sounds of varying pitch and loudness. Youngsters who reveal losses in auditory acuity, especially the high tones, should be referred to an ear specialist.

In the classroom the teacher, by careful observation of students, will be able to spot certain behaviors that may indicate hearing difficulties. Among the more significant symptoms that may be observed by teachers are these:

1. Chronic ear infections.
2. Instructions are misunderstood.
3. Need to have statements repeated.
4. Inattentiveness.
5. Hearing and understanding better up close to teacher than from the seat.

Physical Development: The practice of giving every child entering the first grade a complete physical examination by a physician should be more widely followed. No child should have to struggle along handicapped by physical defects which can be corrected, and which, undetected will limit the child's progress and comprehension.

116

When a complete medical check-up is not possible, the teacher can still pick up many signs which indicate a physical problem. Among the more significant symptoms that may be noticed by teachers are these:

1. Overweight/underweight.
2. Pale, appears to be anemic.
3. Seeming lack of energy.
4. Frequent colds/infections.
5. Gross motor difficulties evidenced by various kinds of clumsiness, such as in walking, skipping, throwing, catching, and other physical activities.

6. Fine motor adaptability problems evidenced by copying difficulties, trouble in using scissors or crayons, or any other awkwardness in motor activities.

Many teachers are becoming familiar with the Denver Development Screening Test developed by William K. Frankenburg, M.D. and Josiah B. Dodds, Ph.D., of the University of Colorado Medical Center. This simple screening device is easily administered and can be used to detect gross motor difficulties and problems with fine motor adaptability.

The Intellectual Factors: Today, most schools give group intelligence tests to entering children. These tests can be administered and scored by the teacher. These group intelligence tests are relatively simple and if they are effective, reading ability is not required. The teacher gives the directions orally, and the children respond by marking pictures with a crayon. These tests usually measure such capabilities as ability to follow directions, memory, fund of factual information, concept development, vocabulary, and ability to recognize similarities and differences.

Following is a list of group intelligence tests most often recommended for use with students just completing kindergarten or at the beginning of first grade:

1. California Test of Mental Maturity, Pre-primary Battery.
2. Kuhlman—Anderson Intelligence Test (Grade 1A).
3. Otis—Lennon Mental Ability Test, Primary K.
4. Pintner—Cunningham Primary Test.
5. SRA Primary Mental Abilities.

Those children who score quite low, or who are thought to be much brighter than the test results indicate, or who because of emotional and social factors cannot take the group test, should be tested on an individual intelligence test.

The three individual intelligence tests used most widely for children in this country are:

1. Revised Standford-Binet Intelligence Scale.
2. Wechsler Intelligence Scale for Children—Revised.
3. Wechsler Preschool and Primary Scale of Intelligence.

The Language Factors: A child's use of language in expressing his thoughts reveals much about his language background and how well that background is suited to the task of learning to read. The level of language usage may or may not represent the level of the child's ideas. A child with high level verbal facility may not have any more mature ideas than the child whose language is inadequate or unacceptable. Two main factors of language power are the ability to verbalize an idea, and the nature of the syntax, or sentence structure.

The child's ability to put his thoughts into words depends upon several different language abilities working together, combined with a certain attitude or feeling of wanting to express himself. Language abilities include adequate vocabulary, a command of syntax sufficient to put the words together in proper relationship, ease or facility in producing the amount of language necessary, and the self-confidence and security to function normally.

A certain degree of facility with language is necessary for success in learning to read. The teacher, then, should know how to assess language facility or language maturity in order to know, first, what to expect from the child in the way of progress; and, secondly, what to do for the child in terms of instructional procedures.

Following is a method for assessing language facility that can be used easily and informally by the teacher.

Evaluating Individual Oral Language: A carefully selected picture is presented privately to each child, who is encouraged by the teacher to "Tell all about it." Everything the child says is recorded verbatim, usually on tape. He may be encouraged with nondirective phrases such as "That's fine. Tell me some more." The child's entire verbal output is subsequently analyzed in relation to ability to verbalize ideas and to sentence structure.

For the purposes of analyzing oral language the constant contact of the classroom can be turned to good use. Instead of observing and analyzing the child's responses to one particular picture, the teacher may observe daily the oral language of pupils in all kinds of situations. This observation can take place during formal recitations in class, during informal activities or even on the playground.

Monroe presented a scale for evaluating a child's language ability in interpreting pictures. She suggested that a picture be selected in which two or more characters are engaged in some interesting activity and that the pupil be asked to tell what the picture is about. His verbal response is recorded and classified as to level according to the following steps:

Step 1. The child merely shrugs his shoulders and does not reply. He may venture to name some of the objects in the picture.

Step 2. The child describes what the characters are doing.

Step 3. The child expresses a relationship between the characters or objects.

Step 4. The child sees the picture as one part of a narrative. He verbalizes relationships of time, place, cause-effect.

Step 5. The child reacts to the mood of the picture, perceives the emotional reactions of the characters, and draws a conclusion or evaluates the actions.[1]

Monroe suggests that children who have not reached Step 3 or Step 4 on this scale have not developed sufficient language ability to interpret a picture in a primer and react to the text that accompanies the picture.

If the child has not reached a level where he can adequately handle language at Steps 3 and 4, he very probably should be in a program of oral language development until he gains sufficient facility to succeed in learning to read, that is, until he achieves reading readiness.

---

1. Marion Monroe, "Necessary Preschool Experiences for Comprehending Reading," *Reading and Inquiry.* International Reading Association Conference Proceedings, vol. 10 (Newark, Delaware: International Reading Association, 1965), pp. 45-46.

Visual Discrimination: All reading readiness tests contain subtests to measure visual discrimination. However, it is believed that the best tests for visual discrimination are those which do not require previous knowledge of letters and words, but use other means of measuring visual discrimination. True tests of visual discrimination are found in the following reading readiness tests:

1. Harrison—Stroud Reading Readiness Test.
2. Murphy—Durrell Reading Readiness Analysis.
3. Reading Aptitude Tests by Marian Monroe.

Auditory Discrimination: A simple, yet efficient, test of auditory discrimination that can be used by the teacher is the *Wepman Auditory Discrimination Test.*

This test consists of 40 pairs of monosyllabic words with 30 of the 40 pairs differing in a single sound, such as the beginning consonant (bale-gale), the final consonant (tub-tug), or medial vowel sound (pat-pet). Ten of the 40 pairs are not different (chap-chap). Each word pair is read to the child who has his back to the teacher. The child is directed to state whether the word pair sounds exactly the same or in any way different.

The primary child with normal auditory discrimination should not make more than four errors on the word pairs that are different. The ten word pairs that are the same are there merely as distractors and are not scored.

Directionality: The best method to evaluate directional confusion (inability to identify left and right correctly), and consistent hand preference, is teacher observation.

Experience: In the classroom the teacher, by careful observation of students, will be able to identify those students with a meager background of experience. Among the more significant indications that may be observed by teachers are these:

1. The child has a very limited range of information.
2. The child does not seem to know basic nursery rhymes and traditional stories.
3. The child does not score well on tests of vocabulary, information and concept development.
4. The child's experience seems to be limited to his immediate neighborhood.

Emotional and Social Maturity: This is one area where the teacher is pretty much on her own for it takes a trained psychologist to administer the tests designed to identify children whose maladjustments have marked them for failure. Teacher appraisal, however, can be a most effective tool for spotting youngsters whose lack of emotional adjustment will hinder their reading success.

Spotting Emotional Instability: Among the more significant indicators of emotional instability are these:

1. Excessive timidity, fearfulness or self-consciousness.
2. Overagressiveness.
3. Temper tantrums.
4. Negativism.
5. Hyperactivity.
6. Excessive dependency.
7. Unusually sensitive to criticism, "cry baby."
8. Specific nervous habits such as hair pulling, nail biting, facial tics, stuttering, or stammering.

Spotting Lack of Self-Reliance: Among the more significant indicators of a lack of self-reliance are these:

1. Excessive demands to be helped.
2. Low tolerance for frustration.
3. Excessive dependency.
4. Quick to give up when faced with a difficult situation.

Spotting Poor Group Participation: Among the more significant indicators of poor group participation are these:

1. Withdrawn, inhibited child who does not speak out.
2. Excessive bickering and fighting with other children; too bossy.
3. Easily pushed around by others in group.

Interest in Books: The child who lacks interest in books will often display a lack of interest in reading. This child usually seems disinterested and distracted when the teacher reads or tells stories. Most significant, however, is the child who shows no interest at all in books or in learning to read.

STAGE III: TRAINING SIGNIFICANT AND VERY SIGNIFICANT READINESS FACTORS

Visual Discrimination: Undoubtedly visual discrimination is one of the most significant factors that contributes to reading readiness, for without it the child cannot tell one visual symbol from the other. Skill in visual discrimination is learned, and can be improved by direct training. The direct training of visual discrimination constitutes one of the teacher's major responsibilities in the child's reading readiness program. It seems to follow that the school must provide as much of this experience as is needed, and different children may need different amounts.

Following is a list of visual discrimination exercises that are in current use in many schools throughout this country:

1. Identification of similar geometric figures.
2. Identification of geometric figures with finer discriminations.
3. Identification of common objects with slight differences.
4. Recognition of similar digits.
5. Identification of letters and small words.
6. Finding a specific letter in words of a sentence.
7. Finding identical elements at the beginning of words.
8. Finding identical elements at the end of words.
9. Recognizing "word families."

There are differences of opinion as to the efficacy of these exercises in visual discrimination. As can be seen from the above list, much of this discrimination training has to do with learning to discriminate pictorial forms and geometric shapes from one another. However, it is not at all certain that such exercises have much effect on learning to recognize letters and words. Instead, research in this area seems to indicate that learning to discriminate geometric shapes and pictorial forms from one another does not have much effect on reading ability.

There appears to be concurrence in the literature that the recognition of a word follows from an identification of its constituent elements, and that a clear view of at least some of the letters of the word is necessary before it can be recognized with confidence.

The few experiments attempted with visual discrimination training, such as the one completed by Wheelock and Silvaroli,[1] seem to indicate that skill in word recognition is directly related to the development of specific visual discrimination skills, i.e., the ability to discriminate words and letters.

When reading readiness testing is begun, only those reading readiness tests that include visual discrimination subtests should be employed. And only those subtests that measure the child's ability to discern similarities in letter forms, to perceive differences in letter forms, and the ability to recognize both similarities and differences in letter and word formations, need to be administered to determine each youngster's specific visual discrimination skills. One such test is the *Lee-Clark Reading Readiness Test.*

When the results of the testing program are evaluated, those youngsters who show a lack of specific visual discrimination skills need to be placed in a program for the direct training of visual discrimination.

Whatever visual discrimination training program the teacher decides to employ, it should be a program that emphasizes the direct teaching of learning to recognize

1. Warren H. Wheelock and Nicholas J. Silvaroli, "Visual Discrimination Training for Beginning Readers," *The Reading Teacher*, vol. 21, no. 2, November, 1967, pp. 115-120.

similarities and differences in letter and word formations. As indicated, material which devotes most of its emphasis to training the youngster to discriminate among geometric and animal forms does not have much effect on learning to discriminate letters and words.

Auditory Discrimination: In any of the major reading programs in use in America today, we are likely to find that first-grade lessons require responses combining visual and auditory discrimination capabilities; consequently, the first-grade teacher is likely to combine and require both visual and auditory responses. It appears unrealistic, however, to assume that all children have acquired the associative-conceptual process of discriminating basic speech sounds by the time they begin major reading programs.

Readiness or preparatory lessons found in most of the major programs make provision for requiring the child to discriminate accurately the sights and sounds in his environment. These lessons, however, are not likely to be built on the letter forms or letter sounds used in later reading lessons.

Silvaroli and Wheelock[2] conducted a study with an auditory discrimination program that helped children to discriminate 33 basic speech sounds more effectively. This training program did not purport to teach phonics, the alphabet, or to improve reading instruction. Its purpose was limited to determining whether this kind of auditory discrimination training would help the beginning reader to discriminate 33 basic speech sounds. The design for this program is described below:

1. Don't use a program of auditory discrimination training with children who don't need it. For those children who do need such a program, 15 minutes a day with the program seems about right.
2. The learning task for children in the program is to make an appropriate response to contrasting pairs of basic speech sounds, within the context of a known word presented via a tape recorder.
3. If the contrasting pair is the same, e.g., **Pen-Pen**, the children display a small square card with the picture of a bell on it. The tape then plays a bell sound to reinforce the proper response. In this manner the child is able to compare his own output against another repetition of the standard.
4. If the contrasting pair is different, e.g., **Pen-Pin**, the children display a small round card with the picture of a buzzer on it. The tape then plays a buzzer sound to reinforce the proper response. In this manner the child is able to compare his own output against another repetition of the standard.
5. The tape should consist of basic speech sounds within the context of words. Each word can be used many times during the training in various combina-

2. Nicholas J. Silvaroli and Warren H. Wheelock, "An Investigation of Auditory Discrimination Training for Beginning Readers," *The Reading Teacher*, vol. 20, December, 1966, pp. 247-251.

tions with other words. The time for the pronunciation of each word should be approximately one second.

6. The typical pattern used throughout is as follows: word (one second); contrasting word (one second); reinforcement interval time to select bell or buzzer card (five seconds); reinforcing second—bell or buzzer (one second); start next pair.

Some suggestions for selecting the basic speech sounds are as follows:

Segment I: Introduce the relatively easy consonant sounds of B P M N in the final position of one syllable words, e.g., **Tab—Tap.**

Segment II: Introduce the relatively easy consonant sounds of D T G Sh in the final position of one syllable words, e.g., **Rush—Rug.**

Segment III: Introduce the more difficult consonant sounds of V F S in the final position of one syllable words, e.g., **Have—Has.**

Segment IV: Introduce the more difficult consonant sounds of V F S in the initial position of one syllable words, e.g., **Vat—Fat.**

Segment V: Introduce the more difficult consonant sounds of Th (voiced) Th (voiceless) R L in the final position of one syllable words, e.g., **Bath—Ball.**

Segment VI: Introduce the more difficult consonant sounds of Th (voiced) Th (voiceless) R L in the initial position of one syllable words, e.g., **Thing—Ring.**

Segment VII: Provide a general review of all consonants previously introduced in both final and initial positions.

Segment VIII: Introduce the short vowel sounds of A E I O U—U in the medial position of words composed of the consonant sounds trained in the medial position of words composed of the consonant sounds trained in the previous segments, e.g., **Bat—Bet.**

Segment IX: Introduce base words with the endings S ED ER ING added, e.g., **Reads—Reader.**

Segment X: Provide for a general review of the medial vowels and word endings previously introduced.

At the beginning of the program the material can be used with the children every day for a period of about 15 minutes per day. When the children have demonstrated some proficiency with the material, usually after two weeks, it is better to go to an every-other-day schedule.

It is important at the outset that you encourage the children to respond no matter how many errors they make initially.

Check to see how the group is doing and watch for children who do not make independent judgments but wait to see what the others are doing.

This is *auditory discrimination training* only. Do not attempt to relate the words students hear to the words or letters as printed. If you do, this is likely to cause confusion and retard the student's progress.

124

The Language Factors: The beginning youngster's language development can be stimulated in a variety of ways by the teacher. She can provide opportunity for each child to speak in turn when working in a small group. Those games in which children have to finish a sentence or a story, played in a group, provide excellent opportunity for practice in talking. The teacher can encourage the children to talk about their work or something else that interests them. There are many games and activities which will contribute to these language skills.

The Peabody Language Development Kit (American Guidance Service, Inc.), contains a manual of 180 daily lessons, stimulus cards, large story cards, plastic color chips, 2 puppets, and a tape of fairy tales and music. This is an excellent program designed to stimulate oral language development.

The Sounds of Language (Holt, Rinehart, and Winston), is based on the premise that a reading selection should be taught as a total linguistic experience from which children can analyze language and later verbalize their understanding of how it works.

Key Vocabulary—The child builds his own individual word list. He dictates each word to the teacher, writes and reads each word. Words are kept by the child and are reviewed frequently.

Rock *Materials* (Melton Book Co., Dallas, Texas), This program consists of 128 lessons designed to help non-English Spanish-Surnamed children acquire the basic syntactical structures of English. Each lesson is supplemented with visual aids, games, seatwork, music, art, etc.

There is continuing development of prepared oral language programs for beginning students which follow the procedures used in teaching English as a second language to adults. These oral language programs emphasize oral exercises in sentence patterns and structural linguistics, and they result in greater fluency in speech and ability to use words to express ideas, and help to move youngsters toward an extended use of standard English.

Directionality: The ability to distinguish right from left, up from down, forward from backward, and directional movement (directionality), and the ability to integrate one's sensory-motor contact with the environment through the establishment of a consistent hand and eye preference (laterality), are fundamental to successful reading. Without adequate development of these directional skills, the child is distracted by frequent reversals, inversions, and word confusions. The child must follow a constant left-to-right movement for successful word recognition and forward progress along the lines of print.

The *Move-Grow-Learn* Program developed by Mariann Frostig (Follett Pub. Co.), is a packet of cards with the description of one psychomotor activity per card. The program teaches directionality and laterality along with body awareness, coordination, agility, strength, flexibility, balance, and creative movement. Cards include exercises and games which require few additional materials. The cards are easy to use. The teacher makes the decision as to which cards in the set she will use.

The classroom teacher, by using imagination, can create variations of these basic directionality and laterality exercises. Keep in mind that the basic purposes of these exercises are to develop recognition of directions, and the pursuit of these directions by coordinated hand-eye movements.

Experience: There is much the teacher can do to provide meaningful, worth-while and varied experiences for those children who come from a meager background of experience.

Visits to stores, factories, museums, fire and police stations, even within the school itself, and to other resources in the community can be helpful. Longer trips outside the immediate community area to farms, the zoo, historical sites, etc., are also possible. The teacher should plan for the development of new vocabulary and concepts during the trip and in later discussions in the classroom.

Pictures, films, film strips, and tapes can help in the development of an enriched experiential background.

Children should be encouraged to share their experience with others in the classroom as a means of enriching awareness and experience.

The classroom itself can be used to provide rich experiences through the reading of stories, plays, and poems to the children. It is also helpful to interpret the meaning of these readings, and to encourage the children to participate in this interpretation.

Treasure Chest (Harper & Row), is a readiness program based on children's literature, and is organized into 20 units designed to cover an entire school year. It covers language arts, science, arithmetic and social studies, and is an excellent program for the culturally deprived youngster.

SUMMARY

When we talk about readiness for reading we are really talking about the *prevention of reading disability.* What we have presented in this chapter is an identification of essential readiness factors. In essence, if schools were able to identify all of the significant factors important to readiness for reading and in turn establish alternatives for helping the learner develop these factors, preventing reading disability might become more of a reality than an abstract goal.

Teachers and administrators should be able to arrange content to match the learning style of the individual child. It is as important to understand *how* pupils learn as well as *what* they learn.

Reading education, in the past, has often been based mainly on the reading program selected by the school, and in many instances has covered only a narrow aspect of the reading area, e.g., phonics, visual discrimination, etc. This chapter identifies the factors which tend to create reading disability in a school situation and uses a series of procedures (working models) to eliminate or reduce the persistent problems which relate to reading disability. Readiness for reading is a developmental stage at which inherited (biological) and learned (environmental) factors should have prepared the child for a program of formal reading instruction. Readiness for reading is a blending of these interdependent factors.

This chapter on readiness for reading was organized around the following constructs:

Stage   I—Underlying Readiness Factors.

Stage   II—Evaluating Significant and Very Significant Readiness Factors.

Stage III—Training Significant and Very Significant Readiness Factors.

Most Development textbooks in Reading Education devote at least one chapter to the topic of Reading Readiness. Research and research reviews also discuss the topic of Readiness. The problem we have observed lies in the wide variety of terms or categories used to organize this vast amount of data. We felt that it might be useful to identify those factors which are most frequently discussed—hence, Stage I. In addition, we felt that if we made simple direct statements about each factor, this would provide you with background for those readiness factors, we will call significant and very significant, which lend themselves to evaluation (Stage II) and training (Stage III). You will find that the factors of age and sex have been eliminated from Stage II and Stage III because they are biological "givens" and cannot be evaluated or trained.

Readiness for reading and the prevention of reading disability can be considered as being synonymous. We attempted to identify those factors which tend to create reading disability in a school situation and presented a series of procedures (working models) to eliminate or reduce the persistent problems which relate to reading disability.

REFERENCES FOR CHAPTER 8

Anderson, Irving H., and Walter F. Dearborn. *The Psychology of Teaching Reading.* New York: The Ronald Press Company, 1952.

See: Chapter 2 (pp. 50-100) "The Concept of Reading Readiness." Deals extensively with the question. "What is reading readiness?"

Artley, A. Sterl. *Your Child Learns to Read.* Chicago: Scott, Foresman and Company, 1953.

See: Chapter 2 (pp. 12-57) "Your Child Gets Ready to Read." As a teacher, you can refer parents to this chapter to help them understand the concept of readiness.

Auckerman, Robert C., (Editor). *Some Persistent Questions on Beginning Reading.* Newark, Delaware: International Reading Association, 1972.

See: A paperback of 175 pages. Read through the entire book.

De Hirsh, Katrina, Jeanette Jefferson Jansky, and William S. Langford. *Predicting Reading Failure.* New York: Harper & Row, Publishers, 1966.

See: This is a preliminary study of reading, writing, and spelling disabilities in preschool children.

Durr, William K. (Editor). *Reading Instruction: Dimensions and Issues.* Boston: Houghton Mifflin Company, 1967.

See: Chapter 2 (pp. 25-27) "Readiness and Beginning Reading." Several excellent articles on this topic.

Harris, Albert J. *How To Increase Reading Ability.* New York: David McKay Co., Inc., 1970.

See: Chapter 2 (pp. 20-59) "Readiness for Reading." An excellent table of reading readiness handicaps and their correction.

Heilman, Arthur W. *Principles and Practices of Teaching Reading.* Columbus, Ohio: Charles E. Merrill Publishing Company, 1967.

See: Chapter 2 (pp. 25-70) "Preparing for Reading." Stresses that preparing for reading implies activity on the part of the child and a deliberate structuring of experiences on the part of the school.

Monroe, Marion and Bernice Rogers. *Foundations for Reading: Informal Prereading Procedures.* Chicago: Scott, Foresman and Company, 1964.

See: The entire book is recommended as a valuable tool for readiness strategies.

Spache, George D., and Evelyn B. Spache. *Reading in the Elementary School.* Boston: Allyn & Bacon, Inc., 1973.

See: Chapters 2 and 3 (pp. 48-142) "Readiness and Reading for Young Children" and "Readiness Training." Provides excellent resources for the teacher.

Zintz, Miles V. *The Reading Process: The Teacher and The Learner.* Dubuque, Iowa: Wm. C. Brown Company Publishers, 1970.

See: Chapter 16 (pp. 373-400) "The Concept of Reading Readiness." A discussion of the factors most important in the child's readiness for learning how to read.

chapter 9

CLASSROOM ENVIRONMENTS

Introduction

At this point we hope that you have acquired basic skills in the areas of word recognition, comprehension, and evaluation. We believe that competency in these basic skill areas will enable you as teachers to make effective instructional decisions in your reading program.

In this chapter we will describe two types of classroom environments we have observed throughout the United States. Space limitations force us to describe them in somewhat oversimplified manner. We feel, however, that the two models we will present are valid as descriptions of the ways most schools and teachers function. We are aware, of course, that there are exceptions within each structure, and that these exceptions, some subtle, some distinctive, affect learning achievements both positively and negatively.

Our purpose in presenting these two generalized models is to lay the foundations for showing, in subsequent chapters, how various reading methods and materials are related to the specific classroom environment in which they are used. We also want to describe, briefly, how and why these two different structures and methods originated, that is, the cultural perceptions and expectations out of which they grew.

We feel that it will be helpful for people who are preparing themselves to teach reading to know something about the historical development of our public school system, how the system is related to the culture, and some of the reactions encountered when departing from tradition.

We also want to describe our two models in a manner that will enable teachers to perceive which type of classroom environment is used, accepted or required in a particular school so that they will be able to make appropriate and effective decisions regarding classroom management, the selection of materials, and the choice of method to be used in teaching students to read.

The model below outlines the basic classroom environments we call Pre-Structured (T-s)* and Emerging (t-s).

Two Basic Classroom Environments		
	Pre-Structured (T-s)	Emerging (t-s) (t-S)
Classroom Curriculum	Textbooks used almost exclusively	Interest/Experience of both teachers and students used almost exclusively
Expected Academic Behavior (Teacher)	Non-decision maker	Decision maker
Teaching Style	Teacher lecture whole group oriented	Large group, small group, individual conferences
Evaluation of Students	Report Cards-(A, B, C or 1, 2, 3 etc.) based on comparative group expectations	Parent Conferences or written reports— based on individual performance
Expected Behavior (Student)	Academically Dependent	Academically Independent
Levels of Learning	*Cognitive* Psycho-motor	*Affective* *Cognitive* Psycho-motor

Under the heading Emerging, we have the third type of classroom environment identified with the letters (t-S). This environment is well known in educational literature, but is not widely practiced in the United States. To be more specific, the kind of emerging environment labeled (t-S) is best described in the popular book, *Summerhill: A Radical Approach to Child Rearing.* By A.S. Neill.[1] "Summerhill" or a similar concept is significantly different from either of the two environments outlined above. We mention this third environment only for the purpose of providing a contrast, and have elected not to deal with it thoroughly because the Pre-Structured (T-s) and Emerging (t-s) environments represent the types of environments found in the public schools of this country.

*T represents teacher and s represents student. The use of upper and lower case letters symbolically represents the relative responsibilities of teachers and students in the two different environments.
1. A.S. Neill, *Summerhill: A Radical Approach to Child Rearing* (New York: Hart Publishing Co., Inc., 1960).

Pre-Structured Environments (T-s)

We will begin by outlining and interpreting the Pre-Structured Model:

Prestructured	
	(T-s)
Classroom Curriculum	Textbooks used almost exclusively
Expected Academic Behavior (Teacher)	Nondecision maker
Teaching Style	Teacher lecture, whole group oriented
Evaluation of Students	Report Cards-(A, B, C or 1, 2, 3, etc.) based on comparative group expectations
Expected Behavior (Student)	Academically Dependent
Levels of Learning	*Cognitive* Psycho-motor

We believe that approximately 95% of all American classrooms can be described by the term pre-structured. If we were to randomly select 100 classrooms at any grade level 1-12, in any school district in the United States, 95 of these 100 rooms would be functioning according to the Pre-Structured Model. We also believe that the pre-structured classroom environment is largely predominant in American education. Consequently, it is the only type of learning environment that is familiar to the majority of teachers, administrators, parents and children.

We will discuss each of the six aspects of the pre-structured classroom as shown in the model. No attempt will be made to evaluate this environment or prove our observations in scientific terms. Rather, we will depart from traditional textbook style and hope that you will enjoy our observations of the pre-structured classroom.

In the above model, the first area is labeled *classroom curriculum.* In the pre-structured classroom, textbooks are used almost exclusively. Recently, Dr. Hillel Black[2] indicated that in American classrooms (1-12) the textbook is used for 75% of

2. Hillel Black, *The American Textbook* (New York Morrow: American School Book, 1967).

each instructional day. Each student attending these grades will own or rent approximately 65 or more textbooks in his 12 years of school. This appears to be a reasonable estimate. At most grade levels a student owns or rents a reader, a science book, a social studies book, a health book, and others. If we multiply five or six books per year by 12, we arrive at the figure of 65 or more books.

To better understand the central position of textbooks in the schools' curriculum, it is necessary only to note some of the common statements teachers make. For example, classroom teachers talk about the need to "get the book covered," or mention that they—or other teachers—are x number of pages ahead or behind in a certain book. Teachers' planbooks generally indicate that daily lesson planning is on a page-by-page basis. Toward the end of the school year or term, some teachers become apprehensive about not getting the book covered. A variety of statements are heard in faculty rooms. For example: "Wow! I'm 115 pages behind and I only have 3 weeks to go." Most teachers feel obligated to use the manual in its prescribed or pre-structured way. In effect the pre-structured curriculum indicates that the school, as an instrument of the community, has decided in advance what the learner should know. It is simply a matter of the teacher and students working through the pre-structured material for a given grade level.

Closely related is an area we call *expected academic behavior—teacher.* In a pre-structured classroom the teacher is not expected to make significant instructional decisions. We used the words, "nondecision maker," and that's precisely what we mean. For example, if a sixth-grade teacher is attempting to cover 39 or more countries in both Asia and Europe, that teacher is not expected to question whether France should or should not be included. The teacher's concern is related to *how fast* France should be covered. The teacher in the pre-structured environment makes decisions about the *rate* at which the material is covered. Rarely is the teacher expected (or allowed) to make decisions regarding the *nature* of the content itself. The sixth-grade teacher in most schools is likely to spend two or three days on one country, two or three on another, a week on another, etc., until the book is covered. Of course, teachers will not find a contract clause stating that they are not to make instructional decisions. The implication, however, that the teacher will not make major instructional decisions is there nevertheless. The assumption, valid or invalid, is that the community knows in advance what the student needs to learn; and the teacher's role is to see that this expectation is fulfilled.

If you are teaching about Europe and Asia and would like to test our observation, raise the following question at your next faculty meeting: "Should I teach my students about Czechoslovakia?" This will stop the faculty meeting cold. It would even be difficult for the principal to answer the question. It would be equally difficult for fellow teachers to answer the question. More than likely they will agree that although it isn't really necessary, the superintendent wants you to teach Czechoslovakia. If you talked to the superintendent, he would probably indicate that he doesn't care, but that somebody on the school board wants it taught. If you were to get the board, the superintendent, the principal and teachers together they would probably agree that it's not a major problem, but would also probably insist that the State Department wants Czechoslovakia taught to sixth graders. Discussions regarding the content of curriculum is not a common occurrence in a pre-structured classroom environment. It is generally assumed that we have a certain amount of content to cover, and the teacher is expected to cover this material in a systematic and interesting way.

A third area in our model is labeled *teaching style.* Let's assume that we're about to enter a pre-structured classroom which has approximately 30 students and a teacher. Probably the teacher would be lecturing to the whole group, and the students would be working from a textbook, a ditto sheet or some type of printed material. We should acknowledge that the lecture style in a pre-structured classroom is fairly efficient. It would be ridiculous to expect the teacher to ask each child individually to turn to page 52. It's much more efficient to just ask the class to turn to page 52.

We also would expect to find the teacher talking a great deal of the time. We estimate that most teachers talk or direct conversations approximately 80% of the time.

A fourth area in our model is labeled *evaluation of students.* Here we find the widely used and well known device called the report card. The report card with its A, B, C or 1, 2, 3, rating indicates where the student ranks within the group. An A or 1 grade generally means that the student was able to keep up with the rate established by the classroom teacher in the materials that were purchased by the district and endorsed by the state. Not incidentally, an A or 1 grade also means that the student is clean and is reasonably punctual. American schools have always been interested in washing and punctuality. We trust that you won't jump to the conclusion that we are against washing and punctuality; we're merely suggesting that many things enter into a reported letter grade which are not necessarily based on pupil achievement or ability.

Before getting into the area labeled *expected academic behavior—student,* we need to ask, "Is it possible for anyone to learn in pre-structured environments?" Our answer is yes. In fact, almost everyone reading this book probably attended pre-structured schools. We believe that students can and do learn in pre-structured schools, and we're interested in what they learn. It is this interest that leads us to the area of *expected academic behavior of students.* Students in this environment are largely expected to be dependent. That all encompassing word, "dependent," suggests that the learner is expected to be dependent on the teacher and the printed material used in the classroom. The learner is not expected to make or participate in instructional decisions. He is there to do what the teacher tells him to do and to do it in the prescribed manner. If the pre-structured task is reading, the student is to read rapidly and answer the teacher's questions. If it is writing, the teacher expects good penmanship, good spelling, good structure, and correct answers to the questions posed by the teacher. Again, we're not suggesting that good spelling, good writing habits, etc., are undesirable traits; we are merely suggesting that "doing what is expected" and "being dependent on the teacher" constitutes what is labeled "learning" in a pre-structured environment. This area of academic dependence is extremely important; therefore, we would like to elaborate by describing common classroom situations. We invite you to join us in our irreverence.

We don't believe that children come to school independent; rather, they come from homes that tend to foster a great deal of dependence. Parents require that children eat in certain ways, dress in certain ways, use certain language. Most of the child's daily activity is prescribed by the parent; the child is expected to do what is requested. In our culture, it is not common to find parents providing alternatives for children. This pattern is carried over into the school. Children, at five or six years of age, enter school and hear teachers saying: "Row 1 may go, row 3 may go, row 4 may not go because Charles was moving." They hear the teacher tell them how to line up, who's to regulate the windows, pull the curtains, etc. Pre-structured schools have schedules for starting and stopping everything. In fact, schools have even scheduled the bodily functions of most children, for recess comes at a specific time each day.

We hope you see the humor of the situation and at the same time recognize that we are not opposed to schedules and order. Schools, like any institution, need a realistic amount of planning to handle lunch schedules, starting times, stopping times, and other matters. Our point is that pre-structured classrooms rarely balance needed order with the provision of realistic, imaginative alternatives for students. We feel that when students are constantly directed in school, they become dependent in other areas and are apt to become rebellious in destructive ways. Yet we frequently find intermediate classroom teachers saying: "I gave them an assignment and they copied directly out of the encyclopedia. When will they ever do something on their own?" Imagine this situation: As the eighth-grade teacher is introducing a lesson on creative writing, he might say, "I'd like you to write a theme on any subject that appeals to you." Up goes a hand and the student asks: "Teacher, what shall we write about?" The teacher is likely to fire back, "Write about anything that you would like to write about, I said this was creative writing." The student is likely to say, "Wow! I haven't had a good idea in eight years." What he means is that he has never been permitted to think and act on his own, yet now he is being virtually commanded to be independent and imaginative. The internal design of the pre-structured environment tends to increase the student's academic dependence, which was started in home situations, and to stifle creativity.

If you doubt our observations about academic dependency, try a quick experiment. Leave your classroom and talk to a colleague out in the hall. Within 30 seconds the noise level will increase in the classroom. Some little joker is jiggling around, someone else is throwing a pencil, down goes a book, a little girl is passing a note. Confusion reigns. The tendency is to go back into the room and say: "I don't understand why I can't leave you for a minute to talk to my colleagues." The students tend to get quiet and feel somewhat embarrassed. If the students are perceptive, and free to express themselves, they might say, "Teacher, you left us alone for 30 seconds and we're not accustomed to being left alone. We have been conditioned to expect someone to tell us what book to take out, what page to mark and how to operate." In the pre-structured room, when the controlling influence of the teacher is removed students are baffled or trapped. They are unable to make decisions regarding what or how to learn, because none of their previous experience has encouraged them to make their own decisions.

The last area in our pre-structured model is labeled *levels of learning.* The pre-structured classroom deals with psycho-motor and cognitive levels of learning. Rather than get into academic disputes over terminology, we would like to present, in simplistic terms, behavioral descriptions of psycho-motor and cognitive levels of learning.

A psycho-motor level of learning refers to performance which is largely automatic. For example, when a person is writing, conscious thought is not required to form letters or words. Much writing is at the habit or automatic motor level. A skilled typist is not typing to determine what letters come next; he has acquired, by our definition, a psycho-motor level of learning, and is using it automatically.

At a cognitive level the learner is involved in thinking or reasoning. Within this level of learning there is a variety of stages and types of thinking ranging from the concrete, or memory stage, to a complicated form of reasoning and logic. At the cognitive level the learner does not have to "act out" or demonstrate that he believes what he is thinking about. It is only necessary to think, reason, and solve problems, The learner is more concerned with "what he thinks about" rather than "what he actually does." We take the position that the pre-structured classroom deals with psycho-motor and cognitive levels of learning almost exclusively.

Now to a question concerning the development of the pre-structured school: Who created it, and why? Some might suggest that it was created by school administrators. Others might suggest classroom teachers, commercial publishers or universities. We believe that no single group created the pre-structured school. It grew out of the perceived needs of our culture. Our culture determined in advance what the learner needed to know, and a pre-structured school environment met this cultural requirement. If our culture needed dependent people, a pre-structured environment served this need. If our culture believed that schools should provide psycho-motor and cognitive levels of learning, the 3R curriculum of *r*eading, *r*iting, and *r*ithmetic was the natural result.

Philosophically, we could find endless arguments about whether the school should lead, follow or reshape the existing culture or society. This is not the place to get into that very important debate. We feel that the pre-structured school, as an institution, contributed to and supported the traditional American culture or society, just as other institutions such as the family, the church, and the school, contributed to and supported the traditional American culture.

If you accept this position, you can understand why the pre-structured classroom is so well understood and accepted by the community. When television programs or advertisements picture students in straight rows with teachers lecturing, we tend to accept this as what school "ought to be." Although it is difficult to understand what a grade on a report card represents, most communities insist on "regular report cards." Dunce-hats, books with a belt around them, ink wells, blackboards, and other traditional stereotypes are well understood by the community.

What will happen to the pre-structured classroom environment if and when the culture or society it serves changes? Obviously, internal conflict and dilemmas will be encountered. As we see it, our culture or society has already changed, and this in turn will force the pre-structured environment to give way to the environment we call Emerging (t-s).

EMERGING ENVIRONMENT (t-s)

We turn now to a description of the Emerging environment:

Emerging (t-s)	
Classroom Curriculum	Interest/Experience of both teachers and students used almost exclusively
Expected Academic Behavior (Teacher)	Decision Maker
Teaching Style	Large group, small group, individual conferences
Evaluation of Students	Parent Conferences or written reports—based on individual performance
Expected Behavior (Student)	Academically Independent
Levels of Learning	*Affective* *Cognitive* Psycho-motor

The emerging classroom environment differs significantly from the environment described as pre-structured. The emerging classroom has a different philosophical base and makes different psychological assumptions regarding how students learn. Greater demands are made on teachers and administrators; and unfortunately the emerging classroom is not widely understood or accepted by the community. We believe that the emerging classroom is largely the creation of educators, and that it serves the double function of following *and* leading the community.

Let's talk about each of the six aspects of the emerging classroom. Again no attempt will be made to evaluate this environment or prove our observations in scientific terms.

As seen in the above model, the first area is labeled *classroom curriculum.* The curriculum of the emerging classroom is based on the interest and experience of both teachers and students. Their common interests do not entirely ignore the expected content of a particular grade level; instead, the teacher and students cooperate in making decisions regarding what is to be learned within a given grade level, and when and how. Using a sixth grade as an example, let's assume that one curriculum goal is to introduce the students to Europe and Asia. In the emerging classroom, the teacher and students might look at the total number of countries involved and decide to deal with

only six countries. They might decide to study three representative European and three Asian countries in depth. This decision would be based on the interest and the experience of both the students and their teacher.

If France was selected as one of the countries to study in depth, the teacher would need to determine the availability of such resources as films, filmstrips, pictures, audio-tapes, reference books, library books, and other materials. Students would have to consider what they would like to know about such a country. This might include geography, famous people, art, culture, music, or other interests. In this type room the textbook serves as a common reference or guide instead of a virtually exclusive resource. (In a later chapter we will attempt to develop three specific stages for developing in emerging classroom).

The next area, *expected academic behavior—teacher,* is closely related to curriculum development in the emerging classroom. The key factor is that *the teacher must be willing to make instructional decisions.* Decisions have to be made regarding curriculum content, classroom organization, classroom management, utilization of materials, amount of time given various topics, and the interests and abilities of the students. The wide variety of decisions must be made constantly. The teacher and students are guided by general objectives and goals, but are not able to predict the exact nature of each classroom experience, nor do they need to.

The emerging classroom places other demands on the classroom teacher. It requires that he function somewhat independently of other teachers, and it is not possible to be ahead of or behind another room. These concepts are irrelevant to the emerging classroom. The teacher must provide a wide variety of alternatives. For example, in introducing and organizing a program of study around the representative country, France, the teacher needs to list a number of questions to be explored and areas to study. France might have unique systems of transportation, industry, and agriculture. Only imagination limits the number of alternatives a teacher could provide students. Obviously, each teacher must have a functional knowledge of a given area. This is the reason for insisting that areas be selected on the basis of interest, experience, and knowledge.

The third area in our model is labeled *teaching style.* Let's assume that we are about to enter an emerging classroom with approximately 30 students and a teacher. The teacher might be lecturing to a large group or be serving as a guide to a small group of students. Or the teacher may be working independently with one student. In any case, we're not likely to find that everyone in the room is working on a particular page or interest at the same time. There would be a wide variety of activities going on in the classroom. Some children might be looking at filmstrips, others working with encyclopedias, others constructing pictures for a scrapbook, or painting a mural. The teacher is generally quite mobile, talking with children and attempting to help them achieve their learning goals. The teacher generally approaches instructional problems by presenting alternatives and urging the student to select the appropriate alternative for himself, in terms of his experiences, his interest, and his need.

The teacher in the emerging classroom tends to talk less, and is generally less interested in controlling conversation than the teacher in the pre-structured classroom. This environment allows the student to assume a great deal of responsibility for how he acts and what he learns.

A fourth area is called *evaluation of students.* In the emerging classroom, parent conferences or written reports based on observed individual performance is the most satisfactory reporting system. (We believe that if a report card is used, it's used largely to appease the community.) These reporting practices require each teacher to be a good observer, concerned with individual student progress. For example, if a student is barely able to speak English, and is in a classroom with native English speakers, this student could not compete favorably. Through the reporting procedure of the emerging classroom, the parent, through an interpreter, might learn that the student is acquiring a greater facility with English, and is attempting to use more English in his conversations. The parent might also learn that although the child was unable to read any English words when he entered school, he has acquired the ability to read several hundred English words. In that same room, we might find an academically talented student. His parents would be told about his individual research project or that he wrote a creative story, or be given some information regarding his work style. Again, we recognize the great demand on classroom teachers because such parent conferences require considerable teacher skills. But the reporting system of the emerging classroom, based on specific recorded data, provides parents with a considerable amount of important information that the standard report card neglects.

The area labeled *expected academic behavior-student* is extremely interesting to us because of the demands placed on students in the emerging classroom. In this room students must make decisions. For example, when the teacher presents learning alternatives which include the study of transportation, agriculture, industry, etc., the student has to decide what he wants to know and how he plans to acquire this information.

We mentioned a "sharing relationship" between the teacher and students. We're not suggesting that if a student decides to study Alaska when the class decided on France, he be allowed to study Alaska. This would be permitted in a "Summerhill" type classroom. What we are suggesting is that in the emerging environment the learner has freedom of choice within agreed upon limits. It provides more choice than the pre-structured classroom, but not complete freedom of choice. Decision making becomes a matter of compromise and joint responsibility between teacher and student. If the student's wishes are not ignored, neither are the teacher's; nor, for that matter, are the community's wishes ignored.

In addition to expecting the student to become academically independent, it is also assumed that *each student will assume more responsibility for his own behavior.* For example, if he elects to learn about several famous landmarks of France, he must accept part of the responsibility to find out about such landmarks. He is not a passive receptacle into which "learning" is poured. How he systematically pursues what he eventually develops or creates pretty much becomes his responsibility. He is expected and allowed to be responsible for the goals he establishes. He may change his goal and elect another course of action. This is perfectly reasonable, but the student must assume his share of the responsibility for setting goals and achieving them.

The final area is labeled *levels of learning.* The emerging classroom, like the pre-structured classroom, deals with psycho-motor and cognitive levels of learning. In addition, it includes the *affective* level of learning. We described psycho-motor and cognitive levels of learning earlier. Now we offer a description of affective levels of learning.

The affective level includes both psycho-motor and cognitive functions or activities, but functions or activities become affective only when the individual acts out the function or activity, that is, when he changes his behavior because of what he has learned intellectually. Specifically, if we asked a person to describe his feelings or tell about the harm that comes from litter, we believe that he is functioning at the psycho-motor and cognitive levels of learning. Learning becomes affective when the individual acts out his ideas and is careful not to throw his gum wrapper in the street.

Another example of the affective level comes from an actual situation observed in a high school. A tenth-grade student was busy collecting names on a petition. When we asked what the student was doing, we were told that he was a member of a small group interested in the general topic on ecology. This group of students found that their legislature was somewhat disinterested in mass transportation. They also found that none of the revenue from the gasoline tax was being used to study the possibility of developing mass transportation systems. The group decided to circulate petitions and send them to appropriate legislative representatives, asking what these legislators were doing about mass transportation and the utilization of the gasoline tax. These functions and activities illustrate affective levels of learning: students were acting responsibly, not just learning abstract concepts.

We believe that you can readily see that the emerging classroom is significantly different from many of our previous experiences. Again, let's imagine ourselves walking into an emerging classroom. The noise level will probably be somewhat higher than what we experienced as students. The students will be generally active. Some students might be preparing a mural, some might be involved in a discussion, others might be making a model.

If a teacher elects to operate this type of classroom in a school that is essentially pre-structured, he should expect a variety of negative reactions from fellow teachers who do not share his orientation and convictions. One could almost hear the teacher next to his room saying, "I used to be able to keep my door open on a warm day, but since that clown moved in I haven't had a moment's rest." The teacher that gets the class next year is likely to say, "It's going to take me all year to straighten out that bunch. They're unruly, undisciplined, and lack respect for adults." One can almost see the look of pain on the custodian's face when he walks into the room. The desks are clustered in groups, rather than straight lines; there are things hanging from the ceiling; there are objects or models all around. Since much of the work is done by children, pictures and bulletin boards lack professional quality. The custodian is likely to run to the principal and insist that he get rid of that teacher because of the messy room.

A teacher told us that one day, while he was engaged in an emerging classroom, a visiting principal happened to come into the room. The principal said: "I see you're taking a break again." The teacher was upset, because she knew that everyone was hard at work.

There was another interesting situation. A mother wanted her boy to go shopping with her at 2:00 p.m. on Friday afternoon. That morning she told the youngster that she would pick him up about 2:00 p.m. The boy threw a small tantrum because his group had agreed to give their report to the class at about 2:00 p.m. The mother could not understand why any youngster would want to go to school, of all places, on Friday afternoon. She had mixed feelings. She was delighted because her boy was excited about going to school, but was confused because she couldn't recall every being eager to attend school. Even so, she took her child to school and agreed to go shopping later. While at school she met a teacher she knew who was deeply committed to a pre-structured classroom. She asked the teacher why her boy was so concerned about not missing school. The teacher told the mother that the boy's interest was probably the result of the fact that students played, cut paper, sat on the floor, and did anything they pleased in "that" room. She quickly pointed out that in her room students work, they copy from the board, they do number facts, and are always "down to business."

Is it any wonder why the mother became confused about the school? As we suggested before, it is necessary that teachers and administrators committed to emerging concepts do an enormous amount of work in the area of parent education, or, as we might call it, public relations. Parents need to understand the nature of this type of education, not necessarily from an abstract philosophical, psychological orientation, but what students are expected to do, how the emerging classroom functions, and why, as simply and plainly as you can communicate. This, you will discover, will also require a great deal of patience and an understanding of why some parents will resist efforts to develop the emerging classroom.

SUMMARY

In this chapter we have attempted to provide a description of two basic types of classroom environments. We hope that these somewhat oversimplified presentations will serve as background data when we present reading programs designed for these environments. We tried to avoid placing value judgments on one or the other environment. The selection of the school environment is a community and school matter. In Chapter 10 we will deal with reading programs and procedures which seem best suited for a pre-structured classroom. In Chapter 11 we will present reading programs and procedures which seem most appropriate in an emerging classroom. We will conclude this Unit (Chapter 9, 10, and 11) by recommending a variety of alternative approaches to teaching reading.

IDENTIFYING PRE-STRUCTURED AND EMERGING CLASSROOMS

Introduction

By now we hope that you have acquired a variety of constructs in the areas of word recognition, comprehension, and individual testing. We also hope that additional constructs in the areas of reading readiness, grouping, group testing, and methods for teaching reading have helped you conceptualize other aspects of the teaching of reading. Finally, in the preceding chapter we presented a description of two major classroom environments (pre-structured and emerging).

All of these efforts have been directed at what we call a "strategy for instruction." The term, "strategy for instruction," refers to our attempt to outline, in the following two chapters, ways in which you can use materials and develop methods and procedures which will be useful and practical in either a pre-structured or emerging classroom, without ignoring the teacher's need to make instructional decisions. We would be inconsistent, after stressing the importance of instructional decision making, if we now provided you with a single or "ultimate" method for teaching reading. It is, however, necessary to be specific about teaching reading; after all, this is what this book is all about.

CLASSROOM CHECKLISTS I AND II

We have developed two sets of questions called Classroom Checklist I and Classroom Checklist II. The questions are designed to help you evaluate or diagnose your teaching situation. The questions deal with professional behavior in your teaching situation, expectations professionals have for children, and common school policies. You will be asked to read each question on both Checklists, and respond with either a yes or no. Classroom Checklist I presents questions related to a pre-structured environment and Classroom Checklist II presents questions related to an emerging environment.

Obviously, these lists are not precise descriptions of your teaching situations, nor do they cover all aspects of any teaching situation. Instead, we believe that if you decide that your situation tends to be more pre-structured than emerging, you should consider our instructional recommendations in Chapter 10. If you decide that your situation tends to be more emerging, you should consider our recommendations in Chapter 11. You might find that neither list relates to your situation; therefore, you might decide to combine recommendations from both Chapters. In short, a strategy for instruction requires you to make instructional decisions while allowing us to be specific regarding reading instruction concepts and methods.

Underlying a "Strategy for Instruction" is our belief that children can learn to read in a variety of teaching situations, and our confidence that good teachers can make productive instructional decisions in a variety of teaching situations.

Complete Classroom Checklist I on pp. 143-144 and Classroom Checklist II on pp. 145-146.

CLASSROOM CHECKLIST I

Check (√) either yes or no after reading each statement. A check of yes means that events or practices, suggested by each statement, occur most of the time in your teaching situation. A check of no means that events or practices suggested rarely occur in your teaching situation.

1. Reading instruction is based on a commercially prepared, sequential reading program.

Yes ☐   No ☐

2. Your district policy requires several report cards each year. The student's grades are usually based on how well he does in comparison to his classroom group.

Yes ☐   No ☐

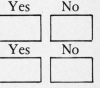

3. Assuming that children are expected to complete the commercially prepared reading program, it is essential to give a variety of directions and keep the group "moving" at a specified rate.

Yes ☐   No ☐

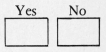

4. School leaders might be uncomfortable if they knew that you decided to use only a portion of the selections in your reader.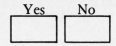

5. Your knowledge of how to teach basic reading is limited.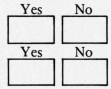

6. Good classroom discipline, as your school defines it, includes the characteristics of quiet children, efficient daily scheduling for each subject, and rules of behavior determined by the teacher.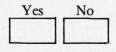

7. Taking field trips, bringing plants or animals into the room, inviting local speakers to the room, etc., are thought to be important. However, this type of activity is considered the exception rather than the rule in your school.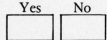

8. Instructional equipment, such as filmstrip machines, tape recorders or record players with headsets, television receivers, etc., are in limited supply.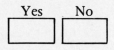

9. In your school it is understood that equipment such as tape recorders, television receivers, film projectors, etc., are to be operated by teachers or aides. (Children might destroy this expensive equipment.)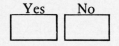

10. More money per child is usually spent on activity books, ditto masters (including paper and fluid) and writing paper, than on construction paper, paste, colored pencils, etc.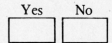

11. Your administrator is likely to act more as a manager than an instructional leader, or more like a "boss" than a co-worker. Stated another way, most decisions regarding the "running" of the school are usually made by the administrator.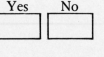

12. Teachers might agree that all forms of parent involvement are necessary (scheduled parent-teacher conferences, active room mothers, informative open house sessions, parent volunteers, etc.) but parental involvement is considered the exception rather than the rule in your school.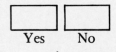

Total responses for Checklist I

CLASSROOM CHECKLIST II

Check (√) either yes or no after reading each statement. A check of yes means that events or practices, suggested by each statement, occur most of the time in your teaching situation. A check of no means that events or practices suggested rarely occur in your teaching situation.

1. You have textbooks in your room. However, all students rarely ever use the same set at the same time.

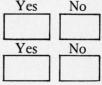

2. The children in your room frequently work in small groups. What they do might be related to a central theme or topic but each group is involved in different activities.

3. The reading program used in your room is different from the ones being used by teachers in other rooms.

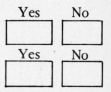

4. A reading skills checklist, carefully used by each teacher, might be all that's necessary to have a sequential reading program in your schools.

5. Most of the professional staff in your school would like to abandon graded report cards and use parent-teacher conferences to provide parents with information.

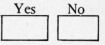

6. You urge students to work together. As a result, the "noise" level tends to increase. Despite this most of the professional staff in your school believes that you are maintaining good discipline in your room.

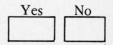

7. Your administrator is regarded as an instructional leader. That is, he or she usually consults you if you are likely to be affected by some decision.

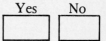

8. Taking field trips, bringing plants or animals into the room, inviting local persons to speak to groups are a common occurrence in your school. In fact, almost every week some classroom is engaged in this type of activity.

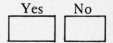

9. Instructional equipment, such as filmstrip machines, tape recorders or record players with headsets, instructional games, aquariums, etc., are given a high budget priority in your school.

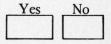

10. Teachers in your building are likely to suggest that expenditures for activity books, ditto paper, etc., be held to a minimum. They would prefer to spend money for other things.

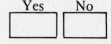

11. As you listen to a student read, you are able to determine if he is having problems attacking words. You are able to determine the specific type of word recognition problems, i.e., consonants, vowels, syllables, etc.

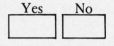

12. You have had an opportunity to meet many local parents because they usually accompany groups on trips, or volunteer as room mothers, or frequently drop in to chat with you.

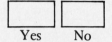

Total responses for Checklist II

If you marked seven or more yes items on Classroom Checklist I, we believe that you are probably teaching in a pre-structured classroom environment and might profit from the recommendations offered in Chapter 10.

If you marked seven or more yes items on Classroom Checklist II, we believe that you are probably teaching in an emerging classroom environment and might profit from the recommendations offered in Chapter 11.

If you do not have responses which suggest either situation, you might elect to use suggestions and methods from both Chapters 10 and 11.

REFERENCES FOR CHAPTER 9

General

Bany, Mary A. and Lois V. Johnson. *Classroom Group Behavior: Group Dynamics in Education.* New York: Macmillan, 1964.

Bloom, Benjamin S. (ed.). *Taxonomy of Education Objectives: Handbook I: Cognative Domain.* New York: David McKay, 1956.

Bruner, Jerome S. *On Knowing: Essays for the Left Hand.* Cambridge: Harvard University Press, 1962.

Flanders, Ned A. *Analyzing Teacher Behavior.* Reading, Massachusetts: Addison-Wesley, 1970.

Krathwohl, David R., Benjamin S. Bloom, and Bertram B. Masio. *Taxonomy of Educational Objectives: Handbook II: Affective Domain.* New York: David McKay, 1956.

Mager, Robert F. *Developing Attitude Toward Learning.* Palo Alto, California: Fearon, 1968.

———. *Preparing Instructional Objectives.* Palo Alto, California: Fearon, 1962.

Moffett, James. *A Student-Centered Language Arts Curriculum, Grades K-13: A Handbook for Teachers.* Boston: Houghton Mifflin, 1968.

Phenix, Philip H. *Realms of Meaning: A Philosophy of the Curriculum for General Education.* New York: McGraw-Hill, 1964.

Raths, Louis E. et al. *Teaching for Thinking: Theory and Application.* Columbus, Ohio: C.E. Merrill, 1967.

Rogers, Carl R. *Freedom to Learn: A View of Education Might Become.* Columbus, Ohio: C.E. Merrill, 1969.

Sanders, Norris M. *Classroom Questions: What Kinds?* New York: Harper & Row, 1966.

Taba, Hilba. *Curriculum Development: Theory and Practice.* New York: Harcourt, Brace & World, 1962.

Torrance, Ellis P. and William F. White (eds.). *Issues and Advances in Educational Psychology: A Book of Readings.* Itasca, Illinois: F.E. Peacock, 1969.

Elementary

Manning, Duane. *Toward a Humanistic Curriculum.* New York: Harper & Row, 1971.

Ragan, William B. *Modern Elementary Curriculum.* (3rd ed.). New York: Holt, Rinehart and Winston, 1966.

Shuster, Albert H. and Milton E. Ploghoft. *The Emerging Elementary Curriculum.* Columbus, Ohio: Charles E. Merrill, 1963.

Secondary

Aikin, Wilfork M. *The Story of the Eight-Year Study, with Conclusions, and Recommendations.* New York: Harper, 1942.

Alexander, William M. (ed.). *The Changing Secondary School Curriculum: Readings.* New York: Holt, Rinehart and Winston, 1967.

Short, Edmund C. and George D. Marconnet. (eds.). *Contempory Thought on Public School Curriculum: Readings.* Dubuque, Iowa: Wm. C. Brown Company Publishers, 1968.

PRE-STRUCTURED CLASSROOM ENVIRONMENT

If you had seven or more yes responses to Classroom Checklist I, you are probably in a pre-structured classroom environment and might profit from the strategies for instruction provided in this chapter.

We begin Chapter 10 by briefly describing five representative types of published reading methods. We believe that these reading methods were designed for use in pre-structured classroom environments. Following this, we will introduce an appropriate strategy for instruction which will serve the teacher in several ways:

- It can be used with any published instructional material (reading, social studies, science, health, etc.)
- It satisfies the basic assumptions of the pre-structured classroom.
- It allows for decision making on the part of the teacher.
- It incorporates many of the constructs presented in previous chapters (see chapter summary for a discussion of how this pre-structured strategy for instruction incorporates many of the constructs presented in this book).

Overview of Pre-Structured Reading Methods

We believe that children can learn to read through the use of a variety of published methods (see Chapter 7). The methods summarized below describe ways in which the teaching of reading is practiced in schools today. These published methods, while not all—inclusive, are representative examples of current methods found in pre-structured classrooms throughout the United States.

Basal Reading Series[1] A basal reading program carried on through the use of a series of basal materials. This series is devoted to the systematic and sequential development of all the skills, abilities, and understandings necessary for interpreting written symbols. As such, it might be characterized by one word, *comprehensive.* It is concerned with growth in *all* aspects of the reading act. These include word perception, comprehension, critical and emotional reaction, and the application and use of reading for recreational and practical purposes. Through the sequential skill program provided in a basal series and the type of content used, children grow in reading as a process in itself, and, through reading, to increasingly higher levels of personal and social development.

1. A. Sterl Artley, University of Missouri, major author for Scott, Foresman and Company.

Three objectives—scope, sequence, and organization—guide the development of a basal reading series. Scope concerns the range of skills that the maturing reader needs to acquire and the content types and themes with which he needs to become acquainted. Sequence refers to the order in which the various elements with which the program is concerned are presented, so that each developmental stage grows out of those preceding, and at the same time serves as a foundation for the ones following. Organization brings into proper relation learners, skills, teaching methods, and instructional materials to provide a program having unity and coherence.

Phonic Method.[2] Reading with Phonics is a system which develops efficiency in word recognition by employing a multisensory approach and a sequential introduction of speech sounds of the English language. All the language arts are integrated to provide broad approaches to use of limited vocabularies.

Reading with Phonics utilizes the 44 most frequently used speech sounds in English. It begins with the teaching of the short sounds of 5 vowels, and progresses to the study of the 10 most frequently used consonants. In each early lesson a consonant is blended with the 5 vowels in pronouncing units or syllables, then with word wholes. Progression is always from known to unknown, from simple to more complex. Words are always attacked at their beginnings, promoting left to right progression.

Reading with Phonics provides the child with a reading vocabulary approximately equal to his speaking vocabulary. Logically, as the child's mastery grows, one compliments the other, providing the key to all basic communication—the foundation for his entire education.

This program of instruction in word recognition is designed for use with *all* basal reading series. It provides exercises and activities related to the entire language arts program—handwriting, reading, spelling, and expression. It has no grade level designation. Since it is a complete phonics program, it may be used in the kindergarten, primary and intermediate grades. It should be introduced in kindergarten or first grade to establish proper word attack skills for independent, fluent readers at the earliest possible age. Reading with Phonics has proven to have great value in the upper grades in creating awareness of the relationship between speech sounds and printed letters, thus providing the disabled reader with a valuable reading tool.

Initial Teaching Alphabet.[3] The Initial Teaching Alphabet (ITA' of 44 characters provides each major phoneme of English with its own symbol, thus eleminating the inconsistent character-to-symbol relationship in present spelling. This alphabet, with its spellings, provides the learner with a consistent alphabetic code. It differs from other phonemic alphabets in both ITA and its spellings were designed to facilitate transition to the regular traditional alphabet, once reading, and language fluency is achieved.

2. Charles E. Wingo, Monmouth College, major author, Reading with Phonics Program.
3. Albert J. Mazurkiewicz, major author for the Initial Teaching Alphabet Co.

Since it is a *medium*, not a *method*, ITA can be used with any method or reading instruction.

The 44-letter ITA alphabet consists of 24 standard, lower-case, Roman letters (omitting "q" and "x"), plus 20 additional characters. Giving each character only one lower-case *form* and one *sound* value eliminates approximately 2,000 confusing irregularities of traditional spelling. The child is not confronted with three separate shapes, "A," "a," " æ," for a single letter and a single sound. In ITA there is only one *shape* for capital, lower-case, or script letters; the difference is in size only. Each character always represents its own sound.

In traditional spelling, the "i" sound is spelled differently in *child, buy, try, eye, file, lie, high, aisle, island, guide* and in other words. This example is but one of many. The regularity of ITA and the more frequent repetion of the fewer syllabic forms enable the beginner to learn the mechanics of reading and writing more quickly so that learning to read—in fact, all learning—becomes, for him, a logical process.

Words in Color.[4] The most important contribution of this method is its full and rapid extension of the linguistic capacities of learners who already speak their language. The natural mental process of combining sounds and related meanings (spoken speech) is extended to include operations on related signs (written speech). The power of reading, writing, and spelling with meaning all language already owned as meaningful speech is developed as a unity. None of these skills is taught separately from the others. All come naturally and spontaneously as by-products of extended linguistic power. Teaching is fully subordinated to learning. The techniques and materials of this method allow the teacher to initiate challenging and enjoyable intellectual games which provide practice, without creating boredom through drill, or strain through memorization, and to generate self-direction and creativity in the development and use of the skills necessary to written language.

Color is far less important than the trade name indicates, since all books and written work from the beginning are in black on white. The use of color does solve quickly and easily the problems created by the ambiguous grapheme-phoneme relationship of English without affecting usual spelling. Thus on the wall charts, color provides a valuable clue, and word imagery is more vivid. The many spellings of each sound occur in the same color, and the many sounds of one spelling occur each in a different color (each of the 47 sounds of English identified has its own color).

Examples:

1. late, way, they, eight, straight, veil, great, pail. Same sound, thus in same color.
2. pat, was, village, any, fatal, swamp, all, ate, care. Different sounds, thus in different colors.

4. Dorothea E. Hinman, Encyclopedia Britannica Press, an author who works with Calel-Gattegno, the developer of Words in Color.

Linguistics in Beginning Reading.[5] The following four statements attempt to indicate the specially stressed features of an approach to beginning reading that applies linguistic knowledge.

1. The six-year-old child understands spoken sentences in which the basic sentence patterns have, as their content, words that he knows. For the beginning reading material, the child must recognize that the written words in the sentence structures are those he already knows when he hears them spoken.

2. As the basic readiness requirements for beginning reading, the child must know the alphabet. He must be able to identify, by name, rapidly and accurately, the individual letters. He must also be able to determine immediately whether two sequences of two or three letters are alike or different in respect to both the individual letters that constitute each sequence and their order within each sequence.

3. English spelling, in its representation of English words, drastically shifted its basic principles from 1450-1600. It moved away from a representation that could be grasped in terms of correspondences between individual letters and individual sounds to a representation through spelling patterns. It made possible the "silent" letters of our etymological spelling as well as the differentiation, by spelling, of words having the same pronunciation.

These developments in English spelling provide a basis for a very different approach to the teacher of beginning reading. It features specifically, even from the very early steps, the making of independent "extensions" of the matrices to build the pupil's ability to read hundreds of words he has never seen written before.

4. Reading for meaning requires the building of situation meanings out of the words and sentences read. Beginning books without pictures compel the pupils to read for meanings rather than guess at words after looking at pictures.

Strategy for Instruction

It is impossible to list here all the methods available to the teacher of reading. We have outlined the Basal Reader Method, The Phonics Method, The Linguistics Method, and the Special Alphabet Method.

It has never been possible in the history of reading in the United States to state that any specific method is better than any or all others. No particular method can be described as a panacea to make every child a superior reader. As we have implied in our insistence that the teacher must make appropriate instructional decisions, a published reading method is only a part of a well-rounded reading program.

Let us assume that in your particular pre-structured classroom environment, your district has purchased a graded, sequential instructional reading program, i.e., a basal reading series. We have already stated that it is possible for children to learn to read in

5. Charles C. Fries, Ann Arbor, Michigan, one of the major authors, Merrill Linguistic Readers.

a variety of teaching situations and that productive instructional decisions can be made by the teacher, regardless of the method used. What then, should you consider in your strategies for instruction?

First of all, the basal reading series you have been provided, at your grade level, contains enough material for the entire school year. Indeed, it is not possible to use all of this material. For example, your particular reader may contain 80 stories designed to develop word recognition and comprehension skills. What instructional decisions do you, as the teacher, make as you determine your strategies for instruction? There are two important elements to consider:

1. Pupils' levels of skill mastery.
2. Pupils' backgrounds of experience and appropriate interest levels.

Before the teacher can adjust reading instruction to the students' needs, the teacher must know what those needs are. It is necessary, therefore, for the teacher to analyze the basic reading skills—word recognition and comprehension—of the students. This has been discussed, in detail, in the first two units of this book. After the teacher has determined the pupils' levels of skill mastery, he should then determine the utility of the skills to be developed in the teacher's manual for any given selection. It would be inefficient to continue working on a particular skill after the students have mastered it, simply because the teacher's manual indicates that this should be done. On the other hand, it would be futile to attempt to develop a skill for which the students have no background simply because the teacher's manual indicates that this is necessary.

It follows, then, that the teacher must make decisions regarding which selections are to be used, based on what the teacher knows to be relevant to her students, given their levels of skill mastery. Although the teacher has been assigned a basal reading series for use with his students, it is his responsibility to make appropriate instructional decisions as to what portions of that series are best suited to the students' needs. As we have pointed out, it would be inefficient and ineffective to try to cover all of the material at a predetermined, inflexible rate.

The pupils' backgrounds of experience and appropriate interest levels must also be considered by the teacher when deciding what selections will be used and what selections will be by-passed. Stories selected should be those which can best be understood by the children, and to which they can readily relate. For example, if a teacher is working in an urban environment, stories that deal with city living and experiences should be selected, rather than stories dealing with rural or farm experiences.[6]

The basal reader provides stories of many types. However, the teacher, taking into account the pupils' backgrounds of experience and appropriate interest levels, must decide which stories will be most utilitarian. The teacher should not use a story simply because it is the next one in the book.

6. We refer you to the Constructs presented in Chapters III and IV on Comprehension.

Directed Reading Activity. In 1944 Betts[7] named the instructional procedure found in most Basal Reader Manuals a Directed Reading Activity (DRA) and encouraged its continued use since it had stood the test of time. Chall[8] concluded that most manuals continue to suggest a four-part DRA. These parts are: (1) Preparation for the story; (2) Presentation of new words; (3) Guided reading and interpreting the story; and (4) Follow-up activities. This procedure has long provided teachers with an organizational plan for presenting reading lessons.

In recent years a different type of directed reading activity has appeared. This procedure, devised by Stauffer,[9] is called the Directed Reading-Thinking Activity. His procedure consists of five parts: (1) Identification of purposes of reading; (2) Adjustment of rate of reading to the purposes declared and to the nature and difficulty of the material; (3) Observation of the reading; (4) Development of comprehension; and (5) Fundamental skill training activities, discussions, further reading, additional study, and/or writing.

The traditional DRA and DR-TA, when examined carefully, establish contrasting teaching-learning situations. However, this is one more example of how educators tend to complicate rather than simplify the teaching of reading. Teacher's manuals, used in most classrooms, present the DRA instructional strategy. If the teacher elects to use the DR-TA as the instructional strategy, is it necessary to purchase reading materials which are designed for the DR-TA? Or should the teacher attempt to adapt the DR-TA to the existing DRA?

Rather than attempt to resolve these questions, we offer an instructional strategy which meets the following criteria:

- It can be used with any published instructional material (Reading, Science, Social Studies, Health, etc.).
- It must satisfy assumptions of the pre-structured classroom.
- It must allow for teacher decision making.

Following is an original short story of approximately 1,000 words entitled *Not for the Bread.* This reading selection can be used in grades 5 through 12. We use it to illustrate how classroom teachers might plan a lesson, and to enable you to perceive the relationship between lesson planning and the Constructs we have presented in previous chapters.

7. E.A. Betts, "Directed Reading Activities," *Educational Administration and Supervision,* 30 (November, 1944), pp. 67-74.

8. Jean Chall, *Learning to Read: The Great Debate* (New York: McGraw-Hill, 1967).

9. R.G. Stauffer, *Directing Reading Maturity as a Cognitive Process* (New York: Harper & Row, Publishers, 1969).

NOT FOR THE BREAD

Beaver Falls is a small town in western Pennsylvania. Beaver Falls is a steel-mill town. Making steel is hard work. It takes hard, tough men to do the work in the mills. For these men it is a lifetime of lifting and loading, of sweat and pain. There are only two ways out of the mills: death or football.

John Namath came to Beaver Falls as a kid. He saw his father go to the mills. And not long after, he followed him there. It was not the kind of a life he wanted for his kids.

In the steel country of western Pennsylvania, football was more than just a game. It was a way to escape the mills. If a kid was tough enough, and hungry enough, and could play football, he could escape from the mills.

On May 31, 1943, a son was born to John and Rose Namath. His name—Joseph William Namath. It didn't take him long to know he wanted no part of the steel mills. "I was afraid I would have to spend my life there," he said. "I dreaded that. I saw my father come home tired and dirty. I hated it."

Once, Joe's father took him to the mill in which he worked. Joe took one look and swore he would never go back. And he never did.

Joe started playing sports when he was young. He was throwing a football when he was big enough to walk.

His brothers played football in their yard. Joe was only five and too little to play, but the boys needed a quarterback. So Joe was it.

He learned to play tough at a young age. He had to catch the ball or get knocked down by his brothers.

But they did educate him. They never let him feel sorry for himself. Joe learned that if you don't have confidence, you can't do anything.

Joe learned that lesson well. He started playing football in the Pop Warner League when he was ten or eleven. He was so small that he couldn't see his pass receivers when the linemen stood up. But even then he believed in himself.

When Joe reached junior high he was still very small. He was only five feet tall, and weighed one-hundred fifteen pounds. Because he was so small he stayed at quarterback.

In high school, Joe's football coach didn't think he was strong enough to play. But Joe went to practice every day. He only got into one play that year, and it was on defense. No other kid in Beaver Falls wanted to play as much as he did.

By the time he was a senior, Namath had grown to 6'1", 175 pounds. That year, 1960, he was the starting quarterback. Up to that time, Joe had spent a good deal of time sitting on the bench. However, he studied what was happening on the field to prepare himself for when he would play.

It was time well spent. When Joe started at quarterback he impressed everybody. He had the ability to call for a change of play at the line of scrimmage when he saw how the other team had lined up their defense. This skill was rare in a college player, much less in a schoolboy.

The year before Namath started at quarterback, (1959), the Beaver Falls' "Tigers" had won four, lost five and tied one. Everyone thought that 1960 would be the same kind of a year; win a few, lose a few.

On the second play of the first game against Midland, Namath put the ball out for his running back. The Tiger blockers crashed into the Midland linemen with straight ahead blocking. Then Joe Willie withdrew the ball and hid it on his hip. Joe ran easily to the outside. He wanted Midland to think he had faked the handoff.

But Namath really *had* faked the handoff. When the Midland tacklers discovered that the man they tackled didn't have the football, they shouted, "Bootleg! Bootleg!" And they went after Namath.

It was too late. Namath was around end and racing downfield. He went sixty yards for the touchdown.

The Tigers won their season opener 43-13.

In their next game, Beaver Falls won 39-7. Joe completed eight of nine passes for 186 yards.

By now the college football scouts were starting to hang around Beaver Falls. Word of Namath's skills had gotten all over the country.

As the season ended, Beaver Falls was undefeated. And what is more, they won their first championship in thirty-two years.

At the beginning of that year no one would have given a dime for Beaver Falls' chances. But then, no one knew about Joe Willie Namath. He made the difference.

After high school, many colleges wanted Namath to come and play for them. Joe finally decided on the University of Alabama. With Namath on their side, Alabama became the top ranking team in the nation.

From Alabama the road led to professional football and the New York Jets.

It was a windy, winter's day in January, 1969. The door of New York's City Hall opened. Mayor John Lindsay walked through a mob of policemen to a platform in the park. There were about 6,000 people in the park, but they had not come to hear Lindsay.

A young man followed Lindsay through the door. The young man looked mod in his sportcoat, long hair, and sideburns. And when he came into the view of the crowd, the people cheered wildly.

"We want Joe. We want Joe," they roared.

"Namath for Mayor. Namath for Mayor."

They had every reason to cheer: Joe Namath had brought them and the New York Jets a World Championship. When the cheers died down, the Mayor read a proclamation which established January 22, 1969 as "New York Jets Championship Day."

One man in the crowd held up a sign:

"Broadway Joe. What else can be said?
He did it for pride. Not for the bread."

As Namath left the platform, mobs of fans rushed at him. "I love it," said Joe. "These are my people. They're young people."

As he moved away from that screaming mob, somebody asked him, "Are you all right?"

"Yeah," said Namath. "Nothing bad every happens to me."

"It's a long way from Beaver Falls, hey?"

"Sure is," said Namath. And then, in a thoughtful way, he said, "Beaver Falls."

I. PREPARATION FOR THE STORY

New Words. The teacher decides what constitutes a reasonable number of new words. In some situations it may be as few as three. In others, it may be as many as 15. The teacher also decides what constitutes a new word, based on her knowledge of her students. (The authors of instructional materials do not know *your* students; they can only generalize.)

In *Not for the Bread,* one teacher selected the following as New Words:

> confidence
> escape
> established
> platform
> receivers

These words were selected as new words by *one* teacher. Each teacher must select words he feels are appropriate.

Concepts. Identifying concepts which might be unknown to the students. Here again, the teacher decides which concepts need to be explored and explained to enable the students to understand the story. The teacher also decides how many concepts will be developed in this particular selection, again, based on the sophistication of her group. Merely describing concepts is not instructionally sound; *the teacher needs to provide indirect (visual aids, etc.) or direct experiences (concrete objects, trips, etc.).*

The fifth grade teacher selected the following concepts for development:

1. steel-mill town	1. used a film on steel making
2. sitting on the bench line of scrimmage faked the hand off "bootleg" play	2. had several students act out in class, one student presented a football diagram for the "bootleg" play
3. New York Jets	3. Students discussed football game seen on TV

Word Recognition Skills. The teacher's knowledge of the students' general level of skill mastery should determine what word recognition skill(s) are to be presented or reinforced at this time.

Our demonstration teacher selected the following phonic generalization for review:

Review the rule that a single vowel in the middle of a one syllable word is usually short: *set, top, but, men,* etc.

Our demonstration teacher might have decided to reinforce the following structural analysis generalization rather than deal with the single vowel skill:

Explain to the students that *y* is usually changed to *i* before a suffix is added. Present the words below and have the students form their plurals. Do the first one with them.

country	countries
story	stories
city	cities
dirty	dirties
university	universities

Dictionary or glossary (only if it applies in the lesson). As you will recall, we encouraged teachers to include only consistent high utility word recognition concepts. Trying to present all word recognition concepts suggested for each selection is not instructionally sound.

Review Chapters 1-5 for the relationship of planning and the constructs used in this book.

II. READING THE STORY

Purpose(s) for Reading Selection. The teacher informs the students why they are reading this particular selection.

The fifth-grade teacher said,

"Joe Namath is a world famous football player. Read this story to see how it was more a desire on Joe's part to escape the hard life of the steel mills than a love for football that brought him to the top of his profession."

Product or Process Questions. The teacher decides upon a reasonable number of questions, and might give them to the students *before* they begin to read the selection. However, it is more important that the teacher decide on the type of questioning approach to use. Specifically, the teacher needs to deal with either a *product* or a *process* questioning approach.

As you will recall, product type questions have predetermined answers: the student must give the answers that are in the Teacher's Manual. These are usually Fact (F) questions which require direct recall of the words in the story.

Product type examples (factual in nature):

Q.   Where was Joe Namath born?
A.   Beaver Falls, Pennsylvania.
Q.   When was "New York Jets Championship Day" proclaimed?
A.   January 22, 1969.
Q.   What University did Joe Namath play for?
A.   The University of Albama.

Product questions related to Inference (I) and Vocabulary (V) usually require more than mere recall of specific words in the story, but again the student must give responses which approximate the answers in the Teacher's Manual.

Product type examples (inference and vocabulary in nature).

Q.   What does the title of this story, *Not for the Bread,* mean to you?
A.   Namath had a great deal of pride in himself and worked hard.
Q.   It is about 400 miles from New York to Beaver Falls. What do you think is meant by the statement, "It's a long way from Beaver Falls?"
A.   It is a long way not in distance, but in terms of what Beaver Falls meant to Joe in terms of his life there, and what happend to him in New York.

If the teacher elects to use a Process type approach, the entire procedure will have to change from a question-answer style to a free-wheeling, open discussion style.

For example, if the teacher wanted to deal with word meanings, several approaches are possible:

multiple meanings of words	words which signal identity
specific meanings of words	words which influence
words which signal time	etc.

159

We repeat the first paragraph from *Not for the Bread*. We'll use the paragraph to briefly illustrate how the teacher might deal with five different word meaning Process approaches.

Beaver Falls is a small town in western Pennsylvania. Beaver Falls is a steel-mill town. Making steel is hard work. It takes hard, tough men to do the work in the mills. For these men it is a lifetime of lifting and loading, of sweat and pain. There are only two ways out of the mills: death or football.

The teacher might divide the class into small groups, with not more than four students in each group. The students might be asked to select those words which have:

multiple meanings

hard	1. firm
	2. powerful
	3. difficult

work	1. employment
	2. labor
	3. solve

etc.

specific meanings

Pennsylvania—a state
football—a game
etc.

words which signal time

January
etc.

words suggesting events happened

making steel
lifting
loading

words suggesting events are happening

Beaver Falls *is* a small town.
It takes hard, tough men.

words which signal identity

these men (men of Beaver Falls)

words which influence

small town
hard work
no way out
Beaver Falls is a dreary place.

These are but a few of the endless possibilities which exist in exploring each paragraph of a story. We're not suggesting that this approach become the only approach to questioning. However, if used on a regular basis throughout the year, it should help the learner recognize some of the underlying processes he invokes and uses when reading independently.

The teacher can turn the Product type questions, usually found in instructional materials, into Process type merely by making simple adjustments.

For example, here is a typical Product type question with several possible answers:

Q.   Football, in Beaver Falls, was more than a game. Why?

Answers:

1. Players make money playing football.
2. It served as a way out of the hard life in the mill.
3. The boys liked basketball.

"Correct" Answer #2

To adjust to a Process type, all the teacher needs to do is **Not Provide** the "Correct" answer. Instead, ask students to respond to each possible answer.

For example, responses to each possible answer might be as follows:

Answer #1

"Players do make money playing football, but not while they're at the nonprofessional level (Beaver Falls)."
"It wasn't mentioned in the story."

Answer #2

"It seems to be the most reasonable answer."
"Success in football is a good way out of a difficult life."

Answer #3

"This story is about football not basketball."
"This is a dumb item."

The main point we wish to stress is that in a Product approach, the feedback to the learner consists of knowing the number of items correct or incorrect. In a Process approach the learner gets feedback about each alternative answer, and also learns that what is labeled "correct" is often arbitrarily chosen.

If sufficient Process training is provided, we believe that students will have a better opportunity to acquire the understandings, ideas, (processes) etc., involved in a Product questioning situation.

Review Chapters 3-4 for the Relationship of Planning and the Construct Uses in this book.

III. REREADING

Students usually are asked to read to solve problems which might result from the discussion and/or questions asked. Have the students rapidly locate the information under discussion or in question. This should correct any confusion which might have occurred during the silent reading.

IV. FOLLOW-UP AND RELATED ACTIVITIES

Oral Reading Activities. The teacher decides upon a purpose for an oral reading of the story. Selections are not read in toto just for the sake of reading each story aloud. As an example of an oral reading activity, the teacher might have several students prepare an oral reading of what they considered to be the most exciting part of the story.

Developing Additional and Related Comprehension and Word Analysis Skills. After a particular skill has been introduced the students will need a good deal of practice to develop the skill. Here the teacher may select a page or pages from an activity book to provide the needed practice.

Teacher/Student Directed Activities. Many times a selection read in a basal reader will suggest extended activities for the teacher/students. For example, the story about Joe Namath may motivate students to want to do wide reading about Namath and football/sports. This wide reading may lead to individual/group projects, etc.

SUMMARY

Assuming that the results of Classroom Checklists I and II identified your teaching situation as pre-structured and that you made the decision to adopt some or all of our recommendations, we would like to summarize by briefly pointing out the relationships between our constructs and our recommended pre-structured strategy for instruction.

Pre-Structured Strategy for Instruction	Construct
Teacher/Administrator selection of a reading method which is appropriate for children and enthusiastically accepted by the teacher.	The improvement of instructional practices occurs when teachers and administrators make appropriate instruction decisions (Chap. 7, pp. 103-110).
	Rationale for classroom environments pre-structured classroom (Chap. 9, pp. 129-147).
Directed Reading Activity	Directed reading-thinking activity (Chap. 10, pp. 149-164.
I. Preparation for the Story	Language symbolizes our world of experience. Print symbolizes our language (Chap. 3, pp. 25-33).
New Words	
Concepts	Experience is basic to all communication (Chap. 4, pp. 35-52).
Word Recognition	The ability to hold the whole word and simultaneously attend to parts within the word (Chap. 2, pp. 7-16).
Dictionary or Glossary	Word recognition lessons should be limited to consistent high frequency word elements in the main areas of "readiness," consonants, vowels, and structure-syllables (Chap. 2, pp. 17-24).

Pre-Structured Strategy for Instruction	Construct
II. Reading the Story Purpose(s) for reading selection Follow-up Questions: Product or Process	The development of comprehension skills requires a balance between process and product approaches (Chap. 4, pp. 35-52). Types of questions (Chap. 6, p. 74). The teacher has the ability to recognize when either a process approach or a product approach is possible (Chap. 4, pp. 35-52).

III. Rereading

IV. Follow-up and Related Activities

REFERENCES FOR CHAPTER 10

Bush, Clifford L., and Huebner, Mildred H. *Strategies for Reading in the Elementary School.* London: The Macmillan Company, 1970.

See: Part 3 (pp. 175-270) "Planning and Organizing Effective Reading (Practical Aspects)." Six chapters on this topic including sources of reading materials and programmed learning.

Dechant, Emerald V. *Improving the Teaching of Reading.* Englewood Cliffs, New Jersey: Prentice-Hall, Inc., 1964.

See: Chapter 14 (pp. 403-475) "Materials for Teaching." Materials for teaching reading, basal readers, readiness materials, booklists, etc.

Hafner, Lawrence E., and Hayden B. Jolly. *Patterns of Teaching Reading in the Secondary School.* New York: The MacMillan Company, 1972.

See: Chapter 9 (pp. 189-226) "Providing for Individual Differences Through Technology and Organization." An excellent section dealing with the logistics of reading instruction.

Harris, Albert J. *How to Increase Reading Ability.* New York: David McKay Co., Inc., 1970.

See: Chapter 6 (pp. 113-137) "Group Instruction in Reading." Presents illustrative plans for grouping for reading instruction.

May, Frank B. *To Help Children Read.* Columbus, Ohio: Charles E. Merrill Publishing Company, 1973.

See: Module 9 (pp. 289-341) "Organizing and Managing Your Reading Program." Outlines an organizational scheme for reading instruction which fits the teacher's own teaching style and her pupils' learning needs.

Spache, George D., and Evelyn B. Spache. *Reading in the Elementary School.* Boston: Allyn & Bacon, Inc., 1973.

See: Chapter 4 (pp. 145-190) "Using the Basal Reading Approach." A thorough, comparative discussion of the basal approach.

Stauffer, Russell G. *Teaching Reading as a Thinking Process.* New York: Harper & Row, Publishers, 1969.

See: Part II (pp. 19-150) "Group Instructions at Various Levels." Presents specific information on the Directed Reading-Thinking Activity Plan.

Wallen, Carl J., *Competency in Teaching Reading.* Chicago: Science Research Associates, Inc., 1972.

See: Chapter 18 (pp. 453-471) "Using Testing and Teaching Strategies with three types of Reading Methods." Discusses prescribed, programmed and creative reading methods.

Wilson, Robert M., and Maryanne Hall. *Reading and the Elementary School Child.* New York: Van Nostrand Reinhold Company, 1972.

See: Chapter 11 (pp. 241-263) "Planning Lessons." Stresses planning as a means of translating theory into procedures for implementation of the theory.

EMERGING CLASSROOM ENVIRONMENT

John Lear, writing about man in the *Saturday Review,* said: "Among the animals of the earth, only man can dream. Other species laugh and cry, love, rage, and kill. Man alone has the power to imagine tomorrow."

Teaching reading in an emerging classroom can be referred to as individualized reading instruction. This approach transcends the traditional method of teaching reading in that it requires and provides for an entirely new relationship between the teacher and the students. It is based on psychological and philosophical concepts radically different from those which gave rise to the pre-structured classroom, as we have indicated earlier.

Proponents of individualized reading instruction envision the time when public education in this country will be oriented predominately toward, and based upon, the concepts which have already resulted in many schools, in the emerging classroom. In any case, if individualized reading instruction is to be either effective or possible, the classroom itself must be physically restructured. That is, the psychological and philosophical concepts, the methods and practices based on these concepts, and the classroom itself must be integrated, conceptually and physically, in what we have called the emerging classroom.

To illustrate, and as a point of departure for this chapter, we begin with a definition which points toward the potential breadth of learning which can be acquired in the emerging classroom in which individualized reading instruction is practical. Schubert[1] defines individualized reading as follows:

"Individualized Reading:

1. Based on the concepts of seeking, self-selection and pacing, the program provides time for the individual child to seek his own reading materials, to read them at his own rate, and to receive guidance from his teacher, who works with him in an individual conference. Group activities are not omitted in this plan, which may include sharing periods, as well as group instruction in specific skills as needed.

2. Individualized developmental reading is characterized by the elimination of systematic instruction using basal readers, using individual reading in a variety of reading materials as the core of method rather than as supplement.

1. Delwyn G. Schubert, *A Dictionary of Terms and Concepts in Reading* (Springfield, Illinois: Charles C. Thomas, 1964), pp. 206-208.

3. An individualized reading program provides each child with an environment which allows him to seek that which stimulates him, choose that which helps him develop most, and work at his own rate regardless of what else is going on.

4. Individualized reading is not a single method with predetermined procedural steps to be followed in formal sequence. This type of instruction does not eliminate group reading; neither does it support a laissez-faire attitude toward instruction. The prime objective of individualized reading is to provide each pupil with a variety of reading situations so that each may progress according to his own growth rate.''

This definition clearly indicates that individualized reading involves much more than the acquisition of standard teaching techniques and the "orderly" use of available printed materials. It transforms and extends the learning experience; and it calls for and allows the creative imagination John Lear described as dreaming in the quotation which heads this chapter. And it makes both teaching and learning, which are complementary, not separate, experiences (except in wholly arbitrary intellectual abstractions). adventurous and exciting.

The concepts of seeking, self-selection and pacing, to recount just a few, place the emphasis not on the group or the "method," but on the individual child and his responsible participation in the learning process.

IMPLEMENTING AN INDIVIDUALIZED READING APPROACH:

At this point it is necessary to consider a very basic question: "What practices or procedures do I use in launching an individualized reading program?"

There are three basic components necessary for the implementation of an individualized reading program:

Stage   I: Room Organization.

Stage II: Unit Themes and Student Activities.

Stage III: Individual Conference and Record Keeping.

Stage I: Room Organization

The primary activity under the heading *Room Organization* is establishing varied and realistic interest-work centers in each classroom or resource area. These interest-work centers could be: an art area (paper, paints, magazines for cutting, etc.); an audiovisual area (filmstrips, records, tapes, head-sets for listening, etc.); a library area (paperbacks, hard coverbooks, etc.); a general project area (reference material, mural making, etc.); and whatever else is appropriate in terms of teacher-pupil interest needs.

The other concern under this heading is helping teachers understand that children need to be taught and permitted to use these areas independently, and to learn to assume full responsibility for their activities while working in these various areas.

In the primary grades some easy centers to start with are:

1. Playhouse—Grocery, Post office, animal den, police station, court house, etc.
2. Art Center—Paints, papers, egg cartons, ribbons, buttons, etc.
3. Library Center—Magazines, books (a wide variety, pictures, words), comic books, children's weekly publications, newspapers, anything that is printed.
4. Writing Center—Story starters, dictionaries (word and picture), A.B.C. writing cards, picture cards, typewriter, etc.
5. Game Center—Variety of board games, etc.

At the upper grade level, in addition to the above centers, the following centers might be included:

1. Skill Center—Word recognition, vocabulary, comprehension, math, spelling, etc. SRA Kits, other skill sheets or kits, etc.
2. Science Center—Aquariums, terrariums, microscope, harmless chemicals, rock collections, etc.
3. Audiovisual Center—Filmstrip projector, language master, tape recorder, record player, projection box, etc.
4. General Projects Center—Bulletin boards, class newspaper, picture collections, etc.

In setting up the various interest-work centers, the following suggestions should prove helpful:

1. Start one center at a time and have it running smoothly before you start the next one.

2. The teacher must supervise the interest-work centers at first, then encourage the children to work independently. The teacher must guide the students to understand the importance of regular, consistent work habits if their learning objectives are to be realized. Although it may seem paradoxical, even contra-dictory, the teacher's goal and reward in this specific responsibility is to enable the students to discover that their freedom to work at their own volition, accept responsibility will result in learning as joy and excitement, not just as duty.

3. Start with a small group of children at a time. Show these children how to perform an activity before you put them into a center. Then name an "expert" for that activity so that if questions arise in the future the children will know whom to ask for help.

4. Rotate materials within the centers and change one or two activities each week. Too many activities carried on too long in a center will result in boredom, and thus defeat the purpose of the various centers.

5. The teacher must assume the initial responsibility for assigning students to the centers. Afterward, other means may be employed. For example, the teacher may set up a simple system of rotating students from center to center. Students might be permitted to make their own choices, provided only that they do not neglect necessary areas of study and experience. A committee of students, elected by their classmates, might make assignments. The completion of a project within one center might well be the time when (1) all the students in that center move to another center; (2) a new project is undertaken by the group without changing centers; or (3) two or three students might exchange places with an equal number of students from another center. What is important to remember and implement here is that the teacher seek to maintain a balance between necessary supervision of the classroom allowing students to develop their own interests and exercise indi-vidual responsibility.

6. Limit the number of children at each center by the number of places at that center. For example, John wants to work at the A-V center. However, he sees four children there and he can see that only four are permitted at one time in that center, so he waits until one child leaves before joining that group.

7. *Do not* use the centers as rewards for completing work or being "good."

8. Be sure that each child is able to function in a center before he is permitted to use that center.

9. The basic notion is: *learning how to learn.*

Before looking into the second stage necessary for the implementation of an individualized reading program, we would like to reaffirm the position that we took in Chapter 9 regarding an emerging classroom. That is, in order for the teacher to be successful with an individualized reading program, that teacher must be committed both philosophically and psychologically to the concepts on which the emerging classroom is based.

Stage II: Unit Themes and Student Activities

Unit themes and student activities are designed to build upon the interests of teachers and children. They are also designed to provide general curriculum content expectations for respective age and grade levels. For example, if a sixth-grade teacher is expected to discuss Europe, the unit approach might result in the selection of only one country, or several representative countries (depending on teacher-pupil interest), and develop, in depth, this content area for several weeks. This greatly expands the traditional textbook approach, i.e., reading several pages, briefly discussing the content introduced, and then answering questions at the end of the selection read, then hurriedly moving on to the next section of the textbook.

The real value of the unit teaching approach lies in the fact that it provides flexibility in curriculum practices. The nonreading child has the opportunity to base his activities on speaking and listening, while the developmental child has the opportunity to base his activities on reading and writing. In short, all ways in which children can learn are natural aspects of a unit teaching approach. Our present practices tend to allow only for teaching-learning activities based on reading and writing, thus excluding other activities.

The Unit is a series of planned, coordinated experiences organized around a central theme or problem. Basically, there are two unit types:

a. *The Teaching Unit:* The teaching unit is composed of purposeful, related activities organized around aspects of everyday living *significant* to the child. It provides for the integration of learnings related to many curriculum areas.

b. *The Resource Unit:* The resource unit is a collection of suggested teaching and learning experiences and materials organized around a selected topic or area.

The basic difference between a teaching unit and a resource unit is one of anticipation or preplanning. The teacher who has been doing unit teaching for several years may have completed two or three teaching units, then realize that these continue to be relevant, so they are used again, perhaps in a slightly modified form. Nevertheless, the teacher has collected materials and ideas, has sources of information, etc., which can still be used. When this happens, you have a resource unit. Or the teacher may have certain areas in the curriculum that must be covered and then prepares resource units to fill these needs.

Unit Development

Approach: Methods to be used to motivate; to stimulate interest in the unit.

Launching: Discuss the unit—talk about ideas to be learned, problems to be solved, and activities. Discuss what needs to be done in order to reach selected goals.

Research: Once these decisions are made, each student will select a committee to work with. Each committee takes on different aspects of the problem—a division of labor.

Pooling: Within each committee, each member takes on certain portions of that committee's total responsibility—a further division of labor. Periodically, the committee meets and the members share whatever information, knowledge, experiences, etc., they have acquired with the entire committee.

Reporting: When the pooling is completed, the committee summarizes what has been learned and then shares information with the class.

Culmination: As a culminating activity, the class then proceeds to do what they said needed to be done in order to achieve their goals.

Evaluation: The teacher—students evaluate the unit and its outcomes. The evaluation should be both quantitative and qualitative. That is, there may be tests covering skills acquired—quantitative. The teacher may note that Mary is able to work well in a group and is becoming more independent—qualitative.

A SAMPLE TEACHING UNIT

The authors of this text have had the opportunity to observe the development of the following teaching unit on growing up (primary grade level). In addition to reporting our observations, we will also indicate other ways in which the unit might have been developed in the classroom. The ways in which units can be selected and developed are, of course, limited only by the teacher's imagination and ability to motivate the students to participate responsibly in all classroom activities according to their individual interests, capacities, and prior experiences.

Approach: For several days, the teacher and students discussed things they liked or disliked. Some of the objects and experiences discussed were: pets, food, television, accidents. The discussions began to center on how people develop friendships. Finally the students decided that they wanted to learn more about themselves as people. Another approach to the unit could have been playing a "Name Sharing Game" in which each student named the other students, adding his own name. Then the students could have learned the song, "Getting To Know You."

Launching: Once the purpose was identified, the students had many questions.

Some of these were: "How tall am I?" "What does my voice sound like?" "Who is the oldest student in the room?"

Research: Before beginning the formal activities necessary to the accomplishment of the purpose selected, both the teacher and the students must do some form of research. The teacher's major responsibility here is to collect the resources and materials necessary for the successful completion of the unit, and preparing for the activities involved in working out the unit. We outline below some activities which might be used in helping the students come to know themselves—and each other—better.

Activities:

1. Place mirrors around the room so that the students can look at themselves.
2. Have the students sketch self-portraits.
3. Have each student write his or her name with black crayon, then color around the name. Have the students identify the letter their names begin with. Then let the students place these on their desks to be used as name plates.
4. Have the students trace silhouettes—one student traces another. Display the silhouettes around the room. (The body and clothes might be colored in later.)
5. If tape recorders are available, let the students record their voices for playback later, so that they can hear how they sound to others.
6. Have the students write the word **Me**, then make a picture of the word.
7. Have the students write their names on folded paper, with the name on the fold. Have them trace around the name, then cut out around the name. They should leave the name attached to the larger paper, so that when the paper is unfolded the name will be outlined within the area from which it was cut.

Resources:

Books:

1. Big Brother—Charlotte Zolotow
2. Is This You?—Ruth Krauss
3. It's Nice to Be Little—John Stanley
4. Just Like You—Leonore Klein
5. Just Me—Marie Hall Etts
6. The Little School—at Cottonwood Corners—Eleanor Schick
7. My Name Is _____ —Lois Buker Muchl
8. One Snail and Me—Emilie Warren McLeod

Music:

1. How Would You Say Hello? The Magic of Music (Ginn 1965) page 7
2. Guessing Song-Music Around the Clock (Follett 1963) page 84
3. I'm a Great Big Boy-The First Grade Book (Ginn 1969-71) page 3

Films:

1. David and the Puppy
2. Dickie Builds a Truck
3. Helping Johnny Remember

In addition to preparatory efforts by the teacher, committees or small groups were set up on the basis of their common experiences or interests.

Pooling: Once the youngsters selected the committee each wanted to work with, a chair person was elected for each committee. The chair person led discussions on each committee member's responsibilities to the committee.

Reporting: Each committee reported to the class what they had discovered. One committee read their report. Another committee used pictures. Another small group put on a brief play.

Culmination: As a class project, write a book—"All About Me." It can be a mixture of all works done on this unit. Student makes pictures and tells the teacher about them and he may write down what he is telling.

> Discuss what he has discovered about school, friends and himself.
> Build models of his school or room as a display.
> Put up a display in the cafeteria.
> Etc.

Evaluation: The teacher evaluated the effectiveness of this unit by doing the following:

> Observed activities in the classroom. Had the child relaxed in the atmosphere the classroom provided? How did he get along with others? Did he share? How much work had each child contributed? Had he worked alone or was he withdrawn from the group?

Following is a list of important considerations that a teacher must bear in mind when setting up a unit teaching approach:

1. Whether the idea for the unit comes from the children, the teacher, or the course of study, it is the teacher's job to make it answer the needs of the children.

2. Do not place arbitrary limits on the unit selected. Allow it to overflow into its natural channels—language, reading, arithmetic, science, spelling, art, music, or literature, if it finds a natural outlet there.

3. All of the experiences in the school day do not necessarily stem from this unit of study. Other activities go on as usual.

4. The unfolding of a unit of work must follow the way most natural to children's growth, not a logical outline as is usual in the adult approach to learning.

5. Not all children need to seek the answer to the same problem. There should be a continuous sharing of knowledge, group with group.

As a final note on unit teaching, it should be pointed out that it would be unrealistic to attempt a unit approach before the interest-work centers are operational and before the students are able to function in them.

When youngsters are first learning to operate under a unit teaching approach, it is a good idea to hand out a ditto sheet as a means of periodical checking, once or twice each week.

The teacher might make a simple ditto sheet based on the sample below:

```
                              Name_____

     Topic_____

     Committee members_____

     _____

     _____

     _____

     I am working on_____

     _____

                              or

     I will work on_____

     _____
```

These periodic checks on students will provide the teacher with a realistic form of accountability. Folders which include these sheets should be kept on each group.

We suggest that before you lead your class in the development and completion of a unit, you do a unit, or some units, as a personal learning experience. This exercise should give you broader insight into the ways in which the unit approach works, and an indication of what can be accomplished through the unit approach.

Stage III: Individual Conference and Record Keeping

The final component of an individualized reading program is the individual conference and record keeping. The individual conference (teacher-to-pupil or teacher-to-small group) and teacher-made records of the details of the conference is by far the most important component of an individualized reading program.

As the children develop a reasonable level of independence with unit activities, and acquire the ability to function in interest-work centers, the teacher then has the opportunity to schedule conferences to guide children in their learning process. Since the activities of the conference are based on the learning needs, background and interest of each child, one can readily understand how this overall approach can be used to enhance the learning achievements of children from radically different backgrounds and kinds of preschool experiences who are often thrown together in a single classroom.

The teacher, through individual and group conferences, becomes aware of pupil needs in word attack and comprehension skills. The teacher can keep records of pupil needs and achievements either in a notebook, chart, or card file; a sample of which is given on the following page.

INDIVIDUAL RECORD

STUDENT'S NAME _Tom Smith_

DATE	ACTIVITY	COMMENT RECOMMENDATIONS
2/10	(Book) Mr. Rush P. 84	His comprehension is O.K. Word Recognition— needs help with Syllables VC:CV and V:CV
2/14	Mr. Rush P. 128	Checked syllables VC:CV and V:CV more practice give syllable quiz next time
2/18	(Book) Black Mare	Book seems too difficult for Tom, suggested he try another
2/22	Black Mare P. 105	Still has difficulty with book but he likes it? — so O.K.

The direct teaching aspect of the emerging classroom is centered in Stage III, the individual conference. Obviously, if the teacher is to direct his complete attention to one student or a small group of students, the total classroom situation must be designed to allow other students to work independently for reasonable periods of time. This is one of the major values of the unit approach; it is designed for this purpose.

The information recorded about each conference with a child, the periodic data collected on his project or committee activities (Stage II), plus general teacher evaluation in the form of comments, will provide a wealth of data for a parent conference or discussion with the building principal.

The comments made on the individual record included references to lessons based on behavioral objectives (i.e., consonant sounds). Many schools and commercial companies are providing teachers with hundreds of single concept lessons which are stated in behavioral terms. These single concept lessons frequently include: a pretest, a subtest, and a posttest. These materials are ideally suited to the emerging classroom and provide the teacher with a realistic number of individual lessons in the areas of word recognition and comprehension.

If single concept materials are not available, then the teacher must identify instructional lessons (usually found in activity books, kits, prepared work sheets, etc.), and have such lessons available for students. Identifying such materials and preparing adequate copies requires a great deal of time. If the teacher needs these materials prepared locally, it is advised that the principal help organize a team of teachers, aides, and parents and provide funds for paper and folders. As with everything in education, if it is of value, it usually requires more time and money.

SUMMARY

Assuming that the results of Classroom Checklists I and II identified your teaching situation as emerging and that you made the decision to adopt some or all of our recommendations, we would like to summarize by briefly pointing out the relationships between our constructs and our recommended strategy for instruction in the emerging classroom.

Emerging Strategy for Instruction	Construct
Teacher/Administrator agreement on the rationale for an emerging or individualized reading approach.	The improvement of instructional practices occurs when teachers and administrators make appropriate instruction decisions. (Chap. 7, pp. 103-110).
	Rationale for classroom environments emerging classroom. (Chap. 9, pp. 129-147).

Emerging Strategy for Instruction	Construct

Implementing an individualized reading program.

Stage I	Room Organization	
Stage II	Unit Themes and Student Activities	
Stage III	Individual Conference and Record Keeping	The ability to hold the whole word and simultaneously attend to parts within the word (Chap. 2, pp. 7-16).

The ability to hold the whole word and simultaneously attend to parts within the word (Chap. 2, pp. 7-16).

Word recognition lessons should be limited to consistent high frequency word elements in the main areas of "readiness," consonants, vowels, and structure-syllables (Chap. 2, pp. 17-24).

The development of comprehension skills requires a balance between process and product approaches (Chap. 4, pp. 35-52).

Types of questions (Chap. 6, p. 74).

The teacher has the ability to recognize when either a process approach or a product approach is possible (Chap. 4, pp. 35-52).

REFERENCES FOR CHAPTER 11

Figurel, J. Allen (editor). *Reading and Inquiry.* Newark, Delaware: International Reading Association, 1965.

See: Sequence VII (pp. 146-170) "Individualizing Reading Instruction." Contains many good articles dealing with individualizing reading instruction at all levels through college.

Hafner, Lawrence E., and Hayden B. Jolly. *Patterns of Teaching Reading in the Elementary School.* New York: The Macmillan Company, 1972.

See: Chapter 10 (pp. 227-244) "Patterns of Individualizing Reading Skill Development." Reports on a comprehensive approach to individualizing reading skill development—the Wisconsin Design for Reading Skill Development: Rationale and Guidelines.

Heilman, Arthur W. *Principles and Practices of Teaching Reading.* Charles E. Merrill Publishing Company, 1967.

See: Chapter 11 (pp. 341-369) "Individualizing Reading Instruction." Presents the point of view that individualized reading represents a new emphasis on evolving classroom practices which fit individual pupil needs.

Lee, Dorris M., and R.V. Allen. *Learning to Read Through Experience.* New York: Appleton—Century—Crofts, 1963.

See: A paperback of 144 pages—an excellent resource for using the language experience approach.

Miel, Alice (editor). *Individualizing Reading Practices.* Columbia University, New York: Bureau of Publications, 1964.

See: A paperback of 90 pages with several excellent articles on this topic.

Rosenzweig, Esther. *Individualized Reading.* Wilkinsburg, Pennsylvania: Hayes School Publishing Co., Inc., 1966.

> This is a guide to independent activities in individualized reading for the intermediate grades.

Smith, Nila Banton. *American Reading Instruction.* Newark, Delaware: International Reading Association, 1962.

> *See:* Chapter 9 (pp. 308-423) "The Period of Expanding Knowledge and Technological Revolution." See those sections dealing with the individualized approach, the linguistic approach and programmed learning.

——. *Current Issues in Reading.* Newark, Delaware: International Reading Association, 1969.

> *See:* (pp. 328-356) "What Are the Advantages and Disadvantages of Individualized Instruction." Presents a position paper on this topic and a pro-challenger reply and a con-challenger reply.

Spache, George D., and Evelyn B. Spache. *Reading in the Elementary School.* Boston: Allyn & Bacon, Inc., 1973.

> *See:* Chapter 5 (pp. 191-217) "Using the Individualized Approach." Contains a concise, well-written section on the principles of individualized reading.

Veatch, Jeannette. *Individualizing Your Reading Program.* New York: G.P. Putnam's Sons, 1959.

> *See:* The entire book is recommended. It presents many excellent articles on this topic.

——. *Reading in the Elementary School.* New York: The Ronald Press Company, 1966.

> *See:* Part II (pp. 61-204) "Classroom Management." Detailed discussions of the independent work period, the individual conference, and grouping.

chapter 12

ROLE OF THE SPECIAL READING TEACHER

The early 1960s ushered in an era of increasing concern for youngsters with reading problems. Many schools in this country began to employ "Remedial Reading" teachers to work with youngsters disabled in reading in a situation outside the regular classroom environment—to provide some reading help, as it were. With the enactment of Public Law 89-10 (Elementary and Secondary Education Act) in 1964, funds were made available to schools to enable the schools to initiate special reading programs where none had previously existed. The demand for "Remedial Reading" teachers greatly increased.

For a description of the role of the "Remedial Reading" teacher during these early years of the 1960s, we have selected the term *assignment.* We have selected the term assignment because it seemed to suggest that many of the key functions of the special reading program were "assigned" or arbitrarily decided by someone other than the "Remedial Reading" teacher. We believe that this assignment concept represents a traditional and frequently illogical approach to correcting reading problems. Special reading programs which might be classified as assignment usually have many of the following characteristics.

The case-load is likely to range from 80 to 120 children per remedial reading teacher per week. The remedial reading teacher is expected to work with groups of eight to twenty children per session. The children are assigned to the remedial reading teacher by the school administrator and classroom teachers. The remedial reading teacher might be expected to work with these assigned children for more than a 30 week period. Children are "helped" in small groups rather than on an individual basis. Individual diagnoses and specific individual treatments are practically nonexistent.

Any given group, in the assignment type reading program, is likely to have a wider range of individual pupil difference than a group in the regular classroom. For example, each assigned group might contain children with psychological, physical, and intellectual limitations. Some of the children in each assigned group may have problems with the word recognition skills, with the comprehension skills, or both word recognition and comprehension skill problems. Other children in each assigned group may have the basic word recognition and comprehension skills, but have developed negative attitudes toward reading. Some of the children may come from subcultures whose language usage is significantly different from the language used in school.

Wide differences in the background of disabled readers and large case loads thus have the tendency to force the reading teacher to utilize a narrow program of word recognition (phonics) development for *all* children. As a result, there is little time for individual record keeping or consultation with teachers and parents.

We believe that an assignment approach has little or no positive effect on most of the disabled readers; the remedial reading teacher quickly becomes overburdened and eventually frustrated. And most serious of all, the remedial reading teacher is not able to help the classroom teachers provide an effective developmental (classroom) program and, thus, *prevent* many reading problems.

Toward the close of the 1960s, we began to discern some perceptible changes in the way special reading programs were being implemented. The term "Remedial Reading Teacher" fell into disuse and the term "Special Reading Teacher" or "Corrective Reading Teacher" became more popular. The outmoded assignment concept began to give way, and was replaced by what we have termed a *referral* approach to correcting the learner's reading problem.

A referral method enables the special reading teacher (SRT) to function as a trained professional, to effectively correct reading problems, and to modify developmental (classroom) reading programs. Special reading programs which might be classified as referral usually have many of the following characteristics:

Group reading achievement and group intelligence tests are used to survey the school population. These test data are charted and teachers are asked to comment on the reading problems in their rooms.

After the initial survey, background information is collected and the SRT selects children to test individually. This specific diagnostic testing then enables the SRT to classify children and decide on the type and probable duration of the individual child's reading problem. For the SRT to be effective he cannot simply apply "arbitrary" methods to all students. That is to say, the effective SRT uses his knowledge and understanding of the reading process to select those techniques, approaches, and methods that best fit each individual student.

To enable the SRT to be sensitive to the various types of pupil needs he is likely to encounter within a given situation, a strategy for classifying varying reader "types" was devised.

A. *The Developmental Reader:* Developmental readers are youngsters who make normal progress in reading. Their capacity to achieve and their current achievement are virtually equal. The developmental reader has no problems in reading. The instructional program is designed to meet the needs of these pupils who are progressing adequately relative to their general capacity to achieve.

The material, the procedures and the tests in the school are adequate for the developmental reader. Reading instruction is provided as an integral part of the educational program at all grade levels. It aims at systematic development of abilities as the child matures and has greater potential for achievement.

The developmental youngsters make up about 65% of our total school population. Approximately two-thirds of American children learn to read and do profit from the reading programs in our schools as they are now established.

All of our frustration has to do with the remaining one-third of youngsters who are exceptional children in one way or the other.

To summarize, the developmental youngster is one who makes normal progress and can easily survive in what we term a public school achievement.

B. *The Corrective Reader:* This is the youngster who has a reading problem which can be corrected in a public school environment. Corrective readers do not usually require clinical instruction unless the reading retardation is compounded by continued inattention to correction and attendant emotional complications.

The causes of the problem can be traced to a lack of readiness when initial experiences with reading were provided, but instruction was continued above the proper level; a lack of adequate background of experience or oral language facility; pressure from the home to achieve, and so forth.

Most corrective readers are boys. Corrective readers have at least normal intellectual capacity. They are, in effect, underachievers. That is, the corrective reader is not achieving at a rate commensurate with his capacity to achieve.

Corrective readers can be subdivided into one of two categories—mild corrective, or corrective. The mild corrective reader usually has the following characteristics:

1. Normal range I.Q. This youngster has the ability to profit from a short-term correction program.
2. He is one or two years behind grade level in reading.
3. He has some reading skills. He usually seems weak in either word recognition and/or comprehension.
4. He might be able to read, but dislikes reading.
5. He is embarrassed over poor reading achievement.
6. He frequently needs a close relationship with a teacher and must experience moderate degrees of success with reading.
7. He does not have a known psychological and/or neurological problem.

The corrective reader usually has the following characteristics:

1. Normal range I.Q.
2. More than two years behind grade level in reading.
3. Needs very specific instruction in word recognition and/or comprehension skills.
4. Is beyond being embarrassed, but usually has a negative self-concept and is unwilling to try because he is convinced of failure.
5. Needs very small group instruction in order to acquire specific skills.

181

6. Needs close relationship with the teacher and must experience success in reading at his instructional level.
7. Does not have a known psychological and/or neurological problem.

C. *The Remedial Reader:* This is the youngster who is virtually a nonreader and is severely disorganized regarding his symbolic organization. The disorganization is rooted in psychological or neurological causes.

The defect is in the ability to deal with letters and words as symbols, with resultant diminished ability to integrate the meaningfulness of written material. It is characterized by difficulty in learning to read despite conventional instruction, adequate intelligence and socio-cultural opportunity.

Despite the fact that he has normal intellectual capacity, the remedial reader needs the assistance of specialists to get at the specific causes of his reading disability. Frequently, this type of youngster fails to attain the language skills of spelling and writing commensurate with his intellectual capacity.

A program that can provide individual instruction on a clinical basis by specially trained personnel is required. The so-called "Dyslexic" youngster would fit into this classification.

To summarize, the remedial reader has the following characteristics:

1. Normal range I.Q.
2. Nonreader. Would need extended help in reading and personality adjustment.
3. Has known psychological and/or neurological problems.
4. Needs special treatment techniques. The usual visual-auditory approaches to the teaching of reading are not effective.
5. The special reading teacher must coordinate her work with other specialists, e.g., psychologist, neurologist, special education teacher, etc.

D. *Language Other Than English:* These are the ESL (English as a Second Language) children. They are the children whose native language is something other than English and may include those children who speak some substandard form of English—a kind of "ghettoese." They can be characterized as follows:

1. Children lack the experience of middle-class children.
2. Sounds (phonemes) and sentence patterns are built from several different languages; therefore, they experience confusion when expressing themselves in school-type language patterns.
3. They need assistance in speaking and listening *before* being taught reading and writing.
4. They are virtually overwhelmed by the typical school curriculum.
5. In academic situations they react like rejected children.

Under a referral approach, it is recommended that mild correctives be helped in groups of five to eight children. Correctives should be helped in groups of not more than three, and remedials on a one-to-one basis. The instructional needs for each of these children will vary. Some children may be in the program for approximately ten weeks, others twenty weeks; still others may be in the program for the entire school year. The SRT is expected to keep a record folder on *each* child. These records should include all previous data and the specific needs of and progress made by each child.

Under this referral approach the SRT is expected to spend three-fourths of his time with disabled readers, and approximately one-fourth of his time as a consultant to fellow teachers.

Administrators, classroom teachers, and parents will have to be prepared to deal with a referral concept in a special reading program.

It should be apparent that the case load for the SRT will be much smaller under this approach and that *all* children with reading problems will not be in the program at the same time. Decisions will have to be made regarding who will be helped, and for how long.

The administrator will encounter the parent who knows the school has a special reading program and wants to know why her child is not being helped—Now! The classroom teacher may expect the poor readers to be assigned to the special reading program while he is working with more able readers during his reading period.

All professionals concerned with the individual reader will have to be in communication in order to provide a consistent program of daily instruction. This is usually quite difficult to maintain in a busy elementary schedule.

The referral approach demands more from the administrator and classroom teacher, and requires that the SRT be a specially trained professional. The initial phases of the referral approach are likely to present a series of new and somewhat unusual problems.

As great an improvement as the referral approach is over the outmoded assignment approach to reading problems, the referral approach is not really workable. In most schools today, the average classroom at any given grade level is still operating at that teaching-grade level.

For example, a fifth-grade level classroom is doing fifth-grade level "work." The youngster with a reading problem who goes to the SRT for 30 to 45 minutes a day for special reading, then comes back to his regular classroom where he spends more than four hours per day doing fifth-grade level "work." There is thus a sharp contrast between what is done in the classroom and what is done when he is with the SRT.

Let us take as an example the case of Ira. Ira is a youngster in Ms. Armstrong's fifth-grade class. In going over Ira's test scores, the SRT notes that Ira has high average intellectual capacity but seems to be reading about three years below grade level. The SRT then calls Ira in for some diagnostic tests. In evaluating Ira's informal reading inventory, the SRT has placed Ira's instructional level for reading at a second-grade level. Because there are no compounding neurological or psychological problems, Ira is classified as a corrective reader and accepted for the special reading program.

Ira is then placed in a group of five other children, all of whom need very specific instruction in the word recognition skills. Ira's group is to meet with the SRT every day for 30 to 45 minutes. Ira must experience success in reading at his instructional level, which is second grade. This instructional level is met while Ira is in his special reading group. But what heppens to Ira when he goes back to his regular classroom?

When Ira gets back to his regular classroom, the teacher announces, "We are now going to have Social Studies (or science, math, whatever). Please open your books to page 23." Ira's textbook, unfortunately, is written on a fifth-grade level. But for Ira to experience success in reading it must be at his instructional level. For Ira, and many other youngsters, this is not a fifth-grade level.

To acknowledge that Ira's instructional level for reading is second-grade level, and then expect him to read fifth-grade level material is, to say the least, frustrating. Yet there are thousands of youngsters like Ira to whom this happens every day.

To provide help with reading for youngsters like Ira is commendable. However, when what goes on in special reading programs is not consistent with everyday classroom practices, the special reading program does not have maximum effect. Indeed, unless the classroom teacher attempts to adjust her instructional practices to meet Ira's special needs, he may experience even greater frustration.

Just as in the 1960s the remedial reading teacher gave way to the special reading teacher, so must the SRT concept give way in the 1970s to a new concept. What is called for is a trained professional in reading who can operate as a *Coordinator* for the total reading program, and who functions essentially as an in-service "Trainer of Teachers."

The role of the *Reading Coordinator* is based on the following assumptions:

1. The improvement of instructional practices in the classroom requires expert assistance which is provided in a systematic manner.
2. The primary concern of the reading coordinator is the *classroom* behavior of the teacher—not the teacher as a person. We recognize that it is impossible to separate the classroom behavior of the teacher from the teacher as a person. However, we believe that concentrating only on the classroom behavior of the teacher will reduce many of the tensions between the reading coordinator and the teacher because the teacher is more likely to accept recommendations for modified classroom behavior. Eventually, the teacher may become changed as a person. The assumption is a complicated one, but the intention is to try to shift the focal point from a counselling relationship to one of a working-partnership relationship.
3. The reading coordinator is a working partner with the classroom teacher. As a partner, the reading coordinator shares equal responsibility for the design of the changes to be made. As in any partnership, both parties must understand why certain behaviors need to be changed, both must want to affect such changes, and both need to derive personal and professional satisfaction from the changes made.

Most public schools are unequipped to deal with, or to accept, the role of the reading coordinator. Most schools make a clear distinction between teachers and administrators. Administrators, i.e., principals, assistant principals, supervisors, have a clear leadership identity in a school situation. They are the ones who are expected to work with teachers. On the other hand, classroom teachers have a clear identity. They are the ones who are expected to work with students. The reading coordinator does not immediately have such clear identity. He is not assigned a number of children to work with, so in the traditional sense he is not a teacher. The reader coordinator is expected to spend most of his time working with teachers, but he is not an administrator in the traditional sense; for up to the present time only administrators were expected to work with teachers. The reading coordinator might better be described, or thought of, as an in-service "Trainer of Teachers" whose specific function in a school is to help bring about the improvement of instructional practices in reading. We believe that the reading coordinator should spend at least 75% of his time working directly with teachers and administrators.

The duties of the reading coordinator will vary from school to school, with some reading coordinators diagnosing and working with children who have reading disabilities. In other situations, the reading coordinator might be expected to work solely with teachers and administrators. Because specific responsibilities are likely to vary it will be helpful to look at some functions which relate directly to "Trainer of Teachers" activities. Three major functions are:

1. Observer.
2. Facilitator.
3. Resource Person.

1. Observer.

In fulfilling the role of "observer," the reading coordinator should be able to determine quickly whether the teacher more closely fits the pre-structured or emerging type. As indicated in previous chapters, if the teacher is observed to operate in a pre-structured manner, then the reading coordinator might suggest better ways to use published material. On the other hand, if the classroom teacher is inclined toward an emerging-type classroom, the reading coordinator might help with a series of recommendations that we made in this area.

In actuality, there is a good deal of overlap between the roles of "facilitator" and "observer." However, the term "facilitator" implies some action or involvement. The term "observer" implies some willingness to assess the teacher prior to moving into the facilitating role. In short, one needs to observe before one is able to facilitate.

2. Facilitator.

The reading coordinator can and should facilitate the total reading program in a school. This can best be accomplished by developing professional and lay understanding of the reading process and instruction in reading. In developing professional understanding, the reading coordinator must take some initiative in bringing ideas to teachers. This can best be done by spending time in classrooms with teachers. The rapport which will develop through a partnership in which classroom concerns and responsibilities are shared will enable the reading coordinator to suggest needed changes. The reading coordinator can increase communication between administrators and teachers when programs for reading instruction are being formulated. Ideally, the reading coordinator should have a relationship with teachers and administrators which would enable him to deal with the communication problems usually found in school situations.

3. Resource Person.

As a resource person, the reading coordinator should be involved in the selection of reading material for classroom use. The reading coordinator has a great deal of exposure to such material, and must be willing to share his expertise with teachers and administrators. However, it is extremely important that the reading coordinator recall our discussions in Chapter 7 (pp. 103-110) regarding methodologies. If the reading coordinator becomes emotionally biased toward a particular set of materials and chooses to ignore the fact that the teacher may not have the same emotional bias, such behavior on the reading coordinator's part could be quite detrimental to the working-partnership relationship that needs to be constantly maintained.

As a resource person, the reading coordinator should be well-schooled in diagnostic testing procedures so as to be able to help teachers identify the specific reading problems youngsters have. The reading coordinator should be equally well grounded in corrective techniques for youngsters disabled in reading and be able to aid the teacher in implementing appropriate corrective techniques.

The reading coordinator, then functions as an "observer," a "facilitator," and as a "resource person" in order to improve instructional practices in reading and to help upgrade the total reading program in the school.

There are many areas that need careful consideration in the dynamic interactions between the reading coordinator and the other professionals in a school setting. We would like to focus attention on three areas that appear to require the immediate attention of the reading coordinator. They are:

1. Sources of anxiety.
2. Implementation.
3. Ethics.

1. Sources of Anxiety.

Classroom teachers are not accustomed to having other adults in their rooms. Traditionally, the principal visited the room on an infrequent basis to make some observations so that he would be able to fill out the annual teacher competency report for the school board. If a classroom became too noisy, which was usually interpreted as "poor classroom control," the principal came in and made some suggestions. Traditionally, the Supervisor (known in some schools as the "Snooper-visor") would come in to check on books or material, etc. In the past, adults who entered the teacher's room were there on an assigned or expected basis. The teacher needed only to wait long enough for the adult to "do something" and then get out. In most cases, the teacher did not expect the adult to "interfere with" the actual instructional program. But the reading coordinator is there in a very positive way to "interfere with" the daily instructional program in reading. This behavior, regardless of the motives which prompt it, will often be threatening to the teacher. This does not mean that the reading coordinator is intentionally threatening; it merely means that he is likely to be perceived by the teacher as a source of threat.

To offset this potentially threatening situation, the reading coordinator must help the teacher recognize that he is there in a working-partnership relationship, and that he believes that the teacher is competent. As we indicated earlier, when the focus of attention centers on the improvement of instructional practices, then the threatening aspects of the relationship tend to diminish. We believe that most teachers are aware of the need for improving and updating instructional practices because of the rapid changes in reading education. If the reading coordinator will focus on this need rather than the possibility that the teacher may feel a certain sense of incompetency, then we believe that the road to removing sources of anxiety may be opened.

2. Implementation.

We believe that implementation of the role of the reading coordinator is achieved more easily when the reading coordinator behaves in a relaxed and informal manner. For example, when the reading coordinator is introduced to a faculty it seems advisable that most attention be given to some of the personal and human characteristics of this person. He likes to play golf, enjoys the theater and music, paints for a hobby, etc. This seems more advisable than going to great lengths discussing the person's professional competencies, degrees awarded, honors, awards, publications, etc. We make this recommendation because it permits teachers to find some neutral opening for discussion. By this we mean, if the reading coordinator is present, it is easier to talk about golf than reading. Informal and easy discussion affords the reading coordinator an opportunity to become acquainted with the classroom teachers, and then lead them into the more sensitive areas of daily instructional practices in reading instruction.

Another important consideration is that the reading coordinator avoid any attempts to seek out the most negative teacher in a building. We have observed in many schools throughout the country a tendency on the part of administrators to be constantly concerned with the "negative" teachers of a faculty. To be more specific, let's talk about a teacher that we call Mr. Miserable. We've observed that every school seems to have a Mr. Miserable on the faculty. This negative teacher has learned to gripe all of the time. He complains about the temperature in the building, the supplies, the children, his own personal life, or anything else that's handy. He's always quick to tell you why something won't work and why something cannot be changed.

We have also noted that the administrators in the school tend to want to convert Mr. Miserable into Mr. Nice. It is our contention that this is practically impossible and counter-productive. The reason we feel this way is that the negative teacher has learned that a good way to get attention and recognition is by being negative. The harder people attempt to bring that teacher around, the more they reinforce his negative behavior. This is why we feel that any attempts to win over Mr. Miserable are counter-productive. It is also counter-productive because the time spent in trying to convert a teacher who has to remain miserable in order to have some type of identity and gain attention is time taken away from a teacher who would respond positively to outside assistance.

We have observed that if you want to be ignored in most schools all you have to do is be competent, cooperative, and do a good job of teaching. In this way, you are likely not to draw much attention from any of your administrators. It is our recommendation that the reading coordinator seek out those teachers who are most positive and most cooperative—the Mr. Nices in the building—and begin working with those teachers to facilitate change. We believe that positive teachers will readily accept suggestions, will remain open-minded in trying out new techniques or material, and, more importantly, the positive person is likely to spread the word about the competency of the reading coordinator. Specifically, one could imagine Mr. Nice in the faculty room telling other teachers how the reading coordinator brought in new material, or demonstrated with children, or came up with some really workable ideas, etc. The other teachers listening to this are likely to be impressed and begin to request this type of help, too.

On the other hand, Mr. Miserable is likely to be in the faculty room downgrading any efforts made by the reading coordinator, and is likely to turn off other teachers because the reading coordinator is viewed as an outsider and a threat that merely disrupts the classroom rather than being helpful.

When this recommendation is presented at in-service meetings, we immediately get the reaction: "Well, what about those poor children in Mr. Miserable's class?" Our response to this reaction is that we feel that the children might fare better if Mr. Miserable is left to the least amount of frustration, i.e., he's better off left alone. For example, the children in Mr. Miserable's room are not likely to be impressed by or to be happy with their teacher. The real problem is not the outside people coming into the room, but that a teacher like Mr. Miserable should be urged to seek a position other than teaching—and we don't know how to effect this. We feel it would be more productive if the negative teacher is left alone and the conditions in the building were positive enough so that the negative teacher might then begin to feel the need to start seeking some of the more positive things that are happening.

As Mr. Miserable listens to fellow teachers talking about new programs, new material, and sees that the only way now to get recognition, identity, or attention is by a willingness to get involved in a positive way toward the reading program, he might begin to develop some positive qualities. If not, at least we can say that the climate in Mr. Miserable's room would continue to be undisturbed. In short, we need to remove the negative person from teaching. If this is not possible, we can begin to create such a positive climate that we might expect that that teacher would seek some change on his own initiative. This might be a naive posture, seen from a counseling point of view; however, it appears to be most realistic given the realities of public education.

After the reading coordinator gains entry into positively oriented classrooms, what he does at that stage is largely dependent on the accumulated experience and training that he brings to his position. How much information and technique can be implemented will obviously depend on the competencies of the reading coordinator. Stated another way, to what extent does the reading coordinator understand basic word recognition and comprehension skill development? To what extent can the reading coordinator diagnose children in these areas? To what extent can he recommend realistic instructional material? To what extent can the reading coordinator help in the overall room climate and overall lesson strategy of the teacher?

These considerations represent only a fraction of the training and experience that must go into the background of the reading coordinator. We hope that the first eleven chapters of this book can provide the reading coordinator with the beginning essential ingredients, however minimal, in the total reading program of the school. Every major component of this book would have to be experienced and expanded upon significantly before one could consider himself a competent, well-trained reading coordinator.

3. Ethics.

Insofar as ethics are concerned, the reading coordinator's first commitment is to the dignity and worth of the teacher he serves. Professional communication with teachers and administrators must be treated as privileged and confidential. The reading coordinator does not report to administrators on the work of teachers. For example, an administrator might inquire about the discipline in a certain room. The reading coordinator senses certain motives on the part of the administrator. It is our recommendation that for ethical reasons the reading coordinator give a neutral response such as: "I really don't know. I didn't notice any unusual behavior when I was in that room." The administrator must not be misled into believing that he has a "scout" available to him in that building. If the administrator feels the need to deal with the continued employment of any teacher, then it is his responsibility to deal with the problem directly, and not expect to use other professionals in the building to do his unpleasant work for him.

The reverse of this ethical concept is also true. A classroom teacher may ask the reading coordinator about what he might have heard regarding some sensitive matter in the school because he knows the reading coordinator has attended some administrative meetings. Again, we would recommend that a similar neutral statement be made. For example, "I can check it out for you, but at the moment I really don't know."

This creates a lonely position for the reading coordinator. He is cut off from intimate conversation with the administrator and the teachers. A certain portion of the reading coordinator's week could be devoted to meeting with fellow reading coordinators from other schools. This would give them all some opportunity to discuss mutual problems and provide some outlets for the consequences of the loneliness that the ethics of the position demand.

SUMMARY

The traditional remedial reading teacher and our best efforts to produce a referral approach special reading teacher will not work to bring about either improvement in children, or the improvement of instructional practices in reading. The ultimate goal, as we see it, has to be the "Trainer of Teachers" in the role of the reading coordinator. We must have someone in each school who constantly helps teachers with the everyday problems of reading programs. Some attention needs to be given to specific disabilities in children, and we believe that this can be most effectively handled by the reading coordinator identifying such youngsters and then making the proper referrals to established professional agencies who appear to be better prepared to deal with extreme cases of pupil disability.

The future role of the reading coordinator needs considerable refinement. We need a national core of such specialists who would be able to describe the classroom behavior, the function, the attitude, the problems, the ethics, etc., relative to such a role. The observations that we have offered in this chapter are merely intended to help point the way toward an urgently needed new role for reading coordinators in public education.

REFERENCES FOR CHAPTER 12

Cohn, Stella M., and Jack Cohn. *Teaching the Retarded Reader—A Guide for Teachers, Reading Specialist, and Supervisors.* New York: Odyssey Press, Inc., 1967.

See: A paperback of 175 pages which is quite practical in its format.

Dechant, Emerald. *Diagnosis and Remediation of Reading Disability.* West Nyack, New York: Parker Publishing Company, 1968.

See: Chapter 4 (pp. 109-139) "How to Organize and Implement Remediation." Helps the teacher to formulate a plan for remediation, outlines principles of remediation, and offers suggestions on how to organize for corrective and remedial reading.

Durr, William K. (editor). *Reading Difficulties: Diagnosis, Correction, and Remediation.* Newark, Delaware: International Reading Association, 1970.

See: (pp. 226-231) "Corrective and Remedial Reading and the Role of the Special Reading Teacher."

Figurel, J. Allen (editor). *Reading and Inquiry.* Newark, Delaware: International Reading Association, 1965.

See: Sequence X (pp. 215-237) "The Specialist in Reading." Contains many good articles dealing with the reading specialist at all levels through college.

Newman, Harold (editor). *Reading Disabilities—Selections on Identification and Treatment.* New York: Odyssey Press, 1969.

See: Chapter 6 (pp. 467-572) "Reading Improvement Programs." A half-dozen well-written articles dealing with this topic.

Otto, Wayne, Richard A. McMenemy and Richard J. Smith. *Corrective and Remedial Teaching.* Boston: Houghton Mifflin Company, 1973.

See: Chapter 15 (pp. 400-434) "The Teacher and Remedial Reading." Contains an excellent discussion of special programs and specialized preparation.

Schell, Leo M., and Paul C. Burns. *Remedial Reading: An Anthology of Sources.* Boston: Allyn & Bacon, 1968.

See: Part Eight (pp. 377-420) "Organizing and Administering a Remedial Reading Program." Many excellent articles on this topic.

Sebesta, Sam Leaton, and Carl J. Wallen. *Readings on Teaching Reading.* Chicago: Science Research Associates, Inc., 1972.

See: Section 5 (pp. 259-296) "Organizing for Instruction: Personnel." See especially, roles, responsibilities, and qualifications of Reading Specialists.

Wilson, Robert M. *Diagnostic and Remedial Reading.* Columbus, Ohio: Charles E. Merrill Publishing Company, 1967.

See: Chapter 11 (pp. 217-230) "Professional Responsibilities and Programs." Discusses the reading specialist and the school program.

Wilson, Robert M. and Maryanne Hall. *Reading and the Elementary School Child.* New York: Van Nostrand Reinhold Company, 1972.

See: Chapter 14 (pp. 301-312) "The Role of the Reading Specialist." Stresses the point that the key to successful utilization of the reading specialist lies in effective communication between teacher and specialist.

PROGRAMMED WORD LEARNING

The specific word recognition elements which are related to our word recognition construct (*"Readiness," Consonants, Vowels, and Structure-Syllables*) are presented in a programmed learning format.

Before you work through the programmed learning material we would like to restate your Performance Objective:

Given groups of words (five words per group) you will be able to name the specific **Consonant, Vowel,** *or* **Structure-Syllable** *elements common to all five words within the group.*

PRETEST

Directions: This Pretest consists of two parts. Part I—Readiness and Part II Consonants, Vowels, and Structure-Syllables. Place your answers on the spaces provided on the right. Check answers.

PART I—READINESS

1. Recognizing the geometric form which is different

    (△ □ △ △) is typical of _____ _____
    lessons.   1. _____

2. Writing saw for was suggests a _____ tendency.   2. _____

3. Hearing likenesses and differences in sounds or words is

    typical of _____ _____ lessons.   3. _____

4. Learning that words proceed from left to right is called

    _____.   4. _____

PART II—CONSONANT, VOWEL, AND STRUCTURE-SYLLABLE

Identify the phonic element which is present in each group of five words. Example: *but trip rabbit dock throb.* Each word contains a consonant, a vowel, and syllable, but the phonic element common to all words is the short vowel sound.

Consonant

5. blaze, study, test, pray, slave   5._____

6. beacon, catch, acre, continue, recognize   6._____

7. might, too, read, bunch, dog   7._____

8. alphabet, hyphen, photo, elephant, Phillip   8._____

9. chair, mother, when, rang, short   9._____

10. gem, generous, strategic, giant, giraffe   10._____

11. pacing, cider, city, mice, cent   11._____

12. knight, lamb, right, clock, often   12._____

Vowel

13. plane, regal, high, escape, poke   13._____

14. ball, false, saw, waltz, claw   14._____

15. voice, town, Roy, proud, scow   15._____

16. school, zoo, boot, tattoo, ooze   16._____

17. tie, Easter, play, row, chain   17._____

18. hint, plug, stab, throb, dent   18._____

19. lord, burst, swirl, Mars, germ   19._____

Structure-Syllable

20. dislike, inland, unhappy, enjoy, retrace   20. _____

21. sooner, clearest, goodly, babyish, freshness.   21. _____

Give syllable-visual-pattern only.

22. acorn, cedar, paper, over, bravest   22. _____

23. yellow, under, aspire, badger, arbor   23. _____

24. little, baffle, ample, title, ladle   24. _____

1. visual discrimination
2. reversal
3. auditory discrimination
4. directionality
5. blends
6. hard c (k sound)
7. initial consonants
8. ph digraph
9. digraphs
10. g sounded as j
11. soft c (s sound)
12. silent consonant

13. long vowels
14. a + l or w
15. diphthongs
16. long oo sound
17. vowel digraphs
18. short vowels
19. r-controlled vowels
20. prefixes
21. suffixes
22. v-cv
23. vc-cv
24. c + le

"READINESS"

The programmed material on "readiness" only deals with three of the 14 factors (see Chapter 8, pp. 111-128) usually associated with readiness for reading. Readiness for reading is concerned with the total development of a young child, therefore, it is important to recognize that the three factors discussed in this portion of the word recognition construct were selected because they are easy to understand and measure. However, if these relatively minor areas are viewed as *sine qua non* of readiness, the reader is likely to get a distorted view of a major developmental stage in the life of a young child.

The "readiness" portion of our word recognition construct deals with:

I. Visual Discrimination

II. Auditory Discrimination

III. Directionality

There are wide differences of professional opinion regarding the development of the learner's visual, auditory, and directionality ability. Therefore, you are urged to learn the key ideas related to these broad "readiness" categories rather than memorize, compare, etc., the minor elements within each category.

I. Visual Discrimination

In addition to being only one of fourteen major "readiness factors," visual discrimination is one of the subfactors in the visual or perceptual area. In addition to visual discrimination, the entire visual or perceptual area deals with such things as visual memory, visual sequencing, etc. We selected visual discrimination because it is the subfactor most commonly taught in the school program.

Essentially visual discrimination involves the ability to see likenesses and differences in geometric forms, pictures, letters, and words. Obviously seeing likenesses and differences in geometric forms, pictures, letters, and words, also requires that one acquire a "visual orientation" and/or "visual relationship." In other words, one must know that, "this ore goes up" or "this one goes that way and this one goes this way," etc.

1. Put an X on the geometric form which is different:

2. Put an X on the picture which is different:

3. Put an X on one of the four letters which is the same as the one in front of the dotted line:

    P :   T   Q   R   P
    C :   O   C   O   Q

4. Put an X on the word which is the same as the one in front of the dotted line:

    big: bag   box   big   but
    house: horse mouse louse house

5. Visual discrimination is only_____subfactor in the visual or perceptual area.

6. Essentially visual discrimination involves one's ability to see

    _____ and differences.

During the readiness for reading stage or at some time early in our life, we all visually reversed forms, pictures, and words. Reversals are normal. However, the length of time needed to overcome reversal tendencies seems related to success in reading.

7. If the learner who tends to reverse letters sees the letter "b," he is

    likely to think, say, or write_____.

8. If this same learner sees the following, what is he likely to think, say, or write?

    p_____

    no_____

    lap_____

    13_____

    saw_____

Margin answers (left column):

P
C

big
house

one

likenesses

d

q
on
pal
31
was

197

9. Is the following statement true or false: "Before training a learner to visually recognize consonants, vowels, or syllables, he should be

true

past the reversal stage." True_____ False_____

II. Auditory Discrimination

Auditory discrimination is also a limited subfactor. What was said about visual discrimination applies to auditory discrimination.

Essentially auditory discrimination involves the ability to hear likenesses and differences in sounds and words.

We are unable to actually provide you with programmed learning items on auditory discrimination because they must be presented orally. We will simulate by asking you to imagine that we are presenting the items orally.

1. If you heard the following sounds, which one would be different? Circle the correct item.

(initial sound)	bat	rat	bat
(final sound)	top	tap	tree
(final sound)	eye	my	did
(medial sound)	hope	top	hop

rat
tree
did
hope

2. Listen to the following pairs of words. Write "same" if they sound exactly the same, or "different" if they sound different in any way:

same
differen'
different
different
same

tip—tip_____
go—no _____
ho—row_____
please—tease_____
hear—here ___ _____

3. Is the following statement true or false: "Before training a learner to auditorily recognize consonants, vowels, or syllables he should

true

be able to hear likenesses and differences." True_____

False_____

III. Directionality

Directionality refers to the learner's ability to understand that English words and letters must be read and written in very specific ways. Words must be read and written from left to right. Letters must be read and written so that they resemble the 26 characters of our English orthography.

You will recall that in our discussion of visual discrimination we referred to reversal tendencies as being normal in young children (especially beginning readers). We believe that reversals are caused when the learner is confronted with the "two-dimensional surface" of print as opposed to his previous experiences in a "three-dimensional world."

1. It follows then that the learner must understand that English

   words are _____ or written from left to right.

2. Is it true or false that the child who has established a left-right "body orientation" is likely to quickly learn the directionality of

   words and letters? True _____ False _____

3. If reversals are normal, can we speculate that young children

   in the Orient make "up and down" type reversals? Yes _____

   No _____

4. "If a third-grade child is consistently reversing letters and words, it makes sense to have him complete the third grade reading

   program rather than helping him with directionality." True _____

   False _____

5. Lessons on consonants, vowels, and syllables should not be introduced until the learner has his directionality clearly estab-

   lished. True _____ False _____

read

True

Yes

False

True

CONSONANTS

Consonant letters and their related consonant sounds (phonemes), make up one of the major letter-form/letter-sound structures of English.

Traditional phonetic programs generally group consonants into the following categories:

    I.   Consonants—single letters

   II.   Digraphs

 III.   Blends

 IV.   Silent Consonants

The reader must recognize that while traditional phonic programs agree on these broad consonant categories, there is little agreement on the specific elements within the categories. Therefore, you are urged to learn the four broad consonant categories rather than memorize, compare, etc., the minor elements within each category.

	I. Consonants—Single letters
	This category usually consists of twenty-one single consonant letters. Fourteen consonant letters have a consistent one-to-one letter-form/letter-sound correspondence. Seven are relatively consistent but each letter has some additional characteristics. An example of a consistent letter is the letter "b," which has one sound. An example of a relatively consistent letter is "c," which may have several sounds (/s/, /k/, /ch/).
21	1. Our English alphabet has twenty-six letters,_____ are called consonants.
14	2. Of the twenty-one consonants_____ have a consistent one-to-one letter form-letter sound correspondence.
b d f h j k l m n p r t v z	3. Fourteen of the consonant letters listed below have a consistent letter-form/letter-sound correspondence. Circle those consonants which have consistent letter-form/letter sound correspondences.

                b   c   d   f   g   h   j

                k   l   m   n   p   q   r

                s   t   v   w   x   y   z

4. Examine each consonant below, circle the seven consonant letters which have relatively consistent letter-sounds. For example, "c" should be circled. At times the letter "c" has a /k/ ("hard") sound, other times it has a /s/ ("soft") sound.

b	c	d	f	g	h	j
k	l	m	n	p	q	r
s	t	v	w	x	y	z

c   g
q   s
w   x
y

5. The underlined words in the sentences below illustrate the additional characteristics associated with seven consonant letters.

a. The sound of "c" in *cent, circle, cylinder* (c followed by e, i, or y) has the ____/ /____ sound. This sound usually is referred to as the "soft c" sound.

/s/

b. The sound of "c" in *canoe, coat, curb, crow* (c followed by a, o, or most letters other than e, i, or y) has the

____/ /____ sound. This sound usually is referred to as the "hard c" sound.

/k/

c. Circle the three words which have the "hard" sound /k/ for the consonant letter "c."

pacify	celebrity	acre
vacuum	income	license

acre
vacuum
income

d. Circle the three words which have the "soft" sound /s/ for the consonant letter "c."

decide	creek	concrete
cypress	narcotic	cigar

decide
cypress
cigar

e. Write the appropriate letter "s" (soft) or "k" (hard) for the following words which contain the consonant letter "c."

1. s

(1) cinnamon_____

2. s, k

(2) bicycle_____ , _____

3. k, s

(3) vacancy_____ , _____

4. k

(4) optical_____

5. k, k

(5) arctic _____ , _____

6. k

(6) peculiar_____

7. s

(7) incite _____

6. The consonant "g" has a regular consonant sound of its own. But when "g" is followed by e, i, or y, it often has the sound /j/ as in jump.

a. The regular sound of "g" (as in go) is used in three of the six words below. Circle the regular hard "g" words:

goose
regular
gas

| goose | regular | gas |
| giraffe | general | wager |

b. Three of the following six words use the /j/ sound of "g," circle the /j/ sounds of the consonant "g":

region
fidget
gem

| region | gold | program |
| grit | fidget | gem |

c. Write the appropriate sound /j/ (soft) or /g/ (hard) for the following words which contain the consonant letter "g."

1. /j/
2. /j/
3. /g/ /j/
4. /g/
5. /g/
6. /j/
7. /g/

(1) giant_/ j /___   (5) wagon _/ /_____

(2) generous_/ /_   (6) gym_/ /_

(3) engage_/ /_,_/ /_   (7) gutter_/ /_____

(4) vagrant_/ /_

7. The consonant letter "s" has a sound of its own but at times the letter "s" uses the sound of /z/. What is more confusing, the reader does not have a clue (similar to the e, i, or y which influences the consonant letters c and g) to determine when "s" uses its regular sound or its sound of /z/.

a. Write the appropriate sound /s/ or /z/ for the letter "s" in each of the following:

(1) has _____   (5) snake _____

(2) girls _____   (6) yes _____

(3) nasal _____   (7) misery _____

(4) side _____   (8) husband _____

8. Thus far, we have discussed fourteen regular consonants and the three consonants (c, g, and s) which interchange with other sounds, this leaves _____ consonants to be discussed.

9. The letter "q" is usually combined with "u" and usually has the sound /kw/. The letter "x" has the sound of /ks/ in most words. Write the appropriate letter "q" or "x." Notice that these letters do not have a sound of their own.

(1) liquid _____   (4) quack _____

(2) next _____   (5) squeal _____

(3) relax _____   (6) equinox ____, ____

10. The final two letters in the consonant category are "w" and "y." We left these until last because sometimes they are used as consonants and sometimes they are used as vowels.

a. The placement of the letter "y" in a word is a simple clue which helps to determine when "y" is used as a consonant and when it is used as a vowel. In the word

beginning — *yellow* the "y" is at the ____________ of the word. In

end — the word *spry* the "y" is at the ______________ of the word.

b. If the word begins with "y," the "y" usually has a consonant sound. If a word ends with "y," the "y" usually has a vowel sound. Say each word below. Listen for the sound of /y/ and write "c" if "y" makes a consonant sound and "v" if "y" makes a vowel sound.

c	yak _________
v	July _________
v	hurry ________
c	year _________
c	young _______

Note: Writers of phonic materials generally require learners to give different sounds to "y" when it is used as a vowel (long i or long e, etc.). We're pleased if you can establish when "y" is used as a consonant and when "y" is used as a vowel.

Frankly, we do not know what to do with the consonant letter "w." In many words it retains its regular consonant sound (wife, wall, beware, etc.). However, it is combined with so many different letters that it seems best to deal with this letter when we present those vowel letters.

Self-Test—Consonants
(See p. 235 for answers)

Study each of the 21 consonant letters listed below. Tell if the consonant letter has a regular sound, if it interchanges with other sounds, or if it is usually combined with one other letter.

letter form	letter sound
b	**Regular Consonant sounds** (list)
c	
d	/ / / / / / / /
f	
g	/ / / / / / / /
h	
j	/ / / / / /
k	
l	/ / / / / /
m	
n	**Interchanges with other sounds** (list)
p	"c" / / or / / "y" _____ or _____
q	(word) (word)
r	"g" / / or / / "w" _____ or _____
s	(word) (word)
t	"s" / /
v	
w	**Combined** (list)
x	"qu" / / "x" / /
y	
z	

II. Digraphs

This category includes five different letter-form/letter-sound combinations. Essentially a digraph sound is made when two consonant letters are joined together to form one sound (or a new sound). For example, the consonant "t" has its own sound, as in top, and "h" its own sound, as in happy. However, when "t" and "h" are joined, as in a new sound, a digraph is produced. The five common digraphs are "ch," "th," "wh," "sh," and "ng."

1. Listed below are twelve words, each contains one of the five common digraph sounds. Write the digraph next to each word:

thick_____; whale_____; chop_____.

bring_____; ship_____; watch_____.

whip_____; hush_____; cloth_____.

ring_____; white_____; young_____.

2. A problem which existed in the consonant category (single consonant sounds) also exists in this category (digraphs). Specifically, writers of phonic materials tend to agree on the category but express different opinions when describing the sounds within the category. We will present some of the unique sounds related to various digraphs and remind you that the ability to recognize a digraph is more important than being overly concerned about all the subtle differences within this category.

a. When "c" and "h" are joined together they form a new sound called a _____.

b. A digraph is formed when we join "n" and _____.

c. T and _____ make the _____ digraph.

d. A digraph is formed when we join "w" and _____.

e. When "s" and _____ are joined they make the _____ digraph.

Left margin answer column:

th; wh; ch.

ng; sh; ch.

wh; sh; th.

ng; wh; ng.

---

digraph

---

g

---

h, th

---

h

---

h, sh

digraph	3. In the word chair we have a "ch"_____. In many words the "ch" digraph usually has the sound of /ch/ as in chair. However "ch" has other sounds which are less common.

a. After each word write *"more"* if the "ch" has a sound similar to the /ch/ in chair. Write *"less"* if the "ch" has some other sound.

<table>
<tr><td>1. more</td><td>6. more</td></tr>
<tr><td>2. more</td><td>7. more</td></tr>
<tr><td>3. less</td><td>8. less</td></tr>
<tr><td>4. more</td><td>9. more</td></tr>
<tr><td>5. less</td><td>10. more</td></tr>
</table>

(1) chilly_____   (6) match_____

(2) church _____   (7) satchel _____

(3) chef_____   (8) character_____

(4) speech_____   (9) achieve_____

(5) chiffon_____   (10) reach_____

/ch/, /sh/ and /k/

b. The "ch" digraph has three sounds: $/\ /$, $/\ /$ and $/\ /$.

c. The more common sound used for the digraph "ch" is

/ch/

the $/\ /$ in a word such as chin.

4. The "th" digraph has two different sounds, usually referred to as voiced or unvoiced. Examples of these are:

voiced "th" digraphs	unvoiced "th" digraphs
teethe	teeth
father	thaw
that	thin

We believe that the distinction between voiced and unvoiced th digraphs is difficult to learn and difficult to teach, therefore, you are urged to learn that th is one of the five common digraphs and ignore all of the attention given to voiced and unvoiced th digraph sounds.

5. Some phonic writers have made these observations about digraphs:

In the "wh" digraph the /h/ "moves" in front of the /w/ and "wh" sounds like /hw/ (examples: what, whip).

Sometimes "n" alone has the /ng/ sound (example: ink).

We could go on and on but such a discussion of these irrelevent differences only tend to cause confusion and detract from the main goal, namely, learning the subcategories presented thus far, **Consonants** and **Digraphs**.

6. Other consonant letters are joined together to form single sounds. However, those listed below have sounds of existing single consonants or are silent.

"ph" usually has the sound of /f/ as in for.

"ck" usually has the sound of /k/ as in trick.

"gh" usually has the sound of /f/ as in enough, or is silent as in night.

a. Listed below are six words which contain digraphs which make existing sounds or are silent. Next to each word mark the sound of this type of digraph:

/f/	phonics	/ /
/f/	gopher	/ /
/f/	laugh	/ /
silent "gh"	night	_____
silent "gh"	dough	_____
silent "gh"	sought	_____

208

Self-Test—Digraphs
(See p. 236 for answers)

Study the digraphs below. Tell if the digraph is regular (makes a new sound), if it makes existing sounds or if it is silent.

ch _____

wh _____

ng _____

th _____

sh _____

ph _____

ck _____

gh _____

III. Blends

This category includes consonants which are combined into two letter and three letter clusters. Blends differ from digraphs (which also join consonants) because each consonant letter in the blend retains some of its regular consonant sound. For example: Say the word blend. You should be able to hear some of the /b/ sound and the /l/ sound. The "bl" in the word blend is a consonant blend.

1. Write the blends next to each word (blends with "l").

pl; fl

play_____   flower _____

pl; gl

complex_____   glove_____

2. Write the blends next to each word (blends with "r").

br; tr

brown _____   tray_____

gr; rt

green_____   hurt _____

3. Write the blends next to each word (blends with "s").

st; spr

stop_____   spring_____

str; sn

street_____   snare_____

4. Write the blends next to each word (blends with "t").

tr; thr

intrude_____   throw_____

tw; tr

twice_____   tree_____

Self-Test—Blends and Digraphs
(See p. 236 for answers)

1. Listed below are ten words. Next to each word write the appropriate word blend or digraph. In some cases the individual word may contain more than one element.

drum_____   this_____

freeze_____   church_____

skate_____   bring_____ _____

shopping_____ _____   house_____

snail_____   score_____

2. Listed below are twelve joined consonant letters (two letter blends, three letter blends and digraphs). Write at least one word using each of the following consonant groupings.

br_____   ch_____   sc_____   th_____

cr_____   gh_____   ch_____   sm_____

spe_____   fl_____   thr_____   ng_____

IV. Silent Consonants

This final category is really more of a miscellaneous category. As in the case of blends we are not providing new sounds; rather, we are presenting consonant combinations which are somewhat unique.

1. The consonant letters "g" and "k" are usually silent when combined with the consonant letter "n." The letter "w" is usually silent when combined with the letter "r."

   a. Say the following words, write the initial sound for each word:

/n/   gnaw _/ /_

/n/   knife _/ /_

/r/   wrong _/ /_

2. The silent letters in the words gnaw, knife, and wrong occur

initial   in the_____ position of the word.

3. In the words patch and stitch, the letter_____is silent.

t

4. In the words limb and comb, the letter_____is silent.

b

5. In the words tight and high the letters_____are silent.

gh

VOWELS

Vowel letters and their related vowel sounds (phonemes) make up another sound-symbol structure of English. Traditional phonetic programs usually group vowels into the following categories:

I. Short Vowels
II. Long Vowels
III. Vowels controlled by the letter r
IV. Diphthongs
V. Long and Short Double oo vowels
VI. Vowel Digraph
VII. Vowels influenced by the letters l and w

The reader must recognize that while traditional phonic programs agree on the above vowel categories, there is very little agreement on the specific elements within these broad vowel categories. Therefore, you are urged to learn the seven broad categories rather than memorize, compare, etc., the minor elements within the categories.

	I. Short Vowels
	This category of vowels consists of five single vowel letters a, e, i, o, and u (sometimes y and w). When these short vowel letters are used in words the reader must associate the sound rather than the name of the vowel letter.
5	1. Our English alphabet has 26 letters,_____ are called short vowels.
y and w	2. Sometimes two consonant letters have vowel sounds, they are _____ and_____.
a,e,i,o, and u.	3. The five vowels are ___,___,___,___, and____.

4. A vowel is short when the _____ of the vowel is associated with the vowel letter.

   a. Listed below are ten words with short vowels and long vowels. Circle the five words which have short vowel sounds.

ape	apple
beg	eagle
ice	igloo
oak	ox
umbrella	Utah

   b. Listed below are eight more words, underline the words which have short vowels and listen for the sound the short vowel makes:

cash	must
dent	bet
clip	fuel
rock	note

5. Sometimes words contain vowel letters that are not sounded (silent) like the *a* in boat. However, most vowel letters are sounded. In fact, every English word or syllable must contain one vowel sound. Pronounce the following word: RMPTF. This word cannot be pronounced because it does not have a vowel sound. You probably had difficulty pronouncing the name of the sorrowful little character in Al Capp's comic strip (Joe BFTSPLK) because his last name does not have a vowel in it.

   a. Words can have long vowel sounds, short vowel sounds, vowels influenced by the letter r, etc. The category (type) of vowel is not important, the important fact is that all English words or syllables must contain at least

     _____ __ vowel _____.

6. Some dictionaries use a symbol called a breve ĕ as in bĕg to identify short vowel sounds.

   a. In the following words mark short vowel letters with a breve "˘" symbol. Some of the words have long vowels and some are silent.

tĕll	tell _____
dēal—a (silent)	deal _____
cōld	cold _____
fūel—e (silent)	fuel _____
wĭck	wick _____
lăsh	lash _____
neither—a (long) i (silent)	rain _____

II. Long Vowels

This category of vowels consists of five single vowels a, e, i, o, and u. When long vowel letters are used in words the reader must associate the name rather than the sound of the letter.

5

1. Our English alphabet has 26 letters,_____ are called long vowels.

2. Long vowels and short vowels use the same letters (graphemes) a, e, i, o, and u. The main difference between these two categories is:

long

_____vowels are associated with the name of the vowel.

short

_____vowels are associated with the sound of the vowel.

214

3. Listed below are ten words with long and short vowels. Write the appropriate word long or short after each word:

[short/a/]   plank _____

[long/i/ (e-silent)]   line _____

[long/e/ (a-silent)]   leaf _____

[long/o/]   bold _____

[long/a/, (y-vowel)]   navy _____

[short/o/]   stop _____

[long/e/ (a-silent)]   steal _____

[short/u/]   gulf _____

[short/i/]   fish _____

[long/u/ (y-vowel)]   duty _____

4. Listed below are ten words with long and short vowels. Write long or short and identify the vowel. Listen for the name (long vowel) or sound (short vowel).

short/u/   pulp _____

long/u/, short/i/   music _____

long/o/   post _____

short/o/   hot _____

short/a/   cap _____

long/a/ (e-silent)   cape _____

long/i/ (e-silent)   life _____

short/i/   mink _____

short/e/   pen _____

long/e/   seem _____

5. Dictionaries use a symbol called a macron, ē as in ēagle to identify long vowel sounds.

In the following words mark long vowel letters (names) with macron "‾" symbol.

e short, echō	echo
e short	dent
fēast (a-silent)	feast
sāle (e-silent)	sale
a short	lash
gōat (a-silent)	goat
mōtive (i-short, e-silent)	motive
tāme (e-silent)	tame
mīce (e-silent)	mice

6. We said that the long vowels ā, ē, ī, ō, and ū are associated with vowel names and that short vowels ă, ĕ, ĭ, ŏ, and ŭ are associated with vowel sounds. You also might have noticed that often times a, e, i, o, and u are silent. Mark the following words with these symbols (‾) long, (˘) short, (x) silent:

rīde, frŏg	ride	frog
sāle, mōmĕnt	sale	moment
plŭs, fāint	plus	faint
fōam, jăckĕt	foam	jacket

216

7. When a word or syllable ends with the vowel e, the e is usually silent and the preceding vowel is usually long. Say each word and think about this widely used phonic rule.

cape	stove
hope	duke
bible	file

Teachers frequently tell children that words such as cape and hope have a magic "e." Cape with the magic e has a long vowel sound /ā/. Cap without the magic e has the short vowel sound /ă/. Add the letter e to the following words and listen to the change in the preceding vowel—short (sound) to long (name):

hate, sale

hat   sal

cape, kite

cap   kit

mate

mat

8. Because long and short vowels are so important in our language, traditional phonic programs have used many ways to describe or identify them. What has been presented thus far can be generalized as follows:

  a. A vowel letter represents more than one phoneme: short

sound

vowel, _____ of vowel; long vowel,

name

_____ of vowel.

  b. Any vowel letter represents short (ă) and long (ā) sounds or names; therefore, vowels cannot have a one-

consonants

to-one correspondence, as do most_____.

c. English words or syllables must have at least one vowel sound; therefore, English words or syllables must have

vowel

_____ sounds (short or long).

d. When vowels are placed between consonants, in words and syllables, they usually have short sounds and are called closed "syllables." Mark (˘) the closed vowels in the following words or syllables:

măp

map

plŏt tĕd

plotted

e. When vowels are placed at the end of a word or a syllable, they are usually long and are called open "syllables." Mark (¯) the open vowels in the following words or syllables:

sō lo

solo

gō

go

f. The following words are divided into syllables, mark (˘) (¯) each vowel, think why some are short and others long.

tō tĕm, hĕl lō

to tem   hel lo

hā lō, răb bĭt

ha lo   rab bit

Self-Test—Short and Long Vowels
(See p. 236 for answers)

Mark the vowels in each of the words below. Use appropriate signs for short and long vowels. Mark silent vowels with an x through them.

1. logic

2. ostrich

3. holiness

4. obtain

5. extreme

6. closet

7. peanut

8. subscribe

III. Vowels Controlled by the Letter R

A third category of vowels can be introduced with this often used generalization: The consonant letter "r" controls the preceding vowel and gives the vowel a sound which is neither short nor long. Examples: c*ar*; p*er*colat*or*; b*ir*d; and t*ur*tle.

Say each word in the example. Notice that the letter "r" has some control on each preceding vowel but degree of control varies. Dictionaries have attempted to deal with this varying degree of control by using such terms as: "half Italian a," "two dot a," "Circumflex o," etc. We believe it is more reasonable to merely learn that the preceding vowel is controlled by the letter "r" and that the sound of the vowel is neither short nor long.

1. Our English alphabet has twenty-six letters; the five vowels

    are_____ by the letter "r."

controlled

2. When a vowel is followed by "r" the vowel sound is neither

    _____ nor _____ .

short, long

    A reasonable name for this category of vowels might be a "vowel controlled by r."

3. Long vowels, short vowels, and vowels controlled by "r" use the same letters (grapheme) a, e, i, o, and u. The main difference between these three categories is:

    Short vowels use the _____ of the vowel.

sound

    Long vowels use the _____ of the vowel.

name

    Vowels controlled by "r" use a sound which is

    _____ long nor short.

neither

4. Listed below are ten words with vowel controlled by "r." Underline this sound and listen to the unique sound of each vowel.

ba<u>r</u>gain, he<u>r</u>mit	bargain	hermit
ste<u>r</u>n, ta<u>r</u>dy	stern	tardy
f<u>or</u>k, <u>or</u>d<u>er</u>	fork	order
bu<u>r</u>n, mu<u>r</u>mu<u>r</u>	burn	murmur
bi<u>r</u>th, sc<u>or</u>ch	birth	scorch

5. Listed below are more words. Write each vowel, tell if it is long, short, controlled /r/ or silent:

/a/ controlled /r/   card _____

/i/ short,
/e/ controlled /r/   trigger _____
/i/ short

/i/ long   wild _____

/i/ controlled /r/   birch _____

/u/ controlled /r/   spur _____

/o/ long, silent   hope _____

/u/ short   pump _____

/e/ controlled /r/   verb _____

wick _____

220

IV. Diphthongs

This category includes four letter-form/letter-sound combinations.

o<u>i</u>l	(oi)	h<u>ou</u>se	(ou)
bo<u>y</u>	(oy)	<u>ow</u>l	(ow)

Essentially a diphthong sound is made when two vowel letters are joined together. For example: the letter "o" is either long, short, or "r" controlled, the letter "i" is either long, short, or "r" controlled, but when "o" and "i" are joined in a word, a new sound—diphthong—is produced.

1. Listed below are eight words. Each contains one of the four common diphthongs. Write the diphthong next to each word.

ow   vowel _____

ow   crown _____

oi   cloister _____

ou   found _____

ou   loud _____

oy   alloy_____

oy   loyalty_____

oi   poise_____

diphthong

2. When "o" and "u" are joined together they form a new sound called a_____.

consonant digraph

diphthong

3. Think back. If we join two consonants (th, sh, ch, etc.) we produce a_____. If we join two vowels (ou, ow, oi, etc.) we produce a_____.

4. Digraphs and diphthongs tend to function alike. They join letters to produce *new* sounds. The difference is that digraphs

vowels

join consonants and the diphthongs join _____.

Learning that vowels can be joined to form diphthongs is not difficult. However, attempting to make a one-to-one letter-form/letter-sound correspondence is difficult. Example, the "ou" in house sounds the same as the "ow" in owl. The "oi" in tabloid sounds the same as the "oy" in boy. The point here is that the sounds (phonemes) remain the same but the symbols (graphemes) change. This is opposite of what we have said about other letters and letter combinations.

Some phonetic writers include the au (author) and aw (crawl) in the diphthong category. Others argue that they should be treated as digraphs and not diphthongs. Rather than enter into the argument we have elected to arbitrarily place them in the "catch all" two vowel category called vowel digraphs and let it go at that.

V. Long and Short Double OO Vowels

When a double oo is used in a word, either a short sound (took) or long sound (fool) is heard.

This category is included because we cannot "fit" these double oo sounds in any other category, yet they occur quite frequently in English words.

1. Listed below are seven words; write the word short if the double oo makes the short sound or long if the double oo makes the long sound.

short; long

proof   boom

short; short

look   book

long; long

wool   goose

short

wood

222

2. The symbols (˘) short and (¯) long also apply as they did in single vowels. Mark the appropriate symbol for these words:

soŏt	soot
foōd	food
moōr	moor
coōl	cool
loōp	loop

VI. Vowel Digraphs

Hey! What's a digraph doing in the vowel area? Frankly, we don't have a reasonable answer. All we can say is that we have many English words which *join two vowels,* yet they do not make new sounds, therefore, they cannot be called diphthongs. We suggest that if two vowels are joined, and do not make diphthongs (new sounds) or double /oo/ sounds, call them *vowel digraphs.*

Vowel digraphs do not make new sounds. Essentially what we have are two vowels together, as in boat, the /o/ sound is heard and the /a/ sound is silent.

We recommend that you ignore the order (first vowel sounded-second silent or first vowel silent-second vowel sounded) or the type of sound the vowel makes (short or long). It seems reasonable to remember that vowel digraphs (two vowels: one is sounded, one is silent) occur frequently and are not diphthongs or double oo sounds.

1. In the following list of words underline the vowel digraph, listen for the vowel sound:

s<u>oa</u>k; b<u>ea</u>t	soak	beat
h<u>ea</u>p; s<u>ee</u>m	heap	seem
t<u>ai</u>l; pl<u>ea</u>se	tail	please

2. Underline the vowel digraph in the following. Notice the interchange of the letters and sounds /ei/–/ie/ (any wonder why "ei"–"ie" words are difficult to spell):

rec<u>ei</u>pt	receipt
f<u>ie</u>ld	field
l<u>ie</u>n	lien
r<u>ei</u>n	rein

3. The same problems occur with "eu" and "ew" words. Underline these sound interchanges and listen to their sounds:

d<u>eu</u>ce	deuce
dr<u>ew</u>	drew
n<u>eu</u>ron	neuron
shr<u>ew</u>	shrew
<u>ew</u>e	ewe

VII. Letter A Influenced by the Letters L and W

The letters "l" and "w" function much the same as the vowel controlled by "r." These letters give the vowel letter a sound which is different from all other categories mentioned. We elected not to include this category with the vowel controlled "r" category because the letters "l" and "w" influence only the letter "a."

1. Underline the vowel letter "a" in each of the following words, listen for the "l" or "w" influence.

s<u>aw</u>; r<u>aw</u>	saw	raw
b<u>all</u>; c<u>all</u>	ball	call

224

STRUCTURE—SYLLABLES

According to Webster's New World Dictionary a syllable is defined as:

"a word or part of a word pronounced with a single, uninterrupted sounding of the voice; unit of pronunciation, consisting of a single sound of great sonority (usually a vowel) and generally one or more sounds of lessor sonority (usually consonants)."

Historically, it is believed that syllables grew out of a need created by the advent of the printing press. Printers needed to "break" words in order to "fit" them on to the printed page.

Some phonetic writers avoid the concept of syllables. They believe that syllables are made up of many sounds and are not even close to a one-to-one letter-form/letter-sound correspondence. Currently some linguists are becoming interested in syllables because of the potential "meaning" relationships believed to be in certain syllables.

Despite the fact that wide disagreement exists regarding the description and use of syllables, every school child is required to: learn how to divide words into syllables, hear the number of syllables and mark the stressed or accented syllables in words.

Rather than enter into endless arguments, we have elected to present three "reasonably" consistent syllable generalizations or rules, discuss the place of accents, and discuss the prefix and the suffix. Thus, this part of the program will deal with:

I. Syllables
II. Accents
III. Prefix
IV. Suffix

Again, we urge you to learn these broad categories rather than compare, memorize, etc., the minor elements within each category.

I. Syllables

It is not difficult to hear the number of syllables in words:

1. How many syllables do you hear in each of the following words?

number of syllables

two	circus_____
one	bat_____
two	problem_____
three	barnacle_____
two	lantern_____
one	gate_____
two	vowel_____
three	consonant_____
three	syllable_____

As you recognize, the difficulty with syllables is not the inability to hear the number of syllables. The difficulty with syllables appears to be our inability to find stable or consistent ways to divide words into syllables.

Phonetic writers use six generalizations or rules for dividing words into syllables. We believe that only three of these "rules" have the greatest application to English words and that at best these three "rules" are only consistent about 60% of the time.

Our purpose in presenting even three "rules" that work slightly better than half of the time, is to provide you with the best of a limited area and to encourage you to be realistic about syllables.

RULE ONE

When there are two consonant sounds between two vowels, the division is usually between the two consonant sounds. The common visual pattern for this rule is vowel consonant—consonant vowel (vc-cv).

1. Underline the syllables in the words below. Listen for the number of syllables and note each vowel sound:

   Example: <u>gob</u><u>let</u> (vc-cv)

<u>par</u> <u>ka</u>   parka

<u>sig</u> <u>nal</u>   signal

<u>sis</u> <u>ter</u>   sister

<u>din</u> <u>ner</u>   dinner

<u>ras</u> <u>cal</u>   rascal

2. The number of syllables in a word is related more to vowels or consonants?

   vowels

3. Essentially in rule one we divide between _____ consonants.

   two

4. The visual pattern for rule one is vc-_____.

   cv

RULE TWO

When there is one consonant sound between two vowel sounds, the division is usually before the consonant. The common visual pattern for this rule is vowel-consonant vowel (v-cv).

1. Underline the syllables in each word below. Listen for the number of syllables and note each vowel sound:

   Example: <u>la</u> <u>bor</u> (v-cv)

<u>spi</u> <u>der</u>   spider_____

<u>pa</u> <u>per</u>   paper_____

<u>so</u> <u>lar</u>   solar_____

<u>ra</u> <u>ven</u>   raven_____

<u>au</u> <u>thor</u>   author_____
   (th=one sound)

2. Divide the following words into syllables. Next to each divided word give the appropriate visual pattern (vc-cv) or (v-cv).

	divided word	visual pattern
mas-ter (vc-cv)	master_____	_____
i-tem (v-cv)	item_____	_____
pi-lot (v-cv)	pilot_____	_____
gar-ment (vc-cv)	garment_____	_____
ham-mer (vc-cv)	hammer_____	_____
prob-lem (vc-cv)	problem_____	_____
ta-per (v-cv)	taper_____	_____
ra-zor (v-cv)	razor_____	_____
sil-ver (vc-cv)	silver_____	_____

RULE THREE

When a word ends with a consonant and the letters "le," the final syllable is formed by dividing before the consonant. The common visual pattern for this rule is consonant plus "le" (c + le).

1. Underline the final syllable in each word below. Listen for the number of syllables and note each vowel sound:

   Example: little (c + le)

twin<u>kle</u>   twinkle

bungle   bungle

un<u>cle</u>   uncle

this<u>tle</u>   thistle

barna<u>cle</u>   barnacle

before

2. Essentially in this rule we divide before or between the consonant?

3. Divide the following words into syllables. Next to each divided word give the appropriate visual pattern (vc-cv), (v-cv), and (c + le):

divided word	visual pattern
lantern_____	_____
rumba_____	_____
vacant_____	_____
trample_____	_____
ankle_____	_____
drugstore_____	_____
acorn_____	_____
father_____	_____

<u>lan</u> <u>tern</u> (vc-cv)

<u>rum</u> <u>ba</u> (vc-cv)

<u>va</u> <u>cant</u> (v-cv)

tram ple (c + le)

an <u>kle</u> (c + le)

<u>drug</u> <u>store</u> (vc-cv)

<u>a</u> <u>corn</u> (v-cv)

fa <u>ther</u> (v-cv)
(th=one sound)

229

Self-Test: Three Syllabic Rules
(See p. 237 for answers)

Listed below are 20 words. Fifteen of the words "fit" three common rules, five words are exceptions. Place fifteen of the twenty words under the appropriate visual pattern (vc-cv), (v-cv), and (c + le).

begin	sterile	corner	climax
humble	fabric	peril	gable
pupil	ventricle	buckle	rabbit
boiling	forest	over	pencil
aspic	cedar	trample	bumble

(vc-cv)	(v-cv)	(c + le)	(exceptions
_____	_____	_____	_____
_____	_____	_____	_____
_____	_____	_____	_____
_____	_____	_____	_____
_____	_____	_____	_____

II. Accents

When we accent parts of words (syllables), we give a stress emphasis or pitch emphasis to the particular part of the word. The marking used to identify the part of the word which is emphasized is (').

We are including accents because teaching and/or learning about accents creates a unique problem.

Every word in every school dictionary divides words into syllables and gives primary (dark marks) and secondary (light marks) accents. We are acquainted with three major word recognition studies, all of which point out that "accent rules" are consistent with and frequently apply to large numbers of words taught in school. Every major reading program includes accent lessons in their intermediate and junior high reading programs.

Despite all of this attention regarding the teaching and/or learning of accents, we are strongly recommending that you avoid the direct teaching and/or learning of accents. We urge this because accent use or how we pronounce words is strongly influenced by "local speech communities." (A "local speech community" is anything you want it to be; a state, a town, a hill community, an inner city, etc.). Therefore, attempts to generalize our infinite accent differences during specific school lessons seem unwise. By direct teaching of accents we mean, statements such as, "place the primary stress (') after the second syllable in the word. . . ."

Indirectly teaching and/or learning that parts of words have different emphasis seems to be a more reasonable approach.

Indirect teaching and/or learning might include:

1. Pronunciation exercises.
2. Dictionary or glossary exercises.
3. Games.

Pronunciation exercises might include how words are said in different "local speech communities." For example, how is the word "father" pronounced in the city of Boston, Mass., rural Arizona, inner city Chicago, Ill.?

Dictionary or glossary exercises might include how to "read" and "use" the pronunciation key.

Games might include the finding of words which are spelled alike but have different pronunciations. For example: present (being at a specified place) or present (a gift).

III. **Prefix**

Some unfamiliar words can be "sounded-out," "decoded," "recognized," "attacked," etc., because the reader has learned the meaning of specific prefixes which are most frequently used in English words. According to Lee C. Deighton[1] the following ten prefixes are frequently used.

apo	intro
circum	mal
equi	mis
extra	non
intra	syn

1. Lee C. Deighton, *Vocabulary Development in the Classroom* (New York: Teachers College Press, 5th ed., 1966), p. 26

1. Knowledge of these ten prefixes will enable you to unlock the meanings in more than 600 English words.

   Next to each of the ten words, listed below, write the meaning of the underlined prefix (you may not know the meaning so just guess. Use the answer to help you learn the meaning).

apo=from

circum=around

equi=equal

extra=more than

intra=within

intro=inwardly,
(on the inside)

mal=bad

mis=wrong
(badly)

non=not

syn=with
(together, at
 same time)

Word	Meaning of Prefix	One Meaning for Word
apogee	_____	The point farthest from the earth in the orbit of the moon.
circumscribe	_____	To trace a line around.
equilateral	_____	A figure having equal sides.
extravagant	_____	Going beyond reasonable limits.
intramural	_____	Within the walls or limits of a city, college, etc.
introvert	_____	To direct one's interest or mind upon oneself.
malice	_____	Active ill will.
misarrange	_____	To arrange wrongly or improperly.
nonchalant	_____	Without warmth or enthusiasm.
syncopate	_____	To begin on an unaccented beat and continue it through the next unaccented beat.

2. One of the two most common English prefixes could not be included above because it has more than one meaning. For example: The prefix "in" might mean *not* as in infallible, or the prefix "in" might mean *in, into* or *within* as in infield.

232

Listed below are six words which include the prefix "in." Write the word *not* if the prefix "in" means not or *in* if the prefix "in" means in, into or within:

1. not; 4. not

2. in; 5. in

3. not 6. not

1. infinite   4. ineffective

2. indoors   5. induction

3. inert   6. indifferent

3. The other common English prefix which has more than one meaning is the prefix "un." For example: The prefix "un" might mean *not* as in unpredictable or it might mean *the opposite of* as unkind. Listed below are six words which include the prefix "un." Write the word *not* if the prefix "un" means not or *opposite* if the prefix "un" means the opposite of.

opposite   1. untied

not   2. unsaturated

not   3. undecided

opposite   4. unload

not   5. unhappy

opposite   6. unlace

IV. **Suffix**

A suffix is an ending which modifies the meaning of a word (usually called a root word). There are about 100 or so common suffixes. These common suffixes modify nouns, adjectives and adverbs. There appears to be approximately 20 suffixes which are most frequently used in English words. We elected to group several of these suffixes under the following 4 categories of meaning:

Capable of being   One who is
State of being   One who does

1. The suffixes "-able" as inserviceable and "-ible" as in credible provide a meaning clue which denotes *capable of being.* The suffixes "-ance" as in disturbance, "-acy" as in intimacy and "-ment" as in development provide meaning clues which denote *state of being.* Below are five words containing suffixes, write the word *capable* if the suffix means capable of being or write *state* if the suffix means state of being:

state	1. amendment_____
capable	2. maneuverable_____
state	3. reluctance_____
capable	4. incredible_____
state	5. democracy_____

2. The suffix "-eer" as in auctioneer denotes one who does. The suffix "-ee" as in devotee denotes one who is. Below are four words containing suffixes, write the word *does* if the suffix means one who does, or write the word *is* if the suffix means one who is:

does	1. engineer_____
is	2. employee_____
is	3. trustee_____
does	4. racketeer_____

Note: The number of suffixes presented above represent a fraction of the common suffixes that could be discussed. The purpose for presenting suffixes was to point out that the suffix is another clue to word learning.

ANSWER KEY

Self-Test   **Consonants**

  p. 205

Regular Consonant Sounds

  / b /   / d /   / f /   / b /
  / j /   / k /   / l /   /m/
  / n /   / p /   / r /
  / t /   / v /   / z /

Interchanges with Other Sounds

  "c"   / s /   or   / k /   "y" *consonant* or *vowel*
  "g"   /g/   or   / j /   "w" *consonant* or *vowel*
  "s"   /z /

Combined

  "qu'   / kw /   "x"   / ks /

Self-Test   Digraphs

    p. 209

ch   —   regular digraph, has three sounds, ch (chair); sh (chef); and k (Christmas). The most common ch sound is the ch sound in a word like chair.

wh   —   regular digraph.

ng   —   regular digraph, usually found at the end of most words.

th   —   regular digraph, has two sounds th voiced (teeth) and th unvoiced (teethe). However, this distinction should be avoided because it is difficult to learn and to teach.

sh   —   regular digraph

ph   —   digraph, usually make the sound of f (fan).

ck   —   digraph, usually makes the sound of k and is at the end of most words.

gh   —   digraph, makes the sound of f (fan) and is often silent when combined with ough, ugh, augh, etc.

Self-Test   Blends and Digraphs

    p. 210

1. drum   — blend *dr*   this   — digraph *th*
    freeze   — blend *fr*   church   — digraph *ch ch*
    skate   — blend *sk*   bring   — blend *br*
    shopping   — digraph *sh*   digraph *ng*   digraph *ng*
    snail   — blend *sn*   house   — neither
                                               score   — blend *sc*

2. Answers to number 2 are too variable, therefore, we did not provide you with the answers.

Self-Test—Short and Long Vowels

    p. 218

    1. lŏgĭc   5. ĕxtrēmĕ

    2. ŏstrĭch   6. clŏsĕt

    3. hōlĭnĕss   7. pēȧnŭt

    4. ŏbtāȉn   8. sŭbscrībĕ

236

Self-Test   Various Vowel Groups:

        Vowel Controlled R
        Diphthong
        Double OO
        Vowel Digraphs
        Letter A—L or W

      p. 225

It is unlikely that you selected words which match the words we used. Compare our words and listen for the sounds. (Note: we underlined the vowels which are representative).

	a	e	i	o	u
vowel controlled r	c*ar*	st*er*n	g*ir*l	c*or*n	c*ur*l
diphthong			m*oi*st	ab*ou*t	
double oo				s*oo*n / b*oo*k	
vowel digraphs	j*ai*l	l*ea*f	d*ia*l	r*oa*d	d*ue*l
letter a—l or w	b*all* / s*aw*				

Self-Test   Three Syllabic Rules

      p. 230

(vc-cv)	(v-cv)	(c + le)	Exceptions
corner	begin	humble	sterile
aspic	climax	ventricle	forest
fabric	pupil	trample	peril
rabbit	over	buckle	gable
pencil	cedar	bumble	boiling

POSTTEST

Directions: This posttest consists of two parts. Part I—Readiness and Part II—Consonants, Vowels, and Structure-Syllables. Place your answers on the spaces provided on the right. Check answers.

PART I—READINESS

Answers

1. Hearing different sounds or words is typical of

   _____ _____ lessons.   1._____ _____

2. Writing 13 for 31 suggests a_____ tendency.   2._____

3. Teaching that words proceed from left to right is called

   _____.   3._____

4. Recognizing the different word (top, top, tip) is typical

   of_____ _____ lessons.   4._____ _____

PART II—CONSONANT, VOWEL, and STRUCTURE-SYLLABLE

Identify the phonic element which is present in each group of five words. Example: *but—trip—rabbit—dock—throb.* Each word contains a consonant, a vowel, and syllable, but the phonic element common to all words is the short vowel sound.

Consonant

5. ladder, wrap, knob, night, kick   5._____

6. glance, certain, cement, bicycle, voice   6._____

7. stratagem, gym, gentle, Ginger, logistics   7._____

8. crack, white, chip, father, shambles   8._____

9. orphan, typhoon, phonics, autograph, phase   9._____

10. dinner, father, bold, listen, go   10._____

11. carry, educate, come, coat, recall   11._____

12. grade, true, clock, replace, best   12._____

Vowel

13. arch, turf, flirt, herb, port

14. chaff, hock, zest, plump, swish

15. leech, oat, cried, waist, gleam

16. wood, crook, foot, hood, nook

17. coil, owl, coy, pouch, broil

18. call, pawn, salt, almost, raw

19. broke, legal, right, gape, tube

13.＿＿＿＿＿＿＿＿＿＿

14.＿＿＿＿＿＿＿＿＿＿

15.＿＿＿＿＿＿＿＿＿＿

16.＿＿＿＿＿＿＿＿＿＿

17.＿＿＿＿＿＿＿＿＿＿

18.＿＿＿＿＿＿＿＿＿＿

19.＿＿＿＿＿＿＿＿＿＿

Structure-Syllable

20. darkest, catcher, needed, homeless, mindful

21. unbutton, disobey, remind, enslave, incorrect

20.＿＿＿＿＿＿＿＿＿＿

21.＿＿＿＿＿＿＿＿＿＿

Give Syllable-Visual-Pattern Only

22. ample, jingle, apple, turtle, ankle

23. monkey, allure, canyon, splinter, angel

24. even, apron, joker, lazy, ration

22.＿＿＿＿＿＿＿＿＿＿

23.＿＿＿＿＿＿＿＿＿＿

24.＿＿＿＿＿＿＿＿＿＿

1. auditory discrimination	13. r-controlled vowels
2. reversal	14. short vowels
3. directionality	15. vowel digraphs
4. visual discrimination	16. short oo sound
5. silent consonants	17. diphthongs
6. soft c (s sound)	18. a + l or w
7. g sounded as j	19. long vowels
8. digraphs	20. suffixes
9. ph digraph	21. prefixes
10. initial consonant	22. c + le
11. hard c (k sound)	23. vc-cv
12. blends	24. v-cv